GOVERNING CALIFORNIA

GOVERNING CALIFORNIA:
Politics, Government, and Public Policy in the Golden State

Second edition

Gerald C. Lubenow, editor

Institute of Governmental Studies Press
University of California
2006

Library of Congress Cataloging-in-Publication Data

Governing California : politics, government, and public policy in the Golden State /
Gerald C. Lubenow and Bruce E. Cain, editors.—2nd ed.
    p. cm.
    Includes bibliographical references and index.
    ISBN 0-87772-4202
California—Politics and government. I. Lubenow, Gerald C. II. Cain, Bruce E.
JK8716.G68 2006
320.9794—dc22   2005034294

Contents

Preface

California existed as a potent myth long before it became a political reality. And, in its political evolution as in its social and cultural landscape, the myths that swirl around the Golden State have played a major role in sculpting reality. Cortes referred to it as "Las Californias," reflecting the belief of early Spanish explorers that California was a series of islands. And, politically, it has come to resemble a series of islands, each with unique interests and characteristics. There are the great urban islands along the coast—San Diego, Los Angeles, and the San Francisco Bay Area—as well as the more amorphous but increasingly powerful archipelagos of the Central Valley and the Inland Empire. Nationally, it is an island on the land, a nation within a nation, a huge demographically diverse, economically rich state that would be, on its own, the sixth largest economy in the world.

Hubert Howe Bancroft and other historians have observed that California evolved largely in isolation, gradually developing many of the characteristics and political attitudes of an independent nation. Unlike upwardly mobile office seekers in America's Midwest, South, or East, the prize most coveted by ambitious California politicians is not a seat in the United States Senate, but the governor's office in Sacramento. Viewed by most occupants as an anteroom to the White House, the governor's office provides a national platform to display one's skills at running one of the most economically powerful, culturally diverse, and politically unruly entities in the world.

"California," observed the *California Political Almanac*, "is the planet's most diverse society. At no time in mankind's history have so many people of so many ethnic and national groups, practicing so many different religions, speaking so many different languages, and engaged in so many different kinds of economic activities, gathered in one place."

Along with diversity, change is a hallmark of California politics—change that often leads to new paths that much of the nation will follow. Things happen first in California, according to the cliché. And, very often, they do. California blazed the political trail to direct democracy, personal politics, disaffection with political parties, the use of professional campaign consultants, and state-of-the-art media techniques. It took the lead on the tax revolt with Proposition 13 and on tough anticrime legislation with the three-strikes initiative. As a result of its deep distrust of politicians, California led the way in cutting salaries, perks, and terms for elected public officials. And in 2004, it crystallized the nation's discontent with politicians by throwing out a governor it had elected just a year before.

This book attempts to explain how this diverse, ever-changing, entrepreneurial, and individualistic collection of people functions politically, how its most important institutions of government operate, and how it makes public policy. There are surprisingly few good books available to individuals interested in California politics and government. There are a handful that draw a useful blueprint of the structure of state government, a few that offer a more exhaustive look at the functional relationship between the various branches of state government, and two or three that provide an excellent statistical picture of the state. Our aim here is to give the student of state politics and government a more analytical and interpretive overview of the machinery of state government, the currents that dominate political discourse, and the primary interest groups that play off one another in the ebb and flow of political life.

Other IGS Press books deal with more specific issues. *Racial and Ethnic Politics in California* addresses the major shifts occurring in California politics as a result of demographic change. *Constitutional Reform in California* deals with the continued interest in academic and political circles in a broad restructuring of California's political system to bring it more into line with the current social reality. And the *California Political Almanac,* whose publication IGS took over in 2005 after *The California Journal* ceased operations, provides the best single source reference on who's who and what's what in state government.

Governing California has a more ambitious goal. Designed primarily for courses in California government and American state and local politics, it will, we are confidant, be informative and useful to a much broader general audience as well. It does not attempt an exhaustive explanation of how the various elements of state government function and interact with one another. Rather, it seeks to provide a conceptual understanding of the major elements of state government, how they have evolved over the years, and how they relate to the crucial problems of the day.

Written by leading scholars and respected practitioners, the essays are meant to be pointed and topical as well as balanced and analytical, to provide a current context as well as an historical framework, and to be prescriptive as well as descriptive. Taken as a whole, the collection of essays seeks not to provide a series of rote answers regarding state government, but to help students figure out the right questions to ask as they try to understand how state government works.

In the book's opening section, former state Senator Patrick Johnston and state budget consultant John Decker examine the state legislature, once a model for the nation, and explain how it came to be the bickering, divided, term-limited, partisan body it is today—and how it manages to function nonetheless. IGS Director Bruce Cain, who also currently heads the UC Washington Center, joins UC San Diego political scientist Thad Kousser and Karl Kurtz of the National Conference of State Legislatures to assess the impact of term limits on the legislature. Former *California Journal* editor and publisher A. G. Block, who currently directs the public affairs journalism program at the University of California Center Sacramento, has updated and expanded the late John Jacobs look at the diverse governing styles of chief executives from Ronald Reagan through Arnold Schwarzenegger. Santa Clara Law School Professor Jerry Uelman has done a similarly exquisite job of touching up the late Preble Stolz' assessment of how the state's criminal justice system functions and how a burgeoning work load has affected the California courts. Revan Tranter, former head of the Association of Bay Area Governments, has updated his analysis of the decline of popular confidence in government, the rise of the tax revolt, and the resulting shift of power from local to state government.

In the opening essay of the second section, former IGS Director Eugene Lee traces the initiative, recall, and referendum to their progressive roots and wonders if the state isn't suffering from an excess of democracy. Morgan Kousser of Cal Tech outlines how technology has turned the redistricting process into a computer game where incumbents always seem to win and minorities frequently lose. And Rachel Van Sickle-Ward and Darshan Goux, two UC Berkeley Ph.D. candidates in political science analyze press coverage of the debates in California's 2004 recall election to address the question "Do Debates Matter?".

The final section on public policy opens with a penetrating analysis of the political impact of immigration by IGS Associate Director Jack Citrin and Andrea Campbell. Megan Mullin, a recent UC, Berkeley political science Ph.D. clarifies the current contours of California's ongoing struggle over water.

I want to thank all the authors who contributed their political expertise and talent to this project. This book is their gift to a new generation of politically active Californians. I thank Jack Citrin and Bruce Cain for their continued support of this project and their ongoing efforts to make the Institute of Governmental Studies a home for the kind of research that makes projects like this possible. With this book, as with so much of the work of the Institute, Ron Heckart and the IGS Library staff have been an invaluable resource. Finally, I'd like to thank Maria Wolf without whose tireless efforts and wise counsel this book would never have come together.

Gerald C. Lubenow
UC Berkeley
December 2005

I.   Part I. Government

Chapter 1

The Changing Legislative Landscape

Patrick Johnston

As rolling blackouts swept across huge sections of California in 2001, blanketing the state in darkness, light bulbs blinked on in the heads of Sacramento's rookie legislators. The state's power crisis freed them of any insecurity they may have suffered in the era of term limits. It was, after all, Sacramento's best and brightest, the sage old hands, the savvy pros, the professional pols, who had voted unanimously to deregulate the state's electrical system in 1996. And each year, as the new millennium wore on, there were fewer and fewer of them around as term limits took its steady toll.

In the years that followed, a remnant of old pros who had designed the deregulation law and a wave of legislative newcomers who inherited the mess had to sort through causes, consequences, and remedies offered by a bewildering array of stakeholders. The energy crisis was the great leveler. It was the issue that deflated the conventional wisdom that the old order before term limits insured better lawmaking than the new order of constant change.

To be sure, the California Legislature is a markedly different institution in the wake of the 1990 voter-approved initiative that restricts Assembly members to three two-year terms and state senators to two four-year terms. But it is not as easy to conclude that a term-limited legislature functions better or worse than its predecessors that were unfettered by the ticking of the clock.

Early Days

In the century and a half since Congress admitted California as the 31st state of the Union in 1850, term limits was only the latest of a host of political, economic, and social cross currents to affect the state's lawmakers. When elections were first held for the 16-member Senate (now 40) and 36-member Assembly (now 80), most candidates were either Democrats or Whigs.

The early legislative sessions were marked by turnover and instability among the members. Some resigned to take other positions in the fledgling state government. Many legislators had come recently to California after serving in elective office in their home states. William Gwin, a former congressman from Mississippi, convinced his fellow solons to select him as one of the new state's two U.S. senators along with the legendary John C. Fremont. Gwin argued successfully that California should have a pro-slavery senator in Washington to balance the abolitionist views of Fremont.

The early days of the legislature, meeting in San Jose, were characterized by contentious debate and considerable frustration as the new state emerged from the control of the U.S. Army and before that the rule of Spain and then Mexico. State Senate Finance Committee Chairman Thomas Jefferson Green, who had served in the legislatures of North Carolina and Florida, invited his colleagues to imbibe at the end of each day thereby earning the first session the nickname, "the legislature of a thousand drinks."

As California grew and the economy developed beyond the gold mining industry, railroads spread across the state and communities came to depend upon them to transport a growing population and move goods to market. Eventually the railroad titans manipulated both the Democratic and Republican parties to choose candidates for the legislature that were friendly to their needs.

By 1910, a coalition of reformers and farmers, resentful of the power of the railroads, combined to nominate and then elect Republican Hiram Johnson the governor of California. Led by Johnson, the self-styled Progressives enacted a statewide direct primary election system to skirt the power of party bosses and their railroad patrons. Soon, individual candidates became more important than the party and its platform. Cross-filing, another Progressive reform, permitted candidates to run on every party's ticket, further diminishing the power of the parties and the political pros.

In 1910, California was virtually a one-party state with the political cleavage separating conservative Republicans from progressive Republicans. Despite the population growth in Los Angeles and the San Francisco Bay Area, a 1926 initiative reapportioned the state Senate based on geography—giving the rural "cow counties" a significant overrepresentation. Assembly districts were drawn based on population.

For a time, partisanship was minimal. There were no party caucuses, and the members of each house appointed members to committees and selected chairmen for them without regard to party affiliation. In the 1930s, the Great Depression and the presidency of Franklin Roosevelt brought a surge of popularity to Democrats in California. State Senator Culbert Olson became the first Democratic governor in the 20th century. And partisanship made a brief foray in the Assembly.

But by 1940, nonpartisanship was once again ascendant with the election of moderate Republican Earl Warren. World War II muted partisan political differences as the legislature pursued patriotic themes including the dismissal of all Japanese-Americans from state jobs as a prelude to their internment in relocation camps. (In 1982, the legislature officially apologized for the hysteria-driven firings and appropriated $5,000 for each victim of the racist policy.)

Insiders

Postwar California boomed as a Mecca of opportunity and prosperity. Many, who had passed through the ports of San Diego and San Francisco as soldiers on their way to the Pacific theater and others, who had come to work in the war industries, including many blacks from the rural South, decided to stay and made the Golden State their permanent home.

The legislature of the 1950s reflected the relative anonymity of earlier editions. It was an institution of insiders. Sessions were short. Pay was modest and the work part-time. Without staff or individual offices, members relied on lobbyists for information and amusement. In an era of relatively slow transportation, legislators lived in Sacramento hotels or bunked with fellow members in spartan rental units. The low pay ($6,000 per year) and isolation from family bred a tight-knit male social fraternity that depended on the generosity of the lobbying corps. At eating and drinking sessions such as Moose Milk and the Derby Club, lobbyists footed the bill for the opportunity to chat with lawmakers. The king of influence peddlers was a burly, bumptious liquor lobbyist named Artie Samish, who was commonly referred to as the "Boss of the Legislature" until he was jailed for federal income tax evasion.

In this clubby atmosphere veteran legislators initiated novices into the rituals of lawmaking. Committee chairmen (there were no women in the Senate and only an occasional widow of a former member in the Assembly) and key committee members from both parties would consult with lobbyists in the evening and vote on bills the next day. Loose voting procedures often allowed a committee chairman to announce the fate of a bill without the presence or recorded vote of the committee members.

What the process lacked in transparency, it made up for in efficiency. Pandering to particular constituencies was minimized. Members were not put on the spot for voting against popular but expensive or unwise bills. The unspoken premise was this: it is in the public's interest for elected leaders to thrash out complicated issues without the excessive scrutiny of the public or the press and without fear of losing the next election. These insiders were an elite handful of part-time lawmakers who were comfortably insulated from what Founding Father James Madison termed "the hot temper of popular opinion."

Members of the legislature had an odd little life that rested firmly on a three-legged base: the camaraderie of fellow members, the munificence of lobbyists, and the silence of the press. Partisanship was less important than relationships with colleagues. The working press was at best tolerant of the Capitol's culture or at worst co-opted by a process that doled out tidbits of information and free drinks in exchange for reportorial discretion in their stories.

Partisans

California was changing by the end of the fifties. In 1958, when Democrat Pat Brown was elected governor, the Senate was still run by the "old bulls" on a conservative and bipartisan basis, but the Assembly had split into partisan caucuses. Then came Jesse Unruh. Elected Assembly Speaker in 1960, Unruh transformed the office into a policy and political power center. He raised campaign funds aggressively from special interests and doled them out judiciously to expand Democratic control of the house by electing members who were politically dependent on him.

The Progressive Era reforms that emasculated political parties ironically allowed Unruh to establish the "caucus" party, a political machine fueled by his firm control of the legislature. Republicans soon followed suit. Competition at elections included challenges to incumbents. Legislative programs needed the Speaker's blessing. Unruh allocated committee assignments and staff patronage on the basis of loyalty from Democrats and cooperation from Republicans.

Responding to this shift of power to the Speaker's office, lobbyists showered Unruh and his successors with campaign money. The cost of campaigns rose dramatically from the fifties to the eighties. In 1958 a total of $968,687 was spent on all Assembly campaigns. By 1988 that figure had grown to $57,177,745—a thirteen-fold increase in constant dollars over the thirty-year period. Even funds directed to other caucus members and candidates were often negotiated with the Speaker. Lobbyists, in turn, focused their advocacy efforts on the leader. As a result, Unruh—and after him, Bob Moretti, Leo McCarthy, and Willie Brown—could single-handedly determine the course and outcome of legislation.

The state Senate did not yield as quickly or as completely to control by the President pro Tempore. The Senate organizational structure conferred authority on a five-member Rules Committee and was less amenable to leadership fiat than the Assembly.

In the 1960s, two major changes accelerated the development of a partisan, professional institution: the U.S. Supreme Court's "one person, one vote" ruling and the institution of a full-time legislature. In 1962 the United States Supreme Court, in *Baker v. Carr,* required states to reapportion their legislative bodies consistent with the Equal Protection Clause of the 14th Amendment which does not permit a state to "weigh the vote of one county or district more heavily than it weighs the vote in another." Suddenly the rural counties lost their dominance in the state Senate. Los Angeles-- with seven million residents-- increased its state Senate delegation from one to seventeen.

The second dramatic change came as a result of a change in the state constitution when voters approved Proposition 1A in 1966. Overnight the legislature went from part-time to full-time with the pay increasing from $6,000 to $16,000 per year. Professional staffing increased in the sixties to provide analyses of issues independent of the governor's administration or lobbyists.

The trend was unmistakable and continued through the seventies and eighties as the legislature became more powerful, more partisan, more caucus-driven, more election-conscious, and more dependent on fundraising from special interests despite a 1974 initiative that required full disclosure of campaign finances and crimped the practice of lobbyists wining and dining legislators.

The eighties saw control of both houses of the legislature in Democratic hands led by the high-profile Willie Brown in the Assembly and publicity-shy David Roberti in the Senate. The state's relentless growth required more schools, roads, public transit, water systems, and prisons. After the passage of Proposition 13 in 1978, local governments were effectively barred from raising taxes to keep pace with the demand for public services. The legislature replaced school boards as the decision maker for education policy and the source of most funds. Similarly, issues involving county programs and city services were debated and decided in hearing rooms of the state Capitol.

The legislature's willingness to preempt local government in spending priorities, employee relations, and infrastructure did not extend to land-use policy. California continued to sprawl as the pattern of suburbanization spread beyond Los Angeles and the San Francisco Bay Area into the agricultural regions of the state. Conflicts with environmental and agricultural interests were seldom mediated by the state. Low-density housing developments with long commutes became the pattern in California. The state tried to cope by boosting transportation funding through the gas tax and passing school bonds. Regional regulatory agencies invented by Democratic legislators and acquiesced to by Republican governors, struggled with worsening air and water pollution.

As the decade drew to a close, the excesses of fundraising mounted. The press, increasingly skeptical and adversarial since the days of Watergate, aggressively pursued potential links between lawmaking and campaign donations. The F.B.I. apparently read the newspapers. The U.S. Attorney in Sacramento authorized a sting operation that sent five former or sitting lawmakers, four staff members, and two lobbyists to prison.

The last hurrah for the halcyon days of legislative hubris was June of 1990 when lawmakers sponsored Proposition 112 that traded the oft-criticized practice of honoraria (lobbyist arranged speaking fees paid to lawmakers) for a commission that set compensation for state officials. Voters approved the change and the new commission promptly boosted legislators' pay from $40,816 to $52,500 (now $110,880).

Newcomers

The end was at hand. Capitalizing on the cumulative bad publicity afflicting the image of the legislature and a national movement to rein in politicians at all levels, supporters of term limits passed Proposition 140 in November 1990. Assembly members are restricted to three terms of two years each. Senators are permitted two four-year terms. The limits are prospective and lifetime. As soon as the law passed, ambitious members began looking for their next office. Nested assembly members, sometimes of the same party, battled to succeed their senator. Deference to colleagues became a nicety of a by-gone era.

As legislators left to run for other offices as soon as the opportunity arose or as a result of term limits, the complexion and the culture of the legislature began to change. Turnover gave rise to more minorities particularly Latinos where the percentage increased from 6% in 1987 to 25% in 2005. Women also experienced a gain from 15% to 30% over the same period, but this appears to be a continuation of a longer-term trend.

Assembly leadership was affected dramatically by term limits. After nearly 15 years of Willie Brown as Speaker, the post was briefly held in 1995 by two renegade Republicans (Brian Setencich of Fresno and Doris Allen of Orange County) supported by Democrats, then for a year and a half a by a partisan Republican (Curt Pringle of Orange County). After the 1996 elections returned Democrats to power in the Assembly, the Speakership went to two Latinos in succession (Cruz Bustamante of Fresno and Antonio Villaraigosa of Los Angeles). After bouncing around for another half dozen years, it went, in 2004, to a freshman Fabian Nunez of Los Angeles.

Term limits dictated a schedule in which the incumbent Speaker steps down in the spring of each election year to be succeeded by a new leader who raises the money and carries the flag for the caucus into the fall elections. Meanwhile the outgoing leader tries to parlay his two-year brush with power into another office:

- In 1998, Pringle was defeated for state treasurer but rebounded by winning election as mayor of Anaheim.
- Bustamante was elected lieutenant governor twice, lost a bid for governor in the special election of 2003, and is running in 2006 for insurance commissioner.
- Villaraigosa was defeated for mayor of Los Angeles in 2001, then elected to the City Council, and defeated incumbent Mayor James Hahn in a 2005 rematch.
- In retaliation for their 15 minutes of fame, the traitorous Republicans, Setencich and Allen, lost their seats in recall elections orchestrated by their own party.
- Willie Brown, who was the lightening rod for the term limit movement in California, left the legislature in 1995 to become mayor of San Francisco.

The Senate's leadership has been more stable. After thirteen years Roberti was succeeded in the spring of 1994 by Bill Lockyer (D-Hayward) who served for four years before stepping down in 1998 to run successfully for attorney general. He was followed by John Burton (D-San Francisco) whose own career included an Assembly stint in the sixties, service in the Congress in the seventies and eighties, a return to the Assembly in 1992, and election to the state Senate in 1996. Burton's long political career and quick ascent to become president pro tempore allowed him to lead the house for a full six years, a record not likely to be broken during this era of strict term limits. Don Perata (D-Oakland) became the Pro Tem in 2004.

Robert Hertzberg (D - Los Angeles) was chosen as Speaker in the spring of 2000 and was replaced in early 2002. He departed the legislature after a tumultuous term consumed by the energy crisis that erupted in the wake of the deregulation movement enacted by lawmakers in 1996, the year before he was elected to the Assembly. Despite his prodigious efforts to help fashion solutions to the skyrocketing prices to consumers, the blackouts caused by shortages, the bankruptcy threats of utilities, and the devastating effects on the state's own budget, Hertzberg's grade as problem-solver can only be an "incomplete" to go with his "A" for effort. Two years on the job and one during the height of the crisis is an insufficient time to tame the multi-faceted problem. He too attempted to win another office, losing the 2005 race for mayor of L.A. to Villaraigosa.

Yet Hertzberg left with a legacy that may be the most enduring contribution a legislative leader can make during the era of term limits. He created an institute to train new legislators and new staff in the skills needed to serve in the state Capitol. Now all newly elected members go to class to learn about procedures and policies that they will encounter on the job. Since professional staff turnover is as rapid as their bosses', the institute conducts mandatory classes for them as well. The program is run on a bipartisan basis with respected Republican and Democratic staff codirectors. The informally dubbed "Hertzberg U" has a formal conference room across the street from the Capitol named after Republican Bill Leonard who helped to create the center.

Although the Assembly training institute is the most dramatic contribution to the institution of the legislature (the Senate mostly relies on the Assembly to train members and staff who often matriculate to the "upper" house), Hertzberg himself suggests the theme of his experience as Speaker is summed up in the word "next." The members are preoccupied with what they can do next—the next committee to serve on, the next committee to chair, and the next office to run for. It is a natural reflection of a short horizon.

While turnover affects the Assembly more dramatically, both houses reflect the new reality. Since 1990 the legislature has begun a permanent and profound process of change. The newcomers are just as bright and perhaps more motivated to serve the public than the old, more sedentary cohort of members. But the knowledge base in the Senate and Assembly cannot possibly compete with the expertise in the executive branch and the lobbying corps. The power of individual members is so temporal, any bureaucratic or special interest can out wait a legislative adversary.

As a practical matter, under the relative stability of the 1970s and 1980s, the legislature relied on the committee chairs to provide leadership on the issues under their jurisdiction. They have the staff and time commitment to become familiar with the context in which bills should be viewed. The committee staff and members retain the institutional memory to apply to discrete legislative proposals. And the chairs tend to wield authority by virtue of the prerogatives of the gavel and the greater knowledge of the subject matter.

In a term-limited environment chairs are appointed after a few weeks or a couple of years in office. They have virtually no time or role model to understudy for. In the Senate, experienced policy consultants still dominate the committee staff ranks; the exodus of veteran staffers in the Assembly leaves the chairs with fewer resources than in the past.

Even in the partisan era of the past, committee chairs were stabilizing forces that influenced major policy outcomes. In the new era, committees behave like discussion groups. Bills pass readily through committees, but policy decision-making shifts more to extraordinary legislative arrangements that render the traditional committee process increasingly irrelevant. These arrangements are the informal institutions of the contemporary legislature.

The Big Five

The Big Five refers to the governor, the Senate president pro tem, the Speaker of the Assembly, and the minority leaders in both houses. In 1991, Governor Wilson called the leaders together to resolve a budget impasse. The closed-door meetings took place after the legislative committees had completed nearly six month of budget writing including the "final" conference committee. They negotiated $7 billion in tax increases and $7 billion in program cuts. The resulting compromise was sold to the members of each caucus as the necessary medicine to cure a $14 billion deficit.

Wilson found the device, dubbed the "Big Five," an effective way to negotiate his policy and budget agenda without the public nitpicking of members or the skepticism of the legislative analyst. Although previous governors and caucus leaders had huddled over thorny issues, the 1991 budget deliberation marks the informal institutionalization of the "Big Five."

Leaders blamed the governor for usurping the budget writing process, but they were co-conspirators who moved their policy and personal priorities ahead of the members. In a term-limited world, the members had less time and expertise to fight the budget wars themselves, so they deferred to their leaders to negotiate both large and small matters with Wilson.

By the time Gray Davis took office in 1999, the state coffers were flush with cash. Leaders were the chief lobbyists to the governor for their members' budget requests. In 2001, tax revenues were drying up due to the slowing economy. Even with strong Democratic majorities and a Democratic governor, the budget was not passed until four weeks into the new fiscal year beginning July 1. Davis did not often choose to negotiate with the Republicans. Many times, Big Five became the three Democratic leaders cutting up the pie and then trying to pick off a few individual Republicans.

In his first year as governor, Governor Arnold Schwarzenegger was anxious to improve the political climate, so he tried hard to resolve nagging differences with the legislature. For its part, the legislature, star-struck with the governor's Hollywood and Kennedy connections, was eager to accommodate the actor-turned-Chief Executive. The Big 5 negotiated the wording on three propositions, which were placed on a statewide ballot in 2004. But their meetings were less productive in the first ten months of 2005. Governor Schwarzenegger tried to pass four initiatives in a 2005 special election effort to by-pass the Legislature. His measures were overwhelmingly rejected by the voters, and on election night he went on television to concede defeat and immediately call for a meeting of the Big 5 to begin again to establish bi-partisan rapport with the Legislature.

Budget Trailer Bills

The annual budget bill contains thousands of individual line items that to-gether fund the operations of the state for the coming fiscal year. Beginning in 1982 Governor Jerry Brown and the Democratic legislature created a parasite called the "trailer bill" that enacted technical changes to statutes in order to im-plement the state budget. The trailer bill was authored by the budget chair and passed without debate and without legislative hearings. This device grew in im-portance as the method of balancing the budget. During the Deukmejian admini-stration the law requiring an automatic increase in welfare grants was routinely suspended as part of a Big Five "budget deal."

In 1987, the state Supreme Court invalidated the multisubject trailer bill on the grounds that the state Constitution provides that "a statute shall embrace but one subject." The response was to add so-called trailer bills to the budget process often without referral to policy committees. Both the governor and legislative leaders used the bypass for expediency.

Faced with serious budget shortfalls in the early nineties, they adopted multi-ple trailer bills: 16 in 1991; 9 in 1992; 21 in 1993; 19 in 1994; 11 in 1995; and 12 in 1996. Even after the recession ended, trailer bills were used for a wide variety of policy purposes such as class size reduction and toxic waste clean up. The Re-publican governor could avoid the gauntlet of a Democratic dominated committee process because he had the leverage of the line-item veto in the state budget. In 1997 there were 20 trailer bills and 32 in 1998.

The election of Democrat Gray Davis didn't change the pattern. Even with healthy surpluses 28 trailer bills were approved in 1999... Members began to self-designate their bills as "trailers" in hopes of leaping ahead in the process and at-taching their policy ideas to passage of the annual budget.

In more recent budgets, the number of trailer bill has dropped dramatically, but only because the legislature has chosen to disregard the Supreme Court's single subject ruling. The size of the trailer bills has grown, as they become more like omnibus vehicles than discrete policy subjects.

Member Requests

All legislators want to deliver for their districts. Historically the federal budget has been replete with district spending items that are collectively referred to as "pork barrel." Presidents tolerated most of this ad hoc budgeting because until recently they did not have the power of the line-item veto. In California, however, the governor's authority to "blue pencil" items from the budget restrained lawmakers.

In his final year Wilson found that dangling the promise of approving pet projects like money for local parks and museums would persuade reluctant members to vote for his budget. Davis himself engaged in micro-budgeting to add specific pork projects like the Billy Crystal exhibit at the Wiesthenthal Museum of Tolerance in Los Angeles and construction of Boys and Girls Clubs (a favorite of one-time ally turned opponent Los Angeles Mayor Richard Riordan). Member requests mushroomed at the urging of local governments and nonprofit organizations. With the ticking of the term limit clock, the immediate political gratification of cutting a ribbon for a new Little League field trumped the tedium of rewriting the tax code.

The budget deficits of 2001 and the years to follow have shrunk the phenomenon of member requests, but legislative augmentations remain high. For example, despite the overwhelming deficit in 2002, the legislature added $1.5 billion to the state budget. The appetite for credit continues in the drafting of state bond proposals that earmark money for local projects.

Suspense File

The legislative process relies on the two Appropriations Committees to prioritize the many spending bills that are approved by the various policy committees such as education, health, and transportation. During the '80s Speaker Willie Brown considered it better internal politics to pass many expensive bills and let the Republican governor take the heat for vetoing them. Passing the buck kept the members happy with the Speaker. Eventually this easy virtue infected the Senate. No member wanted to kill bills of their colleagues just because they cost too much money.

So the Suspense File was created by Senate Appropriations Chairman Dan Boatwright in the mid-80's to hold bills and evaluate them after the budget reveals how much money is available for new programs. Now the chairs of the two Appropriations Committees consult with the leadership of both caucuses in secret and parcel out bills based on the policy need to prioritize spending and the political need to reward or punish members without a public vote.

In a term-limited era, the Suspense File slows down the avalanche of costly measures that cascade from policy committees where neither chairs nor members have much perspective on which bills are most important. In 1999, for example, the total cost of bills sent to Senate suspense was $6.8 billion. After the trimming behind the closed door of Room 211, the price tag was cut to $353 million. The members complain about losing their funding, but the pain is lessened by the practice of passing two-thirds of the bills even though the funding is typically 10% of the original request.

Conference Committees

Conference Committees historically were created to resolve differences between conflicting Senate and Assembly versions of a bill. Three members from each house (two from the majority party, one from the minority) would be assigned to meet publicly and fashion a compromise to be taken to the floor of the Senate and the Assembly.

Over the years legislative leaders have used the conference committee process as a way to bypass the regular committees and handpick members to address complex problems. After the passage of Proposition 13 in 1978, that dramatically cut property taxes, a Conference Committee sorted out the options and devised a new financing scheme for local government. Since then the device has been employed to cut taxes, raise taxes, reform the workers compensation system, rewrite health care statutes, and cope with the energy crisis.

All five of these arrangements have the effect of shifting power from members and committee chairs to legislative leaders and the governor.

Mortality

The force of term limits is centrifugal. New members are not joining the cozy club of the fifties where they are likely to settle in and help to run the state in relative anonymity. Nor are they teaming up with a partisan cult bent on maximizing political power. Instead new members are arriving with a hyperactive sense of their own legislative mortality: learn fast, make laws fast, move up the rungs fast, and look for another office fast.

The California Legislature has evolved. It no longer operates like a private club. It is no longer run mainly for the benefit of partisan caucuses. It is more transparent. It is more individualistic. It also is less potent than the governor and the courts. It is a deliberative body that reflects the diversity of opinion in California. It is likely a more honest institution than many of its predecessors. But constant change dictated by term limits has sapped its institutional power. And it isn't coming back.

Chapter 2

Resolving Differences and Crafting Compromise:
Creating a Budget for California

John Decker

An unlikely pair of state senators, Maurice Johannessen and Steve Peace, huddled around spreadsheets in Peace's Capitol office on a clear Tuesday morning, June 26, 2002. Johannessen, a conservative and reserved Republican, represented the state's northern-most Senate district. Peace, whose district bordered Mexico, was known neither for his conservatism nor for his reserve. The two senators, both serving their last year in the legislature, met to develop a compromise that in all likelihood would be unwelcome to the Senate, the Assembly, and the governor. They were trying to balance a state budget that was said to be in deficit by as much as $35 billion.

Earlier in the month, Johannessen had watched Peace chair the legislature's budget conference committee. In that committee, Peace had distributed binders detailing hundreds of budget cuts for the committee to consider. Line by tedious line, the committee reviewed the cuts, considering every appropriation in the budget. By Sunday, June 24, the committee was within $1 billion of balancing the budget, but it had run out of acceptable lists, ideas, and patience. It adjourned without coming to a compromise solution.

When Johannessen, who was not a member of the conference committee, saw the committee adjourn, he thought he saw a possible compromise. He might be willing to vote for a temporary, two-year tax increase. By suspending for two years a company's ability to deduct its net operating losses, tax receipts could be raised for 2002–03 by enough to balance the budget. As part of his proposed compromise, Johannessen would have required Peace and the other Democrats to accept three budget changes considered key by the Republicans: increase revenue sharing for counties, add funding for public safety programs, and provide an ongoing annual business-tax reduction of about $500 million. The Democrats agreed to Johannessen's compromise, and on June 29, Johannessen joined 26 Democrats to approve the deal and pass it to the Assembly. The Assembly, reluctant to approve the compromise, continued to work on the budget for another two months. In late August, it passed a budget similar to the deal worked out in Peace's office.

In 2002, like all but three of the last 15 years, the legislature passed the budget after the start of the fiscal year on July 1. Figure 1 displays the date when the budget passed both houses of the legislature over the last sixteen years. For each budget, the date of passage is listed on the left vertical axis and the size of the General Fund budget is listed on the right vertical axis. There seems no relationship between the size of the budget and the amount of delay.

These delays must seem confusing—perhaps even inexplicable—to the taxpayer reading the *Los Angeles Times* over her morning coffee. Balancing the state budget should require only those mathematical skills, subtracting and adding, learned in elementary mathematics. After all, households balance their checkbooks. How hard can it be to ensure that the state's income (that is, tax receipts) equal or exceed spending? But the budget is delayed because negotiations become freighted with considerations beyond balancing the books. They become another venue for resolving differences between the governor and the legislature. The tenor and the product of their negotiations not only affect how they manage their conflicts, but their very ability to govern.

Stage Props, Kabuki Theater, and Reality Television: Describing the State Budget

Governor Schwarzenegger declared 2005 "The Year of Reform." One of his reforms was contained in a proposal to make a complex, far-reaching constitutional change of the state budget process. To dramatize the effect of his proposal, Governor Schwarzenegger held a press conference where he stood next to a faucet pouring a four- inch-wide stream of red "ink." After detailing the provisions of his reform measure, he leaned over and closed a spigot to stop the flow. For Schwarzenegger, the faucet—a stage prop—symbolized how the budget was recklessly spilling taxpayer money, and how his reforms would turn off the waste. Though

Figure 1
Comparison of Budget Size and Date of Passage, by Year
Dollars in Billions
1990-91 to 2005-06

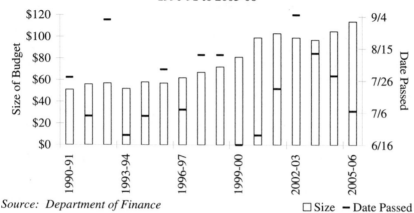

Source: Department of Finance   □ Size — Date Passed

one veteran reporter called the prop and its symbolism "cheesy," the governor was trying to make accessible the obscure and confusing aspects of the budget.[1]

The governor is not alone in trying to simplify budget complexity. Robert Hertzberg, who served as Speaker of the Assembly in 2000 and 2001, referred to his months of budget negotiations as "kabuki theater," suggesting that the negotiations could be completed only after each actor made a series of ritualized moves. Hertzberg was no novice to financial negotiations, having brokered many complex deals in Los Angeles before serving in the Assembly. His legislative counterpart, Senator John Burton, who first served in the Assembly in 1964, said that his budget goal as Senate leader was "to get out alive," as if the six-month long budget process were a season of the reality television show "Survivor." Many legislative and administrative staff refer to the budget as a "game," presumably because the process metes out winners and losers.

Thousands of people are involved in the development, consideration, and passage of the budget bill. They resort to symbols and metaphors to summarize the mind-numbing detail contained in the thousands of documents used when justifying the state's $100 billion annual spending plan. Symbols and metaphors help them to explain the time-consuming process used in developing and adopting the budget legislation. However helpful a metaphor may be in embodying a particular view, it never fully captures the complexity of the process and substance of budget development and implementation. Though there are ritualized aspects of budget negotiations, the completed budget compromise often affects more people than

---

[1] Daniel Weintraub, "Governor's budget talk must return to reality" *Sacramento Bee*. February 27, 2005. E-1

does a theater performance. Metaphors usually do not capture the political trade-offs among spending options, so that while many programs compete for the last budgeted dollar, the signed budget cannot be assessed merely by determining who "won" the last dollar.

Even without referencing a metaphor, those involved in the budget often have divergent interests affecting their view of "the budget." A lobbyist sees—and ex-plains—the budget process differently than does the Director of Finance. The lob-byist is primarily interested in securing funding for a particular program and is not particularly interested in how the program is financed. The Director of Finance is more interested in and responsible for limiting spending to the amount of available revenues.

When Governor Schwarzenegger submits a "budget" on January 10, as re-quired by the constitution, he will forward to the legislature language to be in-cluded in the budget bill. The budget bill authorizes the executive to spend tax money by listing appropriations for each state department, agency, and bureau. Some of the appropriations are for staff and operations while other appropriations finance capital facilities or payments to local governments.

The budget bill provides, in a compact format, specific information about the nature and use of each appropriation. Specifically, it lists each appropriation under a unique numeric identifier, a phrase describing the funding authorized, and the appropriation amount. The legislature may also condition the use of the appropria-tion by adopting statutory language, directing the executive branch to allocate the funds on a different basis than described in state law. It does not provide any detail about the management of the program, the beneficiary or the myriad of policy or political considerations shaping the program.

At a basic level, the budget identifies the relative value of programs, as meas-ured by the amount spent. For example, the 2005 budget appropriates $117.4 bil-lion. Of this amount, about $4 billion is an allocation from the proceeds of bond sales approved by voters for capital projects.

Another $23.3 billion are allocations of earmarked revenues from accounts known as "special funds." Special fund revenues are the proceeds of taxes, charges, and fees levied for narrowly circumscribed purposes. Environmental and resources programs receive about $1.6 billion of these allocations. The revenue for these appropriations is primarily derived from fees. The budget allocates about $8.7 billion from special and federal funds for transportation programs (this amount is supplemented by another $2 billion from the General Fund).

The balance of the budget, about $90 billion, is allocations from the General Fund. Table 1 summarizes the General Fund appropriations by major program area for 2005–06. By far, the legislature allocates the most General Fund revenue to education programs. K-12 schools (kindergarten through high school) received the largest appropriations, totaling about $35.0 billion. Funding for higher educa-tion (including the community colleges, the university systems, and financial aid)

Table 1
General Fund Appropriations, by Major Program Area
As Provided in Budget Act 2005–06
Dollars in Billions

K-12 Education	$35.0
Higher Education	10.2
Health	17.9
Social Services	9.3
Criminal Justice	9.7
All Other	7.9
Total	**$90.0**

Source: Legislative Analyst's Office, California Spending Plan 2005–06.

accounted for $10.2 billion. In total, education accounted for over half of all General Fund spending.

By receiving such a large share of the appropriations in the budget, education funding could be a ready target for reductions in years when the state must cut spending. Proposition 98, a constitutional initiative that guarantees K-12 schools and community colleges a minimum funding level, gives these schools some protection from cutbacks. The university systems and financial aid appropriations have no comparable constitutional protection, making them vulnerable to reductions. They are also vulnerable because the university systems could raise student fees to offset state cuts with new fee revenue.

Health programs received nearly $18 billion from the General Fund. Medi-Cal (local assistance), the state's biggest health program, received $13 billion from the General Fund in 2005–06. In addition, Controller Steve Westly and Governor Schwarzenegger are directing their auditors and law enforcement teams to target fraud within the Medi-Cal program, but neither expects to generate savings of even 5%. To reduce Medi-Cal costs beyond these efforts, the legislature would have to cut reimbursements to doctors, reduce services, or limit participation. Programs for the state's developmentally disabled will receive about $2.3 billion. The legislature appropriated $346 million to the Healthy Families Program, a program subsidizing health care to low-income families.

Social service programs received $9.3 billion from the General Fund. Of this, the supplemental security income program received about $3.5 billion for providing assistance to the poor, senior, and disabled. The CalWORKs program, providing assistance to families with children, received nearly $2.0 billion. The budget appropriated $1.4 billion to children's programs, including foster care, child welfare services, and adoptions assistance. The In-Home Supportive Services program, which assists home-bound people and provides an alternative to nursing home care, received $1.2 billion.

Criminal justice programs received $9.7 billion, primarily for the operation and maintenance of the state's prisons. The prison system has been chronically underfunded in recent years. To reduce costs substantially, the state would probably have to reduce or eliminate the length of prison terms.

The General Fund provides another $1.2 billion for discretionary city and county programs. All other General Fund spending—paying for parks, housing, arts, and general governmental functions—was about $5 billion.

The State Relies Heavily on the Income Tax to Pay for the State Spending

To finance the budget, the state levies taxes, fees, and other charges to generate over $100 billion annually. The state has over 1,000 funds into which it deposits the proceeds of these levies.[2] The largest fund, the General Fund, will receive over 70% of the proceeds of these levies in 2005–06. General Fund revenues are distinguished from all other revenues because they are levied on a wide cross-section of taxpayers and collected without statutory or constitutional limits on their use. As a consequence, the legislature has broad discretion to allocate the revenues to any state purpose. For example, General Fund revenues can be redirected from one program to another. When the legislature eliminated an entire state agency, the Technology, Trade and Commerce Agency in 2003, the savings were redirected to fill financial holes in other state agencies. Because of its volume relative to the other funds, and because the legislature has discretion in allocating them, General Fund revenues command the greatest legislative attention. Three taxes generated over three-quarters of all revenues: The income tax, sales tax and corporation tax. See Table 2 for details.

The single largest stream of state revenue is the personal income tax, and generates $43.6 billion (accounting for about 40 cents of every dollar collected by the state). Wages and salaries generate nearly three-quarters of all reported income. As displayed in Figure 2, other taxable sources are interest and dividends, rents and royalties, net capital gains and net business income, each accounting for about five percent of taxable income in 2002. Business income includes the distribution of profits from partnerships, sole proprietorships, and small corporations. Taxpayers may reduce their taxes if they qualify for and claim various tax deductions (reductions in the amount of taxable income) and credits (reductions in their computed tax).

The income tax system is progressive, which means that rates rise as incomes rise, from a low of 1% to a high of 9.3%. A progressive rate system ensures

---

[2] Department of Finance, "Deficiencies and Section 27.00 – General" *California's Budget Process* Sacramento, CA: Department of Finance. July 2003. 1

Table 2
Estimated State Revenues
General Fund and Special Fund, 2005–06
Dollars in Billions

	General Fund	Special Fund	Totals
Personal Income Tax	$ 42.9	$ .7	$ 43.6
Retail Sales and Use Tax	26.9	4.2	31.1
Corporation Tax	9.1		9.1
Motor Vehicle Fuel Tax		5.1	5.1
Minor Taxes	2.7	4.4	7.1
Regulatory Fees	.3	.8	1.1
Miscellaneous	3.0	9.0	12.0
Totals	**$84.9**	**$24.2**	**$109.1**

Source: Department of Finance.

Figure 2
Source of Taxable Income
2001 Tax Year

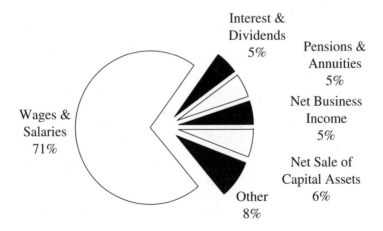

Interest & Dividends 5%

Pensions & Annuities 5%

Net Business Income 5%

Wages & Salaries 71%

Net Sale of Capital Assets 6%

Other 8%

Source: Franchise Tax Board

that taxpayers with higher incomes pay a larger share of their income in taxes than do taxpayers at lower income levels.

Because of the system's progressive tax structure and the distribution of income among taxpayers in the state, the income tax system derives a disproportionate amount of its revenue from a small portion of all taxpayers. This can be demonstrated by ranking the tax returns by tax liability. If the returns are ranked and divided into five equal groups (quintiles) of taxpayers, the tax liabilities for each quintile can be summed. The results of this ranking are displayed in Table 3. The quintile with the lowest amount of income had less than 1% of the tax liability. In fact, of the roughly 13.6 million full-year residents who filed personal income tax returns in 2001, 8 million returns (60%) generated less than 5% of the total tax liability. In contrast, the 20% of taxpayers with the highest incomes reported over 85% of all the income tax liability.

Within the top quintile, taxpayers with the top 10% of income paid 78% of the tax, while the top 5% paid 68% of the tax. The taxpayers with the top 1% of income paid nearly 50% of all the income tax in 2001. By paying for half the income tax, and therefore about one-fifth of all state revenue, the tax behavior of the top 1% of California's wealthiest taxpayers have a strong impact on state revenues. As the wealthiest taxpayers, they generate taxable income in ways where they have discretion about how they realize the income for tax purposes. They even often have discretion about which year they recognize their income for purposes of taxation. If these taxpayers change their tax behavior—or their residency—they can have a large impact on state revenues.

The second largest revenue source, the sales tax, accounts for $31.2 billion (28.5% of total revenue). It is levied on the final sales price of tangible personal property. The law exempts the retail sale of food for home preparation (as opposed to prepared meals), utilities, and prescription medicines. Twenty-seven percent of all sales tax revenue is collected from the sale of machinery and material consumed in the manufacture of consumer goods. That means, nearly three-quarters of all sales tax revenue is derived from retail transactions. The sale of automobiles and parts accounts for 20% of all the sales tax revenue. Transactions at department stores and drug stores generate about 10% of the revenue, as do transactions from restaurants and bars. Sales of building materials and business services account for about 5% each. Figure 3 displays the sources of sales tax revenue, by type of business. The state sales tax rate is typically 5.5% of the sales price, but may be reduced to 5.25% in a year after the state runs large General Fund budget surpluses.

Though retail sales can fall in recessions (sales tax volume fell in 1992 relative to the 1991 levels), the bigger uncertainty about the revenue performance of the sales tax is the long-term trend in consumer practices. In 1945, consumers spent over 65% of their income on goods. By 2002, they spent less than 45%.[3] The

---

[3] Ronald Snell. *New Realities in State Finance*. Denver, CO: National Conference of State Legislatures. 33

Table 3
Tax Liability, by Income Quintile
Listing of the Tax Liability, Tax Year 2001
Dollars in Billions

Returns Ordered By Income	Share of Taxpayers	Share of Tax	Tax Liability
Quintile with Highest Income	20%	85.3%	26.7%
Quintile with Second Highest Income	20%	10.6%	3.3%
Quintile with Third Highest Income	20%	3.3%	1.0%
Quintile with Fourth Highest Income	20%	0.7%	0.2%
Quintile with Lowest Income	20%	0.1%	0.0%

Source: Franchise Tax Board.

Figure 3
Source of Sales Tax Revenue, By Type of Business 2001

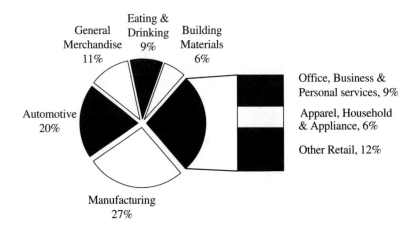

Source: Board of Equalization

economy was evenly split between the purchase of goods and services in the mid-1980s. Since then services have accounted for a greater share consumer spending. Because the sales tax is levied on the transfer of tangible goods, it will generate less revenue as Californians purchase an increasing amount of services instead of tangible goods. As a result, the sales tax base is not likely to expand as fast as the overall economy. Over time, the sales tax base will erode, causing the legislature to consider adjusting the sales tax base to increase the tax's productivity or supplementing the revenues of the sales tax with revenue from services.

Revenue derived from the Corporation Tax accounts for $9.1 billion, about 8.3% of total revenues. The law levies an 8.84% rate on corporate profits.

Motor vehicle fuel taxes are per-gallon levies primarily imposed on the sale of gasoline, diesel, and alternative fuels. The rates, 18-cents per gallon were set by the voters in a 1990 statewide referendum, and generate $5.1 billion (about 4.7% of total state revenues).

Minor revenues generate about $7.1 billion. They include the motor vehicle registration fees ($2.8 billion), insurance taxes ($2.3 billion), cigarette tax ($1 billion), and alcohol tax ($300 million) annually.

The regulatory taxes and fees generate $1.1 billion from the levies associated with particular industries and businesses.

Table 2 shows "miscellaneous revenues" collectively generating about $12 billion (11% of revenues). This total includes fees for services rendered by the state, interest on investment earnings (earnings derive from transactions when the state lends its excess cash to the market on a short-term basis), revenues transferred from local governments for state programs, and revenues from fines. Individually, none of these revenue streams are large.

State finances are highly dependent on the performance of the personal income and sales taxes. They account for about two-thirds of all revenue, and they are both sensitive to changes in the economy. When the economy expands, the income tax revenue tends to grow at a faster rate than the economy. As the economy slows, the income tax base can contract faster than the economy. As the economy heats up, the state can get an unsustainable boost in revenues. When the economy slows, those revenues are likely to fall. A challenge for the state is to use properly the changes in income tax revenue that result from economic cycles: When income tax revenues exceed economic performance, the state should probably use the revenue windfall for one-time investments. When the economy slows and revenues fall, the state may need to raise revenues or cut spending on a temporary basis.

How Is the Budget Put Together?

The constitution divides fiscal responsibility between the legislative and executive branches. This division requires that the branches collaborate. Indeed, from a practical perspective, if legislators are to budget successfully, they must understand the statutory requirements of the administration and the costs of financing departmental duties. For his part, Governor Schwarzenegger is responsible for ensuring that the administration meets the intent of the legislative appropriations and the statutory responsibilities.

Section 12 of Article IV of the State Constitution details the executive and legislative responsibilities. Paragraph (a) requires the Governor to submit annually a proposed budget, with an itemized statement of revenues and expenditures, to the legislature on or before January 10. To fulfill this responsibility—and to identify its priorities and challenges—the administration begins working on its January submission in the previous April. Prior to submitting the budget to the legislature, the Department of Finance requires departments to develop baseline estimates for their costs associated with maintaining current programs, and to document justifications for budget expansions or reductions. The constitution requires that when the governor submits the budget proposal in January, he or she place in bill format the recommended expenditures (that is, propose a budget bill with specific appropriations). To the extent that the executive recommends total expenditures in excess of estimated revenues for the year, the constitution requires the administration to recommend sources for additional revenues.

While it requires the governor to make recommendations for the budget in early January, the constitution reserves to the legislature the control of the submission, approval, and enforcement of budgets. The constitution does not direct the legislature about how to organize itself for review and development of the budget, making the legislative budget process a creature of legislative control and tradition. Statutory law and administrative practice define additional responsibilities for the executive entities, while legislative traditions and internal rules circumscribe how the legislature reviews and amends the bill. Though particular aspects of the annual legislative process vary from year to year, the process has taken on a rhythm and pattern over time.

In all, the legislature takes between six and eight months to pass the budget after the governor submits recommendations in January. Given the mix of constitutional requirements, statutory directives, and legislative custom, the legislative budget process can be confusing and maddeningly obscure. Figure 4 summarizes the key dates in the legislative budget process.

After the governor proposes the budget, the legislative analyst, the legislature's nonpartisan budget expert, begins a six-week review of the proposal. In mid-February, the analyst publishes two documents reviewing major aspects of the governor's proposal and providing context for the state's fiscal condition. *The Analysis of the Governor's Budget* describes the governor's spending plan, typically by department or agency. Often, the analyst will recommend the legislature modify or reject specific aspects of the governor's plan. The *Perspectives and Issues* provides a broader view of the budget, by discussing the underlying economy, revenue trends, expenditure trends, and major fiscal issues.

In March, each house of the legislature begins its public review of the budget by referring the governor's budget proposal to its budget committee, the specific committee charged with holding public hearings to review and amend the governor's budget proposal. To manage the vast amount of detail associated with the

Figure 4
Key Dates in the Legislative Budget Process

January 10	Constitutional deadline for governor to recommend a budget. The Department of Finance releases the *Governor's Budget* and the *Summary of the Governor's Budget*
Mid February	Legislative Analyst releases *The Analysis of the Budget*
Early March	Legislature begins hearings on budget
March 15	Statutory due date for corporations to file tax returns
April 15	Statutory due date for individuals to file tax returns
May 14	Statutory due date for governor to submit May Revisions
Early June	Budget conference committee begins
June 15	Constitutional deadline for legislature to pass budget
July 1	Fiscal year begins

budget items, each budget committee divides the work among four or five sub-committees. The subcommittees have jurisdiction over a broad range of related program areas. The Senate and Assembly have five subcommittees, each covering a broad programmatic area. For example, the Senate has subcommittees dealing with education (including higher education), natural resources (including resource stewardship and environmental protection), health and human services, public safety, and general government. The chair of the budget committee appoints the chair of each subcommittee and assigns legislative staff to support the work of the subcommittee.

During this public review period, the legislature can modify the governor's budget and insert its priorities. For example in 2001, Senator Peace, chair of the Senate budget committee, challenged the governor in public. On January 10, 2001, Governor Davis proposed an $82.9 billion budget, spending about 4% more than the previous budget. After the release of the budget, tax collections began to falter, failing well short of the governor's revenue assumptions. By February, it appeared that the budget would have to be lower than proposed by the governor. So, on March 2, Senator Peace convened a meeting of the full budget committee. Arguing that the state's economy was slowing and revenues would be lower than anticipated, he proposed that the full committee delete funding for all of the governor's new initiatives, saving about $2 billion. In the event the governor's revenue estimates proved accurate, Peace was confident that the Senate could find different ways to spend the $2 billion than had the governor.

When the subcommittees began their deliberations, some immediately restored the cuts made by the full committee. To keep the budget balanced, the subcommittees had to cut from other base programs to finance the augmentations. Most often, however, when the subcommittees did augment programs, they did as

Peace had predicted: They added to the budget to reflect their own, rather than the governor's, priorities.

But the 2001 budget was not typical. In most years, the legislative budget committees[4] start with the assumption of adopting the governor's budget as proposed in January. Making this assumption means that, if a subcommittee wants to deviate from the governor's January proposal, it must propose an amendment to what the governor recommends. Typically, the subcommittees hold at least one hearing per week between the beginning of March and the middle of May. Every budget item assigned to the subcommittee may be heard before the end of May at least once, but a hearing is not necessary. If a department is not heard by the subcommittee, its proposed budget is deemed adopted.

Before each hearing, the subcommittee staff write an analysis, referred to as an "agenda," describing any major proposals contained in the governor's budget. In the agenda the committee consultant may provide analysis of the budget and provide context for the proposal. The consultant may include issues raised by the analyst in the *The Analysis of the Governor's Budget,* or by members of the legislature and their staff. Typically, analyses are available at the hearing and on the two committees' websites after the hearing.

When the governor proposes a budget in January, he or she must make assumptions about how much revenue the state will collect over the next 18 months. These revenue estimates cannot be made with precision. This is in part because two of the state's major taxes are collected three months after the governor proposes a budget. The corporation tax, which accounts for about 10% of the General Fund revenue, is due on March 15. The income tax, due on April 15, accounts for about half General Fund revenue. After these two taxes are paid and the returns processed, the Department of Finance can re-estimate the revenues based on the actual collections. The governor releases the newer estimates on or before May 14, as required by statute. Since 1991, the new estimates have raised or lowered revenue expectations by as much as 7.5%, increasing or reducing the amount of money available to balance the budget. Figure 5 shows the change from December and May for selected years from 1991 through 2000.

At the same time that the governor revises the revenue estimates, he or she will adjust the January spending proposal to reflect the changes in likely revenues. In recent years, these new budget proposals, known collectively as the "May Revision," have contained significant changes to the January proposal. The subcommittees consider these proposals during the last two weeks of May. The budget subcommittees can complete their work as early as the third week of May (as they did in 2005), but typically work until the end of the month. Around May 31, they report their work to the full budget committee for consideration. After the full

---

[4] For anyone interested in advocating before the subcommittees, two guides may be of interest, see: Rachel Lodge, Rebecca Gonzales and Jean Ross, *Dollars and Democracy: an Advocate's Guide*, Sacramento, CA: California Budget Project, 2003, and California Senate Rules Committee, *The Budget Process: A Citizen's Guide to Participation* (Sacramento, CA: Senate Publications) November 2003.

Figure 5
Changes in Revenue Forecasts
Comparing December and May Forecasts
December and May 1991 to 2000 (Selected Years)

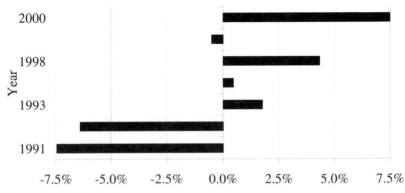

Source: Legislative Analyst

committee adopts the subcommittee reports, the budget bill is amended and referred to the floor for a vote by the full house.

The state constitution requires the budget bill be approved by a minimum of
two-thirds of the membership in each house. For the Senate, this means the bill
must garner 27 votes. The budget requires 54 votes for passage from the Assembly. The two versions of the budget will differ in significant ways from each other
and from the governor's proposal, as each version reflects different priorities and
interests. To resolve the differences, the houses convene a conference committee
consisting of three members from each house. Typically, each house appoints two
members from the majority party to serve.

The legislature's internal rules govern the conduct of conference committees.
They may consider only those provisions of a bill that were approved by one or
the other house. This rule is intended to prevent the conference committee from
developing a compromise that has not been considered and approved by at least
one of the houses. Two members from each house must approve the conference
committee before it is submitted to the houses for approval.

Once the conference committee develops a compromise, it amends a bill,
known as the conference committee report. The report is sent to each house simultaneously. The houses may not amend the report. If the house rejects the report, a
new conference committee, that is a conference committee with different membership, must be appointed.

The conference committee usually refers to each house a set of bills which make
statutory changes to implement the budget. This set of bills is known as "trailer
bills," as they "trail" the budget.

Though the constitution directs the legislature to pass the budget no later than June 15, there are no sanctions against the legislature for failure to meet the deadline. As displayed in Table 4, the legislature has not passed the budget by the deadline since 1986–87.

The governor may reduce or eliminate appropriations before signing the budget. The authority to reduce appropriations within the budget, often referred to as "line-item veto authority," lets the governor reduce or eliminate specific appropriations without requiring the veto of an entire budget. Governors have interpreted the authority, granted under Section 10 of Article IV of the state constitution, to authorize the veto or amendment of budget control language.[5] The legislature, by a two-thirds vote in each house, can restore funding (and presumably, language) with a subsequent vote (known as a "veto override"), but it has not done so since 1979. Consequently, the governor typically has the last word in appropriations levels contained in the budget bill. Table 5 displays the number and value of vetoes from 1991 through 2003, documenting the broad variation from year-to-year.

Shifting Fiscal Authority

Though the governor and the legislature must collaborate annually on the budget, conflicts often arise because of the very nature and purpose of the budget. Revenues are limited—even in a $100 billion budget—so some programs will be insufficiently funded, and some important programs will receive no funding. If the budget is to be balanced, the governor and legislature must agree to limit the amount of money spent. They must set priorities from among competing interests.

The institutional tension develops from the shared responsibility for crafting and managing the state's fiscal condition. Stark and divisive differences can rise because the legislature and governor lack consensus about how program performance should be evaluated and which programs have the greatest value. In this environment, conflict can be "endemic"[6] to the annual development, review, and adoption of the state budget. Within the executive branch, there are conflicts among programs and between the Department of Finance and agencies. Within the legislature, conflicts rise between the houses and between the political caucuses.

Though neither branch can act autonomously on major fiscal matters, the balance of control shifts between the branches over time. Sometimes the tension between the branches of government is so great it overrides partisan affinities, as was the Democrats' experience in 1999. After the 1998 election, Democrats held every statewide office and 60 percent of the Senate and the Assembly. Democrat

---

[5] Rebecca LaVally, *Money and Power: A Look at Proposed Budgeting Changes in the Taxpayer Protection Act of 1992.* Sacramento, CA: Senate Publications. March 1992, 18

[6] Rubin, *op. cit.*, 30

John Decker

Table 4
Date of Budget Passage
and Total Appropriations (General Fund and Special Funds)
1986 to 2005
Dollar in Billions

	Total Appropriations	Date Signed
1986–87	$ 38.1	6/12
1987–88	40.5	7/1
1988–89	44.6	6/30
1989–90	48.6	6/29
1990–91	51.4	7/28
1991–92	55.7	7/4
1992–93	57.0	8/29
1993–94	52.1	6/22
1994–95	57.5	7/4
1995–96	56.8	8/2
1996–97	61.5	7/8
1997–98	67.2	8/11
1998–99	71.9	8/11
1999–00	81.3	6/16
2000–01	99.4	6/22
2001–02	103.3	7/21
2002–03	98.9	9/1
2003–04	98.9	8/2
2004–05	105.3	7/31
2005–06	113.4	7/11

Source: Department of Finance.

Table 5
Number and Value of Governor's Vetoes
General Fund and All Funds
1991 through 2005
Dollars in Millions

	General Fund		All Funds	
	Number	Value	Number	Value
2005–06	40	$ 114.5	93	$ 319.7
2004–05	21	80.1	40	115.6
2003–04	11	1.01	19	47.20
2002–03	41	219.4	88	247.9
2001–02	109	498.9	170	658.3
2000–01	119	1008.7	181	1,794.2
1999–00	106	521.3	149	833.2
1998–99	113	1360.0	182	1,942.7
1997–98	43	298.4	103	336.8
1996–97	32	80.4	64	87.9
1995–96	8	2.1	65	166.5
1994–95	30	33.2	78	77.0
1993–94	28	3.8	85	32.2
1992–93	49	732.6	107	982.4
1991–92	40	76.7	84	193.5

Source: Department of Finance.

Gray Davis won election over his Republican challenger by a 20 percent margin. Despite these advantages, on June 20, 1999, Governor Davis—apparently out of frustration in dealing with the legislative Democrats over major issues such as health care and the budget[7]—told the editorial board of the *San Francisco Chronicle,* that "People expect government to reflect the vision I suggested. Nobody else in the legislature ran statewide. [The legislator's] job is to implement my vision. That is their job."

These comments stung the Democratic leadership in the legislature. Surely, they reasoned, the legislature has an independent role in developing the budget? Rather than merely acceding to the governor's ideas, the legislature should be consulted. After reading the governor's comments, each house deleted some of

---

[7] Robert B. Gunnison, "Davis Says He Calls All the Shots. Legislature's Job Is 'To Implement My Vision'" *San Francisco Chronicle,* June 21, 1999. A-1.

the governor's highest priority issues from the budget, including the governor's favorite tax proposal to exempt teachers' income from the personal income tax.

Recently, the executive branch has exerted greater control over spending and revenue decisions. In December 2003, the director of finance, Donna Arduin, notified the legislature that the administration would increase appropriations to immunize local governments for losses associated with a reduction in local revenues. Arduin contended that the $2.7 billion appropriation was consistent with statutory provisions delegating certain appropriations to the governor. Controller Steve Westly cut checks to the local governments for the higher reimbursement. However, the administration's actions appeared to the analyst to "represent a major revision to legislative policy" and therefore an impermissible use of delegated power. (Later in the year, the legislature adopted statutory language to do by statute what the governor had done by executive order.)

In another case, the administration raised taxes without a vote of the legislature. In 2003, the Vehicle License Fee (sometimes called the "car tax") was eliminated as a result of a court case. The Department of Motor Vehicles, which administers the tax, promulgated emergency regulations to re-impose the tax, at the rates in effect prior to the court decision. According to an analysis by the Assembly Budget Committee,[8] the Department of Motor Vehicles raised annual vehicle taxes by about $1.7 billion through this administrative regulation.

Though the executive seems to assert greater influence over fiscal policy than it did 10 years ago, this shift in fiscal influence may prove to be temporary if the legislature re-establishes its traditional and constitutional prerogatives. To make a more permanent change in the institutional balance, Governor Schwarzenegger advocated for the Live Within Our Means Act, which was considered by the voters as Proposition 76 in a statewide election on November 8, 2005. Though it was defeated by a wide margin, the act represents the governor's best ideas about how to improve the state's fiscal management.

The proposition would have made a number of broad changes to budget negotiations. Of particular relevance were those provisions granting the governor authority to reduce appropriations unilaterally. The governor would declare a "fiscal emergency" (resulting from budgeted revenues or reserves falling below estimates) and propose budget-balancing solutions. If the legislature did not pass legislation to act on the governor's proposal within 30 to 45 days, then the governor would have the power to reduce spending. In some ways, this authority to cut appropriations is like the governor's current authority to reduce appropriations at the time he or she signs the budget.

The proposition also would have authorized the governor to order changes in statutory law and contracts to implement these "emergency" reductions. Unlike anything in current practice, these provisions—if invoked—could allow the gov-

---

[8] Dan Rabovsky, *Concurrence in Senate Amendments, AB 1457*. June 18, 2004. 3

ernor to make changes in entitlement benefit levels, according to the legislative analyst.[9]

Despite the strong views expressed by its advocates and opponents during the election, it is not clear the proposition would actually have helped the state cope with difficult budgets. While the proposition would have given the governor authority to declare an "emergency" and make unilateral reductions, it did not *require* these actions. More fundamentally, the state's fiscal difficulties are not the product of a failed process and would not be changed by adoption of provisions like those contained Proposition 76. The state's fiscal problems result from the inherent difficulty of eliminating services now considered essential, or of raising taxes.

Budgeting and Governing

The state budget will continue to be a challenge for the governor and legislature. In November 2005, the legislative analyst estimated that for each year of the foreseeable future, state spending commitments will exceed the state's statutory tax streams. Cumulatively, and after accounting for the state's reserve requirements, these spending patterns generate a five-year deficit of $27 billion on June 30, 2011, for an annual operating deficit of between $5 billion and $6 billion

In looking at the 2005–06 baseline General Fund budget, the likely targets for spending reductions can be deduced. Assume that the state must fund its baseline allocations for K-14 schools, to the retirement systems, criminal justice, and debt. The balance of the budget—for the university systems, health, social services, resources and general government programs—will cost about $43 billion. If the state were to cut $6 billion from these programs, each area would have to be reduced by an average of 14%.

Where will the state face the greatest pressure to increase spending? Looking at future expenditure patterns, General Fund spending will rise from $90 billion in 2005–06 to $117 billion in 2010-11, a 5.4% annual growth rate. Most (84%) of the increased spending in 2010–11,will be attributable to four categories: K-14 schools, Health Programs, Social Services and bond debt payments. Figure 6 displays the relative effect of cost pressures by major program. It graphs the 2005 base and the estimated increase in 2010.

K-14 spending will grow the most, increasing from $36.2 billion in 2005–06 to $47.8 billion in the 2008–09, for a gain of $11.6 billion over the five years (a 5.7% annual growth rate). Neither the governor not the legislature are likely to relish cutting schools.

The Medi-Cal budget will increase from $13.0 billion to about $17.2 billion (a 5.8% annual increase). The increase reflects a growing Medi-Cal population and rising medical costs, but it does not reflect any programmatic expansions. To

---

[9] Legislative Analyst. *Proposition 76: Key Issues and Fiscal Effects.* Sacramento, CA: Legislative Analyst's Office. September 30, 2005.

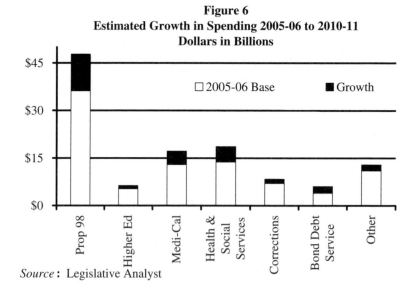

Figure 6
Estimated Growth in Spending 2005-06 to 2010-11
Dollars in Billions

Source : Legislative Analyst

reduce growth below the estimate, therefore, the legislature would have to reduce eligibility, reduce Medi-Cal reimbursement rates, eliminate services, shift costs to some other private or public entity, or find ways to increase efficiency in the provision of services.

Other health and social programs, including assistance for the developmentally disabled and the indigent, will grow from $13.8 billion to $18.7 billion (a 6.3 percent annual growth rate).

Costs for servicing the state's bond debt will rise from less than $4 billion in 2003–04 to over $6 billion in 2010–11, an average annual increase of over 9%. These increased debt costs are primarily the consequence of recent changes in the way the state finances its annual operating costs. Though the state can defer making its debt payments, it cannot erase them.

An alternative to spending reductions is tax increases. As the source of two-thirds of General Fund revenue, the income and sales taxes have the greatest potential for generating new revenue. Minor general taxes, such as the cigarette and alcoholic beverage tax, do not provide significant revenues to the state, so they are unlikely to be of much significance if the state were to use them for generating greater revenue. For example, even if the state were to double the "sin taxes" on alcohol and cigarettes, the change would generate less than $1 billion. Likewise, for the current fee-for-service programs: Even if it were practical to raise the fees, the amount of revenue raised would be less than $1 billion.

In the state's recent history, there have been limited tax increases. When faced with a budget deficit which he believed to be as high as $35 billion in 2002, Governor Davis proposed an $8.3 billion tax increase. His proposal raised the state sales tax rate by one cent for a revenue gain of $4.6 billion, income taxes on the state's wealthiest taxpayers for a revenue increase of $2.6 billion, and the cigarette taxes by $1.10 per pack for a $1.2 billion revenue gain. The legislature did not adopt Governor Davis's tax increase, though it accepted the smaller temporary tax increase negotiated by Senators Peace and Johannessen. Since 2002, the legislature has adopted legislation reducing tax shelters by $1 billion and suspended two tax credits for a temporary tax increase of $250 million. If the legislature and governor are unwilling to raise taxes permanently, they must find away to balance the budget by shifting costs or cutting programs.

A stable, long-term solution is elusive. The compromise crafted by Senators Peace and Johannessen (discussed at the beginning of this chapter) provided balance for a single year.

But the stakes are large. The annual budget negotiations are the state's primary means for setting priorities, providing essential services, and improving the quality of life in California. The choices made in the budget affect not only the current services and programs, but investments in the state's future schools, health and roads. Though the institutional differences can seem beyond bridging, the governor and legislature have in the past collaborated to provide for the state's current and future needs. When the executive and legislative branches work together to address the present unwieldy and difficult budget problem, they do more than balance accounts: they strengthen their ability to lead and to govern the state.

Suggested Sources

In addition to the books and articles cited in the footnotes, other sources for reading about the California budget include:

Annual Material Released about the California Budget

California Department of Finance. *Governor's Budget*. Sacramento, Calif.: Department of Finance.

California Department of Finance. *Budget Summary*. Sacramento, Calif.: Department of Finance.

California Legislative Analyst's Office. *Analysis of the Budget Bill*. Sacramento, Calif.: California Legislature.

California Legislative Analyst's Office. *Perspectives and Issues*. Sacramento, Calif.: California Legislature.

California Legislative Analyst's Office. *California's State Spending Plan*. Sacramento, Calif.: California Legislature.

California Legislative Analyst's Office. *California's Fiscal Outlook*. Sacramento, Calif.: California Legislature.

Other Material on Budget Issues and Policy

Angelides, Phil. November 2003. *California at the Fiscal Crossroads*. Sacramento, Calif.: State Treasurer's Office.

Angelides, Phil. April 1, 2004. *State of California Various Purpose General Obligation Bonds*. Sacramento, Calif.: State Treasurer's Office.

Angelides, Phil. October 2005. *Debt Affordability Report 2005*. Sacramento, Calif.: State Treasurer's Office.

Bowman, David, John W. Ellwood, Frank Neuhauser, and Eugene P. Smolensky. 1994. "Structural Deficit and the Long-Term Fiscal Condition of the State." *California Policy Choices*, ed. John J. Kirlin and Jeffrey I. Chapman. Los Angeles: University of Southern California.

Cain, Bruce E., and Roger G. Noll, eds. 1995. *Constitutional Reform in California*. Berkeley, Calif.: Institute of Governmental Studies Press.

California Budget Project. February 2004. *What Would Proposition 56 Mean for the State's Budget Process?* Sacramento, Calif.: California Budget Project.

California Budget Project. June 21, 2005. *Limiting the Future?* Sacramento, Calif.: California Budget Project.

California Citizens Budget Commission. 1995. *Reforming California's Budget Process*. Los Angeles: Center for Governmental Studies.

California Legislative Analyst's Office. May 2004. *Overview of the 2004–05 May Revision*. Sacramento, Calif.: California Legislature.

California State Controller's Office. June 25, 2003. *Expenditures Under a "No Budget" Situation.* Sacramento, Calif.: Controller's Office.

Ellwood, John W., ed. 1982. *Reductions in U.S. Domestic Spending.* New Brunswick, N.J.: Transaction Books.

Krolak, Richard. 1990. *California's Budget Dance.* Sacramento, Calif.: California Journal Press.

Meyers, Roy T., ed. 1999. *Handbook of Government Budgeting.* San Francisco, Calif.: Jossey-Bass Publishers.

Meyers, Roy T. 1994. *Strategic Budgeting.* Ann Arbor, Mich.: University of Michigan Press.

National Conference of State Legislatures. 1992. *Legislative Authority over the Enacted Budget.* Denver, Colo.: National Conference of State Legislatures.

Ruben, Irene S. 1997. The Politics of Public Budgeting: Getting and Spending, Borrowing and Balancing. Chatham, N.J.: Chatham House.

Schick, Allen. 1995. *The Federal Budget: Politics, Policy, Process.* Washington, D.C.: Brookings Institution.

Schick, Allen. 1990. *The Capacity to Budget.* Washington, D.C.: Urban Institute.

Schick, Allen. 1980. *The Federal Budget: Politics, Policy, Process.* Washington, D.C.: Urban Institute.

Snell, Ronald K. 1996. *State Provisions Addressing Late Budgets.* Denver, Colo.: National Conference of State Legislatures.

White, James, and Aaron Wildavsky. 1989. The Deficit and the Public Interest: The Search for Responsible Budgeting in the 1980s. Berkeley: University of California Press.

Wildavsky, Aaron, and Naomi Caiden. 2001. *The New Politics of the Budgetary Process.* New York: Addison Wesley Longman.

Internet Sites

Assembly Budget Committee: asm.ca.gov
Assembly Republican Fiscal Staff: asm.ca.gov
California Budget Project: cbp.org
California Department of Finance: dof.ca.gov
California Legislative Analyst's Office: lao.ca.gov
Public Policy Institute of California: ppic.org
Senate Budget and Fiscal Review Committee: sen.ca.gov
Senate Republican Fiscal Staff: sen.ca.gov

Chapter 3

California:
A Professional Legislature after Term Limits

Bruce Cain, Thad Kousser, and Karl Kurtz

In the 1960s, California was among the first states to convert its legislature into a full-time, professional body. Almost three decades later, it became one of the states pioneering legislative term limits. Aside from the fact that both trans-formations occurred through initiatives, they share little else in common. Proposition 1A, supported by leaders from both parties like Governor Pat Brown and gubernatorial candidate Ronald Reagan, was designed by Assembly Speaker Jess Unruh to modernize and strengthen the state's part-time legislature and, not incidentally, buttress his own power. It passed in 1966 by an overwhelming 75%–25% margin.[1] Proposition 140, designed by a politically disenchanted Los Angeles County Supervisor and by antitax activists, took aim at the Democratic houses and at the self-described "Ayatollah of the Assembly,"[2] the powerful, flamboyant and

---

[1] See Bell and Price (1980, 187–92) for a discussion of the initiative and Unruh's role in its passage.

[2] This quotation is cited in Anthony York, "Bedlam by the Bay," posted on Salon.com on August 5, 1999.

seemingly entrenched Speaker Willie Brown. The term limits campaign quickly polarized along party lines, and anti-Sacramento sentiment fueled by a long FBI corruption sting pushed the initiative to a slim 52%–48% victory.[3] Although it did not enjoy the consensus support among the state's leaders or voters that Proposition 1A had, Proposition 140 would soon transform California's Legislature just as dramatically as the professionalization movement had a quarter century before.

Even before term limits removed legislators from office, the initiative's effects on the legislature began to be felt. One of Proposition 140's other provisions mandated significant cuts in legislative expenditures, in order to remove "political staffers" and reduce "patronage" (according to the ballot statement of its backers). Instead of cutting the size of political staffs, the legislature essentially subverted the initiative's stated intent by eliminating funding for many nonpartisan experts. While overall staffing levels only declined by 12.5% from 1988 to 1996, professional organizations such as the Legislative Analyst's Office, the Senate Office of Research, and the (now defunct) Assembly Office of Research lost between 33% and 100% of their positions in the immediate wake of Prop. 140.[4] Since their futures in Sacramento were guaranteed to be if not nasty and brutish then certainly short, veteran legislators began to leave voluntarily, bringing a record number of special elections from 1991 to 1995. Those who remained faced short time horizons. They reacted by neglecting some of the less glorious legislative tasks such as oversight, as evidenced by sharp declines in the number of audits that they ordered and the number of requests for information on executive branch operations that they wrote into budgets. The 1995–1996 session, held on the eve of term limits implementation, featured a chaotic series of leadership battles as Willie Brown recruited a series of puppet speakers from the other side of the aisle to help him cling to power even as Republicans won a majority of Assembly seats. It finished with an end-of-session stalemate.

The bulk of our analysis of term limits begins in 1996, the first election in which Proposition 140 prevented many assembly members and senators from running for reelection.[5] Term limits opened up 22 of 80 Assembly seats and 12

---

[3] See Price (1992) for analysis of the Proposition 140 campaign generally.

[4] The overall staffing figures come from two surveys conducted by the National Conference of State Legislatures, and the numbers for California's three expert staffing organizations were obtained by our research assistant, Kelly Yang. This analysis and all of those that follow in the case study are explained in greater detail in our 2004 report prepared for the Public Policy Institute of California, titled *Adapting to Term Limits: Recent Experiences and New Directions*.

[5] Due to a renumbering of Senate seats after the 1990 redistricting and a seat switch with a political ally, Senate President Pro Tempore David Roberti earned himself the distinction of being the first legislator in the nation to be removed from office by term limits, in 1994. It was in 1996, though, that term limits took full effect.

of 40 Senate districts.[6] The new members who won them would only be allowed to compete for three two-year terms in the Assembly and two four-year Senate terms. They were free to move from one house to the other after completing their service, but once they reached their limit, they were banned from that house for life. Many of the termed-out assembly members indeed ran for the Senate, where veterans of both houses like John Burton, Ross Johnson, John Vasconcellos, and Byron Sher continued to exert great influence until November 2004. While a few senators moved in the opposite direction, the Assembly has been dominated by new members who never served before term limits.

These divergent patterns allow us to explore not only how term limits has changed Sacramento but why these changes occurred. One way that limiting terms can affect a legislature is by bringing in a flood of fresh but inexperienced members. Term limits can also influence legislative behavior by shifting legislators' incentives, shortening their time horizons. Senators about to be kicked out of Sacramento feel this most acutely. Differences between the two houses, as well as comparison with past legislative behavior and with trends in California's congressional delegation provide important lessons about the impact of term limits. Using both separate and combined house analyses, we explore Proposition 140's effects on the composition of California's Legislature, its internal institutions, and the policymaking process. We conclude by reporting how the legislature has sought to adapt to the profound changes brought by term limits.

I. Composition of the Legislature

One of the primary goals of the term limits movement was to change legislatures by repopulating them, not only with new members who brought fresh perspectives but with a new type of legislator. This new member would not be the typical career politician likely to be captured by bureaucrats and lobbyists, but instead would return us to the days of the citizen legislator.[7] The new breed could also be more diverse, as old, white, male incumbents were removed from office to open up opportunities to new groups. Increased turnover is a natural effect of term limits in a state where membership was highly stable, and Figure 1 shows that it has indeed been high since Proposition 140 went into full effect in 1996. But more important is examining the characteristics of new members to determine whether term limits has significantly altered the composition of California's Legislature.

---

[6] Assembly information taken from National Conference of State Legislatures (1999) and Senate figures taken from documents provided to us by the Secretary of the Senate's office.

[7] See Petracca (1991) for an example of this justification in the debate over term limits, and Cain and Levin (1999) for a review of the literature supporting and opposing term limits before their implementation.

Figure 1. Turnover Levels in California's Assembly and Senate

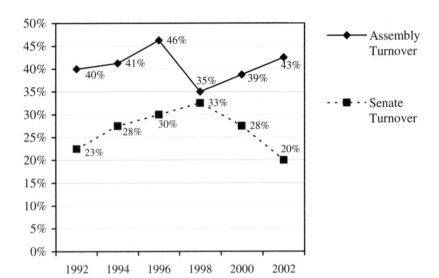

Note: Turnover levels report the percentage of new members after each election. Senate figures report turnover as a percentage of the entire body even though only half of senators are up for reelection in a given election. Data taken from Moncrief, Niemi, and Powell (in press).

A. Representation of Women and Minorities

At first glance, the most radical change that Proposition 140 appears to have brought to Sacramento has been the rapid increase in the number of women and minority legislators elected since 1990. *Los Angeles Times* reporter Eric Bailey reflected conventional wisdom when he explained that "There is no doubt that the law ... produced a statehouse more diverse in gender, ethnicity and professional background. The Legislature now looks 'more like California'" (Bailey 2004). It is undeniably true that today's legislature includes more women, Latinos, and Asian-Americans (though fewer African Americans) than the body did in 1990. Yet these changes may also be the results of demographic shifts, two rounds of redistricting, and the increasing electoral viability of female candidates.

As a statement of cause and effect, conventional wisdom deserves a closer look. In this section, we attempt to sort out the impact of term limits from other explanations of the recent increase in legislative diversity. Disentangling the effects of term limits from these trends is a difficult but not hopeless task. Much can be learned about the gains that women and minorities made by looking closely at their timing, the legislators who were replaced, and parallel patterns in California's congressional delegation.

Unlike most other term limits states, California has seen changes in the gender and ethnic composition of its legislature during the era of term limits passage and implementation. Figures 2 and 3 show that representation of Latinos and Asian Americans grew throughout the past decade as the number of white and black legislators declined. In 1990, white legislators held 69 of 80 Assembly seats and 34 of 40 Senate districts. These figures dropped to 54 and 27 after the 2002 elections, with the representation of minorities groups rising from 14% of all legislative seats to 33% over this period. Blacks held nine seats in the two houses when Prop. 140 was passed, but hold only six today. Increases in the number of Latino legislators in both houses and Asian Americans in the Assembly have indeed changed the face of California's Legislature. The percentage of Sacramento seats held by women has grown from 19% in 1990 to 29% in 2002.

The key question is whether term limits is responsible for these trends. In order to determine how much credit limits should get for the rise in women's representation, we present a historical look at the timing of victories by new female legislators in Figure 4. From 1972 to 1990, women's representation climbed slowly. An average of two new Assemblywomen were elected every two years and one new female senator every four years. Since 1990, this rate exploded to an average of eight new Assemblywomen per two-year cycle and five new women per four-year cycle in the Senate. Before attributing all of this increase to term limits, though, note the timing of the largest surge in women's representation. Figure 4 shows how much of this increase occurred as a result of the 1992 election, often dubbed the "Year of the Woman." Four years before Prop. 140 brought its first set of forced retirements, 15 women were newly elected to the two houses. National events likely increased the propensity of high quality female candidates to run, and the 1991 Special Masters' redistricting gave them the opportunity by creating many open seats.

Still, after dropping in 1994, the number of new female legislators grew sharply after the implementation of term limits, bringing in 28 new assemblywomen and 11 new female senators over three elections. Whom did they replace? From 1996 to 2001, 71% of new assemblywomen replaced a term-limited member, 25% replaced someone who ran for another office, and only one (Wilma Chan) defeated an incumbent. Contrast this to the 1990–1995 period, in which 23% beat an incumbent, 23% replaced an incumbent who retired or passed away, and 27% won a new seat created by redistricting. The remaining 27% replaced a member running for another office, probably in anticipation of term limits. Using this calculus, 18 of the 25 assemblywomen newly elected from 1990 to 1995 did not owe their victory to term limits, establishing a "natural rate" of increase in women's representation. Over the next three elections, 27 assemblywomen won seats that were directly or indirectly vacated due to term limits. Comparing these

Figure 2. Racial and Ethnic Composition of the California Assembly, 1990–2002

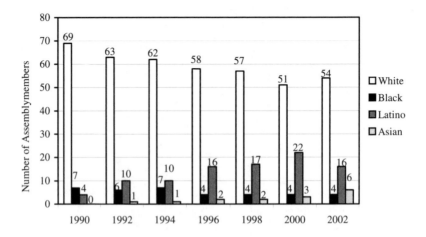

Data collected from appropriate editions of the *California Journal*'s Roster and Government Guide.

Figure 3. Racial and Ethnic Composition of the California Senate, 1990–2002

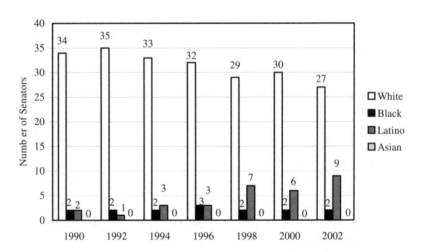

Data collected from appropriate editions of the *California Journal*'s Roster and Government Guide.

Figure 4. Women Newly Elected to Assembly and Senate, 1972–2001

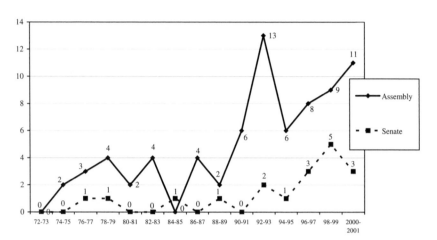

Data collected from Secretary of State's election records and the *California Journal*'s Roster and Government Guide by Kelly Yang and reported fully in Yang (2002b).

figures lets us estimate that nine Assembly seats were opened up to women by term limits over the course of three elections.[8]

A slightly different story can be told about minority representation in the legislature. Here, the dramatic increase in minority legislators was ultimately the product of underlying demographic change. California's Latino and Asian-American populations grew dramatically in the eighties and nineties. Since much of this growth came from immigration, there was a delay in the political implications of the growth as immigrants had to become naturalized and then mobilized into the political system. In a conscientious attempt to comply with the Voting Rights Act, the 1991 Special Masters' redistricting created many more "majority-minority" districts, districts in which Latinos, especially, constituted a majority of the voting age eligible population. From 1990 to 1995, primarily because of redistricting, 17 new minority assembly members and four new minority state senators were elected to office.[9] When term limits took effect

---

[8] Data for our analysis of newly elected women and minority legislators was published initially in Yang (2002).

[9] To count minority legislators, we first relied on directories that included photographs. While this was sufficient to count the number of black and Asian-American officials, gauging Latino representation is often difficult. We used supplemental information such as Latino caucus membership, official biographies, lists provided by ethnic organizations, and press coverage to make final determinations, and did not count those with Portuguese heritage as Latinos.

from 1996 to 2001, minority gains rose to 33 new members in the Assembly and 9 new minority senators.

Again, we look at the veterans these new members replaced in order to make an estimate of how much of the effect can be attributed to term limits. In the early 1990s, 11 of the 17 newly elected minority assembly members won their seats for reasons not linked to term limits, setting a natural rate. After term limits, 15% of new members beat an incumbent or replaced a retiree, but 85% (28 of 33) took seats opened up by term limits. By this measure, Proposition 140's implementation resulted in a boost of 17 new minority legislators. It is important to keep in mind, however, that term limits removed women and minority legislators even as they opened up seats for other women and minority candidates. During the nineties, 10 women and 19 minority legislators were termed out, and the loss of members like Willie Brown was costly for the influence and expertise of minority legislators.

The final way in which we seek to isolate the impact of term limits upon the composition of California's Legislature is by comparing trends in the Assembly and Senate to those in the state's congressional delegation. This comparison is particularly apt in California's case because of the size of its congressional delegation; currently at 53 members, it is in between the size of the state Senate and the Assembly. Members of Congress do not face term limits.10 As we have noted, from 1990 to 2000, the share of state legislative seats held by women grew from 19% to 29%. Over the same period, the percentage of California's U.S. House seats occupied by women rose from 7% to 31%, an analysis that does not even count the 1992 election of Senators Barbara Boxer and Dianne Feinstein. This suggests that term limits may not be responsible for any of the increase in women's representation.

Figure 5 shows that the number of minority members that the state has sent to Washington has grown, though the shift has not been as great as the changes brought to Sacramento. In 1990 and 2000, we compare the composition of California's population to the breakdown of its state and federal representatives. According to the 1990 census, 26% of Californians were "Hispanic." Only 6.7% of the state's members of the U.S. House and 5% of its state legislators were Latino. Asian and Pacific Islanders made up 9.3% of the population but held 4.4% of House seats and no state legislative districts. With 7% of the state's residents, blacks held 8.9% of U.S. House seats and 7.5% of Sacramento seats (State of California, Department of Finance 1999). Minority representatives did better competing for congressional districts than they did in state contests.

By the 2000 census, Hispanics accounted for 32.4% of the state's population, 11.5% of its congressional delegation, and 23.3% of its state legislators. Asian and Pacific Islanders had grown to 11.2% of residents, stalled at 3.8% of U.S. Representatives, but taken 5% of the seats in the legislature. Blacks, with

---

[10] Although Proposition 140 was intended to apply to California's congressional delegation, the U.S. Supreme court rules in its 1995 *U.S. Term Limits, Inc. v. Thornton* decision that states could not limit the terms of their federal representatives.

Figure 5. Racial and Ethnic Composition of California's Congressional Delegation, 1996–2002

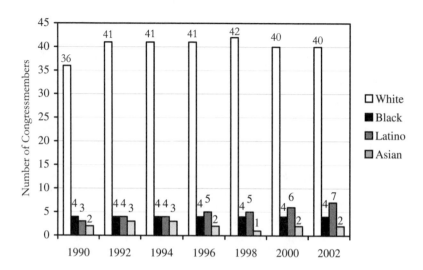

Data collected by Matt Tokeshi from the second through sixth editions of the *California Political Almanac, Congressional Quarterly's Who's Who in Congress* (2001), and *The Almanac of American Politics* (2004).

6.4% of the population, held 7.7% of congressional seats and 5% of state districts (State of California, Department of Finance 2000). For Latinos and Asians, whose numbers were rapidly growing over this period, term limits seem to have made seats in Sacramento more attainable than positions in Washington. Yet for blacks, whose share of the population shrank, term limits left the gains of the 1970s and 1980s vulnerable at a time when congressional seats provided safe havens.

Overall, term limits increased the turnover rate in the California Legislature. Where there was an underlying trend amplified by redistricting, the more rapid churning of officeholders created increased opportunities for demographic shifts to manifest themselves. This point is most clearly demonstrated by the dramatic increases in the Latino legislative caucus since 1990. Where there was no consistent trend, term limits by itself did not generate one, as evidenced by the case of female representation.

B. Changes in Partisan Composition

One hope that may have been in the minds of some term limits supporters in California was that in addition to fundamentally altering the democratic process, limits would diminish the fortunes of the Democratic Party. Yet while Willie Brown may be gone, his party remains in firm control of Sacramento. Table 1 demonstrates that the only recent lapse in Democratic control came before the implementation of term limits, when a nationwide "Republican Revolution" gave California Republicans a one-seat edge in the Assembly following the 1994 elections. After struggling to consolidate their leadership of the chamber for much of the session, Republicans surrendered control of the Assembly when term limits took effect in 1996. Since then, they have not seriously challenged the Democratic Party's majority. During each of the first three post-term limits elections, Democrats strengthened their control of both houses of the legislature.

Table 2 shows why term limits have not changed the aggregate partisanship of California's Legislature: switches in party control in any individual district are rare. In the 1992 elections, the first held after redistricting reshuffled members and districts, many seats changed hands in this game of political musical chairs. Republicans surged to capture nine Assembly seats and four Senate seats in the 1994 contests, but have captured only six districts during the four elections of the term limits era. Democrats picked up seats over this period, too, performing better in districts where nobody was termed out than in seats opened up by limits. In general, however, the vast majority of legislative districts in California are so politically safe that incumbency status is not needed to hold onto them. Members are typically replaced by someone from their own party when they are termed out, although the impact of partisan surges may be magnified in open seats. Again, the lesson seems to be that term limits accelerate existing trends but do not create representation patterns on their own.

C. Other Changes in Legislator Characteristics

In order to observe how term limits changed other characteristics of California legislators, we can compare the career histories of those who entered the Assembly and Senate during the 1980s with those of members first elected in the 1990s. The first lesson is that new members are on average younger in the term limits era than rookies were before Prop. 140 passed. The mean entry age dropped from 47 to 42.[11] This understates the shift in the average age of *all* legislators, since term limits has brought in far more of these new, young members. It also obscures an emerging difference between the ages of men and women, with

---

[11] Data on turnover and average ages of entry was collected by Liz Barge and initially published in "Term Limits Affect Legislative Career Paths," *Institute of Governmental Studies Public Affairs Report*, Vol. 42, No. 3, Fall 2001.

Table 1. Democratic Seat Share in the California Legislature Following Elections

Election	Assembly Percentage	Senate Percentage	Overall Percentage
1992	60%	58%	59%
1994	49	53	51
1996	55	60	58
1998	60	63	61
2000	63	65	64
2002	60	63	61

Table 2. Seats Changing Parties in the Legislature

	Assembly				Senate			
	Untermed		Termed		Untermed		Termed	
Election	D to R	R to D	D to R	R to D	D to R	R to D	D to R	R to D
1992*	13	15	*	*	4	1	*	*
1994*	9	1	*	*	4	0	*	*
1996	0	4	1	1	0	1	2	2
1998	0	3	0	1	0	1	0	0
2000	0	0	0	2	0	0	0	0
2002	0	0	2	0	0	1	1	0

Notes: Redistricting switched Assembly seat numbers in 1992 and Senate seat numbers in 1992 and 1994. Data collected by Annette Eaton from Barone and Cohen (2003), *Congressional Quarterly* (2001), *California Journal Press* (1997), and California Senate, Assembly, and Secretary of State websites, accessed in June, 2004 at http://www.sen.ca.gov/, http://www.assembly.ca.gov, and http://www.ss.ca.gov/elections/ elections.htm.

women more likely to enter the legislature at an older age after raising their families. Several female legislators we spoke to suggested that this created a difference in the perspectives of male and female legislators, influencing how they worked (i.e., giving women a less confrontational style) and their legislative interests (i.e., female legislators take more interest in family and education issues).

Another observation may surprise those who expected that term limits would bring a new sort of citizen legislator to Sacramento: namely, limits have not halted political careerism. The good news for term limits proponents is that the number of new members who were former legislative staffers dropped from

40% in the 1980 to 1990 period to 16% from 1991 to 2000. The bad news is that there was an increase in the number of local officeholders who ran for and won legislative seats in the post-term limits period. This proportion rose from 52% to 64%. In other words, local officeholders as well as amateurs from the private sector were the primary beneficiaries of the new opportunities that term limits created. Given the expense of running for office in California's large legislative districts, it was difficult for large numbers of inexperienced, nonwealthy candidates to succeed in winning legislative seats.

Finally, by tracking what legislators have done after term limits removed them from office, we see that most exiting members are still responding to reelection incentives or other political motives. In the term limits era, a political career is more dynamic in the sense that it requires changing offices more frequently. The modal career path now is from a local office (i.e., city council, board of supervisors, special district, school district, etc.) to the Assembly, then the Senate, and finally to higher office or to local government. While the number who go to local government is still small, it is a more commonly chosen path in the post-term limits era than before. Wherever termed-out legislators go, it is not back to the plow in the way that the admirers of Cincinnatus had hoped. In the first three elections after term limits were implemented, at least half of the assembly members who were termed out in 1996 ran for another office (Yang 2002a). Fully 95% of assembly members termed out in 2002 remained involved in politics, either by starting another campaign, being appointed to an administration post, or by becoming a registered lobbyist (Osborne 2004). California's Legislature has been composed of career politicians since Proposition 1A's professionalization made that type of occupation possible, and Proposition 140's term limits have done nothing to change this.

II. Institutions

A. Leaders

A major concern of many Proposition 140 opponents was that the shortness of the imposed limits would greatly weaken legislative leadership, eventually destroying the discipline and effectiveness of the California Legislature as a whole. As it turns out, the problem has proved to be particularly acute in the Assembly. With only six years of maximum service, Assembly leaders have very little time to prepare for, and even less time to hold, key legislative positions. Since limits took effect in 1996, the end of the first term limit cycle, there have been five Speakers, each serving for less than two years. Their tenure in office follows a regular cycle: it lasts for two budgets and an election. The Speaker is now retired by tradition before the last election of the Speaker's final term so that there is no conflict between the Speaker's role as chief fundraiser for the caucus and any personal fundraising he or she must do in order to get elected to another office. The choice of Fabian Nunez as speaker in 2004 is an important departure in the sense that he was elected Speaker in his first term, and thus will have a chance to serve for a longer period of time. Of course, the downside of this is that he is the least experienced Speaker in recent history, having served less than one term when chosen.

The situation in the Senate is far more stable. There have only been two president pro tempores since 1996. Moreover, since most of the new senators have served for at least a term in the Assembly and typically more, the Senate leaders to come will likely continue to have much more experience than the Assembly leaders. This experience differential puts the Assembly at a disadvantage in the "Big Five" negotiations, when the governor and the four leaders of the Republican and Democratic caucuses meet to hammer out the budget framework.

We see the same patterns by extending the analysis to the set of top leaders in each house (this includes the Speaker and president pro tempore, the Speaker pro tempore, floor leaders, caucus leaders, and whips). Table 3 reveals two important facts: leadership turnover is higher in the Assembly than in the Senate, but in most years there is significant leadership turnover in both houses. In and of itself, this would not bother term limit proponents since it was precisely the length and stability of Willie Brown's speakership that fueled their desire for reform. But even Republicans, who had by and large supported Proposition 140, told us in interviews that the inexperience and instability of leadership was a problem for both parties.

B. Committees

There has been an essential evisceration of the hearing process. . . . Nothing dies anymore, and there are no rules.—Former senator who served in the executive branch.[12]

Although nearly every legislator and Sacramento observer has a distinct theory about how committees have changed and why, the consensus is that the committee system has broken down, especially in the Assembly. But is there really evidence that committees have become less powerful? To verify this trend, and to explore what might be driving it, we collected records of how committees have treated thousands of randomly sampled bills over the past two decades. For a more complete discussion of our methods and findings, see Cain and Kousser (2004). The research design in this analysis —comparing matched sessions before and after term limits, and paying attention to Assembly vs. Senate differences—uses bill histories to examine trends in committee gatekeeping. "Gatekeeping" occurs when a committee does not pass a bill that is refer-

---

[12] Interview by authors, February 25, 2002.

Table 3. Turnover of Legislative Leaders

Election Year	Assembly Leadership Turnover	Senate Leadership Turnover
1992	2 of 6	3 of 7
1994	4 of 6	1 of 7
1996	6 of 9	5 of 7
1998	6 of 8	5 of 7
2000	6 of 8	2 of 7
2002	8 of 8	3 of 7

Note: Figures are taken from comparisons of leadership rosters reported in appropriate editions of the *California Journal*'s *Roster and Government Guide*, 1992 through 2004.

red to it, effectively killing the measure.[13] Because this opportunity to block the progress of legislation gives committee members the chance to control the Legislature's agenda in their policy domain, it is one of their key powers. The other significant privilege that committees are granted is the ability to shape bills by amending them. Committees do not monopolize this power, since floor amendments are in order and authors have the right to amend their own bills unilaterally at any point. Still, the most substantive amendments are usually made in California's legislative committees. Analyzing gatekeeping and amendments reveals how active committees have been in serving their traditional functions.

For each of the four committees in each house, we track the histories of 30 Assembly Bills assigned to the committee and 30 Senate Bills.[14] Over four sessions, our sample includes data on 1,888 randomly selected pieces of legislation.[15] We aggregate the actions of all of the committees in a given house here because they showed similar patterns. We simplify our presentation further by combining findings from the two pre-term limits sessions as well as the two post-term limits sessions, since the effect of term limits is quite constant over time. Levels of gatekeeping and amendment activity are similar in the 1979–80 and 1987–88 sessions, but shift in nearly identical ways from these years to the post-Prop. 140 sessions with which they are matched. Comparing separate de-

---

[13] Although there are procedures to discharge bills from California committees, they are used only in the rarest of cases.

[14] We took these histories from the appropriate editions of the printed *Assembly Final History* and *Senate Final History*, published by the California Legislature. Since the beginning of our analysis, these histories have been constructed from a uniform set of forms that committee staff fill out reporting the actions taken by committees, giving us confidence that figures are comparable across committees and over time.

[15] Over four sessions, four committees in two houses hearing at least 30 bills from each house might have combined to hear 1,920 bills. Our sample only includes 1,888 because some committees were assigned fewer than 30 bills from the other house in some sessions.

scriptions of each pair demonstrates this.[16] Since the actions of California committees appear to fall into pre-term limits and post-term limits patterns, this is how we present the data.

Table 4 demonstrates how often a committee's members exercise their gatekeeping powers. It combines Assembly and Senate data for each era (the 1979–80/1987–88 sessions before Prop. 140 passed, and the 1997–98/1999–00 sessions afterward), and includes bills heard in their house of origin as well as bills that have made it to the second house.

Committees killed 23.8% of the bills assigned to them in our pre-term limits sample, but only 16.5% after Prop. 140 took effect. In both eras, most of these failing bills died a silent death when supportive committee members, anticipating the preferences of their colleagues, did not ask for a vote on a bill,[17] and a handful of bills were withdrawn by a pessimistic author. The major lesson of this table is that regardless of their methods, committees exercise their gatekeeping power less frequently after term limits than before.

One reason that term limits may have weakened gatekeeping is that inexperienced legislators do not have the expertise to identify problematic legislation, and thus kill fewer bills. An alternative explanation of reduced gatekeeping might be that term limits makes legislators more likely to defer to a colleague because they feel less responsible for the long-term consequences of bad policy and more anxious to preserve their collegial relationships in the short term at any public cost. Comparing the actions of Assembly committees, whose members are inexperienced but have reasonably long time horizons, with Senate committees filled with veterans on their way out will give us some insight into these competing explanations. If inexperience is to blame for the decline in gatekeeping, the sharpest decline should be in the rookie-filled Assembly. If deference is at work, senators with short time horizons should account for the drop.

Table 5 shows that Assembly gatekeeping drastically decreased after term limits, but that the Senate gatekeeping decline, though statistically significant, was somewhat smaller. The sharpest drop in gatekeeping is for Assembly Bills heard in Assembly committees. Before term limits, assemblymembers killed 36.3% of their colleagues' proposals, but this proportion fell to 23.3% after Prop. 140. The overall decline in gatekeeping is smaller for the veteran Senate (6.2 percentage points) than it is in the Assembly (8.4). Senators today are nearly as tough as they were before term limits on the bills proposed by fellow senators (a 5.6 point drop that is not statistically significant), evidence that they are not placating their colleagues. The most dramatic drop in gatekeeping by Senate committees comes in their consideration of Assembly Bills (a 6.7 point, statistically signifi-

---

[16] See Enemark and Cross (2002), Abrams (2003), and Wong (2003).

[17] California Assembly committee rules require a committee member to make a motion to pass a bill and for one other committee member to second this motion, while the Senate only requires a single motion.

Table 4. How Often Do Committees Exercise Gatekeeping Power?

	Before Term Limits	After Term Limits
Bills Assigned to Committees	958	930
Bills Passing Committee	730	777
Bills Held in Committee or Failed Passage	213	141
Bills Withdrawn by Author	15	12
% of Bills Passing	76.2%	83.5%
% of Bills Dying	23.8%	16.5%

Figures based bill histories listed in appropriate editions of the Senate and Assembly Final Histories, collected by Dan Enemark, Drew Cross, Matt Abrams, and Christina Wong.

cant decline), which did not get a very thorough screening in Assembly policy committees either. The overall lesson, though, is the nearly universal drop in gatekeeping in both houses.

Committees now screen less legislation than they did before term limits, and while the biggest change has come in the Assembly, this trend is present in nearly every one of the categories examined in Table 5. There has not been a similarly large increase in the percentage of introduced bills that become law. So where does gatekeeping take place? Our data shows that policy committees have been replaced in their gatekeeping function to some extent by appropriations committees and to a larger extent by governors wielding their veto pens.

C. Staff and Lobbyists

The diminished experience of the legislators would matter less if it were offset by a more stable, well-trained, and experienced staff. There is evidence that staff are more formally, and thus possibly better trained as a result of the newly formed C.A.P.I.T.O.L. Institute (discussed in our conclusion), but there is less staff stability and experience. As before, the problems seem to be more severe in the Assembly than in the Senate. The high turnover among members in officeholding and on committees causes parallel staff turnover as staff follow their member to another committee and eventually to the other house.

Table 5. Gatekeeping in California's Policy Committees

When Committees from this House...	Hear Bills from this House...	Percentage of Bills that Fail in Committee	
		Before Term Limits	**After Term Limits**
Assembly	Assembly Bills	36.3%	23.3%
	Senate Bills	16.8%	12.4%
Senate	Senate Bills	28.9%	23.3%
	Assembly Bills	13.0%	6.3%
Overall	House of Origin Bills	32.6%	23.3%
	Other House Bills	14.9%	9.1%
	Assembly Committees	26.6%	18.2%
	Senate Committees	21.0%	14.8%
	Total	**23.8%**	**16.5%**

Figures based bill histories listed in appropriate editions of the Senate and Assembly Final Histories, collected by Dan Enemark, Drew Cross, Matt Abrams, and Christina Wong. Boldface indicates that the proportion of bills reported before term limits in any category differs from the proportion reported after term limits, at the 95% confidence level in a conventional test of significance.

In a study under our direction, Brokaw, Jobson, and Vercruyssen (2001) find that the average tenure of chief consultants to the Assembly's standing committees declined from 8.7 years to 4 years from 1989 to 2000, but staff tenures in the Senate rose from 5.3 years in 1990 to 7.8 years in 2000. Compounding the turnover problems, the legislature further weakened staff expertise by choosing to cut nonpartisan and policy staff in favor of political and personal staff.

When Prop. 140 mandated staff cuts, according to lobbyist Ken Emanuels, "The Assembly took that right out of their policy staff, and fired the experienced, expensive people, hired more, very inexperienced, very inexpensive staffers, and mostly campaign people. In the Senate, the old-time staffers, who have been around a while and understood the nuances, remained. And the difference is like night and day for us."[18] The Legislative Analyst's Office lost over half of its staff between 1990 and 1993, and the Assembly Office of Research was completely eliminated by 1996. By contrast, the Senate Office of Research experienced the least severe cuts among expert agencies.

The weakening of staff has forced members to be more dependent on outside groups for bill-drafting expertise. Newer members are less likely to have staff with "in the building" experience and more dependent on outside help. When asked to estimate what fraction of his bills were suggested by lobbyists and outside groups, one first-term legislator told us that he thought it was over 90% the first year, but then quickly added that he since added more experienced staff and reduced the number to 70%.

Disparities in the tenure of staff may also allow interest groups more influence in the Assembly. A Senate committee consultant thinks that lobbyists are the force behind bills more often in the Assembly than in the Senate, and an Assembly consultant concurred.[19] "For the majority of the committees, most legislation goes right over their head on the Assembly side," said lobbyist Ken Emanuels. "So that gives lobbyists plenty of opportunity to move very significant legislation, which is very poorly understood, at least through one house."[20] Interest group representatives are not uniformly thrilled with these developments, though. When healthcare lobbyist Beth Capell was asked if she works harder after term limits, she replied, "Yes, and I was one of the people that was foolhardy enough to predict that lobbyists would work harder for less result."[21] Strategist Donna Lucas noted one important obstacle: "Lobbyists used to know all the players; they'd been through it before. Now, there's a whole new set of players."[22]

---

[18] Remarks by Ken Emanuels, Emanuels and Associates, at "Ten Years into Term Limits: Academic Findings and the View from the Legislature," Institute of Governmental Studies Conference, Sacramento, California, May 17, 2001.

[19] Interviews by author, Sacramento, California, July 24, 2001.

[20] Remarks by Ken Emanuels, Emanuels and Associates, at "Ten Years into Term Limits: Academic Findings and the View from the Legislature," Institute of Governmental Studies Conference, Sacramento, California, May 17, 2001.

[21] Remarks by Beth Capell, Capell and Associates, at "Ten Years into Term Limits: Academic Findings and the View from the Legislature," Institute of Governmental Studies Conference, Sacramento, California, May 17, 2001. Proof of Capell's claim to have predicted this effect is provided in Capell (1996, 67): "This weakening of legislative structures will force most external players, including interest groups, to expend substantially greater resources for a return diminished in effectiveness and predictability." In this work, Capell also correctly anticipated a "rich get richer (p. 81)" effect, in which interest groups with many resources will prosper while the influence of most lobbyists wanes. Observers in many states have noted this phenomenon.

[22] Remarks by Donna Lucas, President and CEO, NCG Porter Novelli, at "Ten Years into Term Limits: Academic Findings and the View from the Legislature," Institute of Governmental Studies Conference, Sacramento, California, May 17, 2001.

III. Legislative Process

A. Partisanship and Civility

Partisanship continued to increase in the California Legislature after the passage of Proposition 140, and some have suggested that term limits is at fault. This idea is certainly plausible in the sense that since legislators do not serve together long enough to develop strong bonds, partisanship might flourish. In the words of one veteran senator, "The single biggest effect of term limits is increased partisanship. You don't know your colleagues well, and you don't treat them as part of your future. The new members are more like staff in their partisan attitude, and staffers have always been more vitriolic."[23] Other observers believe the problem resides with leadership. "These days, there is less of a long term relationship between those two party leaders, with a much lower percentage of bills passed on consent," observed a committee consultant.

However, is term limits really to blame? We looked for evidence of this in the following way: we compared the ideological extremism (measured by AFL-CIO labor vote scores) of new and veteran members in 1997 controlling for the party registration in their respective districts. The result was that the legislators' AFL-CIO scores were closely predicted by the party registration of their districts, and moreover, that this was as true of new as it was of veteran members. So the data did not support the idea that the new members coming in at the end of the first term limit cycle were more ideological than those going out. We also tracked members of the class of 1996 over their first three sessions, comparing their voting records to those of the class of 1986. The surviving members of both groups drifted to the extremes over their careers. Term limits, by shortening careers, seems to have halted a trend that would have polarized the body even further. Of course, voting records are not the only way to measure partisanship, which may manifest itself in other ways. But polarization in voting behavior is perhaps the most consequential expression of partisanship, and term limits did not increase it.

B. Balance of Power

> The governor will usually be an experienced politician and have more media exposure. Willie Brown could hold his own with [Gov. George] Deukmejian and [Gov. Pete] Wilson, but because leadership will turn over every few years, they are at a disadvantage. This adds to the power of a governor who already has constitutional powers.[24]— Legislative staff member who formerly worked in the executive branch.

---

[23] Interview by authors, Sacramento, California, 25 February 2002.

[24] Interview by authors, by telephone, August 2001.

On the budget, members will be much more interested in their pork after term limits, because they don't have time there to do something tangible on the bigger scale. They are much more susceptible to getting picked off with pork.[25]— Legislative staff member.

The most powerful weapon that California's Legislature possesses in its frequent battles with governors is its ability to tighten—or to loosen—the state's purse strings. As such, budget battles provide political scientists with ideal episodes to study relations between the two branches. The question is whether term limits has sharply curtailed the legislature's ability and/or willingness to rewrite the governor's budget proposals. Because legislators could make many consequential changes to a governor's education proposals without changing total spending in this area much, we look at budgets at the finest level of detail preserved in official documents: i.e., program requirement items. An ideal research strategy would record every item in a governor's budget and compare it with the amount that the legislature finally passed for that item. Since that was not feasible, we identified three key program areas to track over four budget cycles: health care, higher education, and business services.[26] What these areas have in common is that state officials exercise considerable discretion over their spending levels; they are not driven entirely by caseload shifts or governed by initiatives that tie the hands of policymakers. Both governors and the legislature have the ability to set expenditures at levels that reflect their preferences. These areas reflect some of the breadth of a state government's responsibilities and are supported by different constituencies and parties.

This analysis looks at four budgets written in the four comparable sessions that we introduced in our analysis of committees. Matching up the 1980–81 fiscal year budget with the 2000–2001 spending plan gives us the opportunity to observe legislative oversight during eras of unified government. Democratic-majority legislatures negotiated with Democrat Jerry Brown over the second budget of his second term in 1980 and with Democrat Gray Davis over the second budget of his first term in 2000. Both were written during years of significant fiscal expansion. General Fund spending in 1980–81 was 13.3% higher than in the previous fiscal year, whereas expenditures grew by 17.4% between the 1999–00 and the 2000–01

---

[25] Interview by authors, by telephone, August 2001.

[26] We define higher education programs as the University of California, Hastings College of Law, the California State University, the California Maritime Academy, California Community Colleges, and the Student Aid Commission. Health Care funding in California, under our definition, went toward the Emergency Medical Services Authority, the Office of Statewide Health Planning and Development, and the many programs of the Department of Health Services. Business Services covers the Department of Alcoholic Beverage Control, the Department of Corporations, and the Department of Economic and Business Development (which later became the Department of Commerce and then the Trade and Commerce Agency).

budgets.[27] Democrats also controlled both houses of the legislature when budgets for the 1987–88 and 1997–1998 fiscal years were written. California government was divided, though, in each of these sessions. Republican Governor George Deukmejian was beginning his second term in 1987 and Republican Pete Wilson neared the end of his second term in 1997. Spending growth was sluggish in both periods, with state spending rising by 4.8% in the first of these budgets and 7.7% in the second. These four cases give us two pairs of pre- and post-term limits budgets constructed under roughly similar political and fiscal circumstances.

Focusing on our three selected portions of the budget, we began by recording how much a governor proposed spending on a given budget item in January, and then noted how much the final appropriation deviated from this figure. Looking through appropriate editions of the governor's budget for each cycle, we recorded General Fund spending levels from many "Program Requirements" tables. For instance, Gov. Jerry Brown recommended spending $1,781,724 in General Fund[28] money on the Hastings College of Law's "Instruction Program" during the 1980–81 fiscal year. In the next fiscal year's budget, the final deal between the executive and legislative branches set spending on this item at $1,997,594. This change altered the executive proposal by 10.8% of its final value. It was added to all of the other changes made to the governor's higher education, health care, and business services budgets in order to compute the totals reported in Figure 6.

The effect of term limits on the legislature's budgeting power is stark. In both pairs of comparable cases, the legislature changes half as much of the governor's budget after term limits as it did before. The magnitude of this trend is the same under divided and unified government,[29] and represents billions of dollars in legislative discretion that is no longer exercised.

---

[27] Expenditure data is drawn from the Department of Finance's "Historical Data: General Fund Budget Summary" chart from the www.dof.ca.gov website. Note that although spending growth was strong in 1980–81, the state at this time was establishing a new fiscal relationship with local governments to counteract their revenue losses from Proposition 13. This led Gov. Brown to begin his budget message with "Today I submit a budget for difficult times." Tighter finances during this pre-term limits budget should result in the legislature making fewer changes in 1980–81 than during the flush year of 2000–01, biasing our results against finding that term limits has led to less legislative oversight of the budget.

[28] "General fund" refers to the portion of a state's coffers that does not come from federal grants or from specialized state funds that are often dedicated to specific purposes. Since it is the source of funding over which California officials exercise unfettered control, we generally analyze General Fund spending exclusively in this analysis. In order to study some policy areas over time, however, we did not differentiate when General Funds were replaced by discretionary sources such as university general purpose funds, the Alcohol Beverage Control Fund, or the State Corporations Fund.

[29] We should note that, counter to our intuition, changes made to the executive proposals are greater in eras of unified than divided government. This may be because these were also years of greater fiscal growth, giving the legislature a larger surplus to play with. It may also be yet another piece of evidence that the constitutional provision that

Figure 6. Declines in the Changes Made to the Governor's Budget

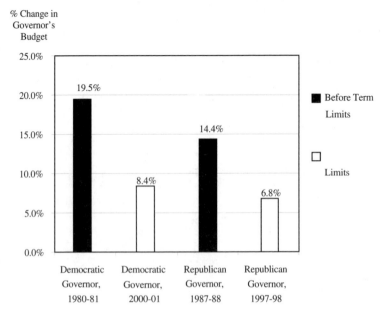

"% Changes" represents the ratio of the total line-by-line changes made by the Legislature to the total final appropriation levels in health care, higher education, and business services. Figures are taken from appropriate editions of the Governor's Budget.

Conclusion: Adapting to Term Limits

Given the high level of professionalism in the California Legislature and the drastic nature of the term limits imposed on it (i.e., comparatively short terms and lifetime bans), term limits should have had an effect in California if it had an effect anywhere. Clearly, that proved to be true. Leadership, the committee system, staff support and power *vis-à-vis* the governor have all diminished in measurable ways. But for better or worse?

Very few state legislators and staff we spoke to, including those who succeeded termed out incumbents and Republicans who had supported Proposition 140, believe that term limits has improved the legislature. Moreover, no one who cares about California government can be comforted by the fact that term

---

requires a two-thirds vote in each house to pass a budget gives the legislative minority a remarkably powerful voice. Democratic leaders most likely wished to alter dramatically the spending plans proposed by Republican governors Deukmejian and Wilson, but this inclination was tempered by the requirement that they compromise with their Republican counterparts in the legislature.

limits has weakened legislative effectiveness. Our assumption in this discussion is that voters did not seek to destroy legislative capacity when they approved Proposition 140 (though some pro-term limits activists explicitly sought to weaken legislatures). Rather, we think that they hoped for more turnover and for greater legislative competence at the same time.

To some extent, the legislature has naturally adapted to term limits. But for these adaptations, things might have been a lot worse. Consider, for instance, bicameralism's role in the post-term limits era. During the constitutional revision deliberations of the mid-nineties, there was serious discussion of reducing the legislature to one house. Bicameralism made sense, some argued, prior to the "one person, one vote" decisions in the sixties, because one house was based on equal population and the other on geographical units like counties in the so-called "federal model." But when the state Senate seats were changed to the same equal population standard used for Assembly districts, and especially when two Assembly seats were "nested" into one Senate seat under the two Special Masters' plans, there was little difference in the interests represented by the two houses. A study by David Brady and Brian Gaines found little difference in the voting patterns in the two California legislative houses after the reapportionment revolution. (Cain and Noll 1995) Moreover, conference committees that were assigned the task of reconciling different versions of bills passed in the two houses often became arenas for last minute legislative skullduggery. This led experienced legislators such as Lucy Killea and Barry Keene to conclude that either a unicameral legislature on the model of Nebraska or a parliamentary system such as in Britain would be preferable.

But term limits has given bicameralism a new reason for existence. The lower house is the entry point and the training ground for most new legislators, while the upper house serves as the more experienced counter-balance. Evidence of this can be found in the comparative experience levels of committee chairs and senior staff, and amendment activities in the two houses. This compensation (i.e., Senate experience offsetting Assembly turnover) was not planned or mandated by Proposition 140. It happened naturally as legislators pursued a logical career path from the Assembly to the Senate.

Another natural adaptation is that legislators have learned that they need to mix experienced (i.e., inside-the-building) staff with campaign loyalists. Those who filled their Sacramento offices with novices quickly found themselves at a disadvantage, relying heavily on lobbyists for expertise and guidance. But conventional wisdom soon corrected this flaw. Other staff compensations occurred by accident. For instance, we discovered evidence that inexperienced Senate committee chairs were often paired with more experienced committee staff. When we inquired as to whether this was a strategy of intentional compensation, we discovered that it was instead the artifact of less prestigious committees often having more stable staff (i.e., because there was less competition for these positions); hence when the newer senators got the less prestigious committees, they inherited more experienced staff.

But aside from these natural adaptations, what more can the legislature do to make itself effective under term limits? There are two possibilities: improved staff and member training, and alterations to California's term limit law.

There is no doubt that member turnover has led to greater staff turnover. Most staff in California are personally hired by the legislators and committee chairs whom they serve. As new members replace termed out incumbents, they bring new staff into the process. As they move from the Assembly to the Senate, legislators take their experienced staff with them, perpetuating the imbalance in experience between the two houses. This then results in a tendency for the Senate to override the Assembly on legislative matters (e.g., the asymmetry of amendment activity and the doubling of high-jacked Assembly Bills in the Senate noted in Cain and Kousser, 2004) and causes unnecessary tension between them. One solution is to mix more experienced staff with new staff as we have discussed. The Assembly might accomplish this through changes in personnel policies or salary levels. In recent years, this has also meant retaining a stable of experienced staff in the Assembly Speaker's office or in the Assembly majority staff. These experienced staff apparently shadow and monitor the less experienced committee and personal staffs.

The model of experienced staff advising less experienced legislators is one that many new legislators will be familiar with from their experience in local government. In the Unruh era, the concept of a professionalized staff meant nonpartisan policy staff, similar to the city manager model in local government. In the modern era, legislative staffers have become more partisan after the bipartisan legislative tradition broke down with the tax revolt of 1978. Short of some new consensus being forged, the legislature will likely continue building its experienced staff corps within the party caucuses. Still, the need for neutral expertise is apparent. Almost all of those we spoke to felt that the bill drafters in the legislative counsel and the policy specialists in the Legislative Analyst's Office had important functions in the term limits era.

However, the reality is that even with a determined effort to keep experienced staff, there will always be a lot of staff turnover. Hence, there needs to be an effective way to train new staff. Under Speaker Robert Hertzberg, the Assembly took steps in this direction by establishing its C.A.P.I.T.O.L. Training Institute (the California Assembly Program for Innovative Training and Orientation for the Legislature). Along with this program, Speaker Hertzberg developed manuals and documents that would make a permanent record of received legislative wisdom and practices. All of the staff and legislators we interviewed believed that this program was a welcome addition.

Legislators for the most part only attended the first couple of C.A.P.I.T.O.L. sessions. In those sessions, they learned the basics about how to set up a staff and deal with travel, facilities, and Assembly publications and resources. They got some process and ethics training, and heard presentations about the committees. The sessions also served as an opportunity for legislators to introduce themselves to one another. There were subsequent training sessions on bill writing and the budget, but it appears that legislators have a limited appetite for formal training sessions. For the most part, they would prefer to pick things up more informally from peer mentors.

A few of the legislators told us that they only attended the first few days of the C.A.P.I.T.O.L. Institute. One felt that the really valuable information about legislative tactics and how to deal with other members came from conversations with more senior members. Another, a Republican, felt that the Institute did nothing to overcome the forces of partisanship since "partisanship results from the issues not the presence or absence of personal bonds."

For staff, formal training is clearly very important and should be continued. Some of the current topics in the C.A.P.I.T.O.L. training include: the budget process, how to staff legislation, training to be a chief of staff, practical management issues, scheduling tips, constituent casework, and techniques for field representatives. The legislative and budgetary training are critical on the Assembly side. The more training staff have on these matters, the less the legislator's office as a whole must depend upon lobbyists and outsiders to provide expertise and knowledge.

One clear weakness in the training is in the area of oversight. As our earlier findings show, term limits have reduced the amount of oversight activity as measured by the number of budgetary supplemental requests for information from state agencies and by requests for Bureau of State Audit reports. The failure of the legislature to do effective oversight could result in more agency waste and less compliance with the intent of laws passed. One way to improve the legislature's oversight capacity would be to add more staff training in this area.

Finally, it is quite possible that California may need to consider some amendment to its term limits law in the future. The most promising proposal politically would be to define an overall legislative term limit equivalent to or slightly less than the effective overall limit that is currently 14 years, but allow members to serve it in one or both houses. This would allow some members to stay in the Assembly and assume leadership positions or develop policy expertise. If only a few of the members do this, it could help redress the current bicameral imbalance. Term limits are for the foreseeable future permanent, but they can be adjusted to improve legislative effectiveness.

References

Abrams, Matt. 2003. "Increased Amendments in California Make a Case For—or Against—Term Limits" *Institute of Governmental Studies Public Affairs Report,* Vol. 44, No. 1, Spring 2003.

Bailey, Eric. 2004. "Age Before Duty," *Los Angeles Times,* June 8, p. A1.

Barone, Michael, and Richard E. Cohen, eds. 2003. *The Almanac of American Politics 2004.* Washington, D.C.: National Journal Group.

Bell, Charles G., and Charles M. Price. 1980. *California Government Today: Politics of Reform.* Homewood, Ill.: The Dorsey Press.

Brady, David, and Brian Gaines. 1995. "A House Divided? Evaluating the Case for a Unicameral California Legislature," in *Constitutional Reform in California: Making State Government More Effective and Responsive,* ed. Bruce E. Cain and Roger G. Noll. Berkeley, Calif.: Institute of Governmental Studies Press.

Brokaw, Brian, Keith Jobson, and Paul Vercruyssen. 2001. "Knowledge and Power in the Post Term Limits Era: The Effects of Term Limits on Committee Chief Consultants in the California Legislature." Paper completed for UC Berkeley's PS 171: California Politics, Prof. Bruce Cain, Spring 2001.

Cain, Bruce E., and Marc Levin. 1999. Term Limits. *Annual Review of Political Science.* 2:163–88.

Cain, Bruce E., and Thad Kousser. 2004. *Adapting to Term Limits: Recent Experiences and New Directions.* San Francisco, Calif.: Public Policy Institute of California.

California Journal Press. 1997. *California Political Almanac, 1997–98, Sixth Edition.* Sacramento, Calif.: California Journal Press, and earlier editions.

California Journal Press. 2004. *Roster and Government Guide.* Sacramento, Calif.: Statenet, and earlier editions.

California Legislature, 2001. *Assembly Final History, 1999–2000 Session.* Sacramento, Calif.: California Legislature, and earlier editions.

California Legislature, 2001. *Senate Final History, 1999–2000 Session.* Sacramento, Calif.: California Legislature, and earlier editions.

Capell, Elizabeth A. 1996. "The Impact of Term Limits on the California Legislature: An Interest Group Perspective." In *Legislative Term Limits: Public Choice Perspectives,* ed. Bernard Grofman. Norwell, Mass.: Kluwer Academic Publishers.

Congressional Quarterly. 2001. *Who's Who in Congress 2001.* Washington, D.C.: CQ Press.

Davis, Gray. 2001. *Governor's Budget, 2001–2002.* Sacramento, Calif.: Department of Finance, and earlier editions.

Enemark, Dan, and John Cross. 2002. "Term Limits Have Changed California's Legislative Behavior." *Institute of Governmental Studies Public Affairs Report,* Vol. 43. No. 2, Summer.

Moncrief, Gary, Richard G. Niemi, and Linda W. Powell. Nd. "Time, Term Limits, and Turnover: Trends in Membership Turnover in U.S. State Legislatures." In press in *Legislative Studies Quarterly.*

National Conference of State Legislatures. 1999. Members Termed Out 1996–2000. Denver, Colo.: National Conference of State Legislatures.

Osborne, Nathan. 2004. "California's Termed-Out Legislators—Where Do They Go?" Paper completed for Political Science 102G: The Laws of Politics, UC San Diego, June.

Petracca, Mark. 1991. Pro: It's Time to Return to 'Citizen-Legislators.' *San Francisco Chronicle*, 26 March.

State of California, Department of Finance. 1999. Race/Ethnic Population Estimates: Components of Change for California Counties, July 1970–July 1990. Sacramento, Calif.: Department of Finance.

State of California, Department of Finance. 2003. Race/Ethnic Population Estimates: Components of Change for California Counties, April 1990 to April 2000. Sacramento, Calif.: Department of Finance.

Wong, Christina. 2003. "In California, the Governor has become the Legislative Gatekeeper." *Institute of Governmental Studies Public Affairs Report*, Vol. 44, No. 1, Spring.

Yang, Kelly. 2002a. *Percentage of Termed-Out Members Who Run for Other Office*. Institute of Governmental Studies Research Brief, April 9.

Yang, Kelly. 2002b. "Term Limits Get Too Much Credit for Boosting Female and Minority Representation." *Institute of Governmental Studies Public Affairs Report*, Vol. 43, No. 2, Summer.

Chapter 4

The Governor: Managing a Mega-State

John Jacobs and A. G. Block

The Office of Governor

The most important thing to understand about the governor of California is that he (so far it has always been a he) is the chief executive officer of a mega-state with nearly 36 million people and a $90 billion-plus annual budget that by itself is the fifth or sixth largest economy in the world. That very fact leads to the second most important thing to understand: by definition and under usual conditions, anyone elected governor of California automatically joins the short list of people routinely mentioned as potential candidates for president or vice president of the United States.

Republican Arnold Schwarzenegger, elected in an historic 2003 recall election that ousted incumbent Democrat Gray Davis, has temporarily changed California's presidential dynamic. Ambition aside, Schwarzenegger was born in Austria and therefore is precluded by the U.S. Constitution from serving as president or vice president. Once Schwarzenegger leaves office, however, California's governor will once again assume his or her place on the short list.

In the 10 national elections between 1948, when then-Governor Earl Warren was GOP nominee Thomas Dewey's vice presidential running mate, and 1984, when former Governor Ronald Reagan sought his second term as president, Californians were on the national ballot every year but 1964 and 1976.

Besides Warren and Reagan, California native son Richard Nixon was on the ballot five times, twice for vice president in 1952 and 1956 and three times for president, a 1960 race he lost to John F. Kennedy, and successful presidential bids in 1968 and 1972.

Governor Jerry Brown ran for president three times without gaining his party's nomination, in 1976, 1980, and 1992, and Governor Pete Wilson ran for his party's 1996 nomination but was forced to withdraw early. Since Reagan, only one governor—Republican George Deukmejian—was resolutely not interested in higher office. Vice President George Bush wanted Deukmejian as his running mate for 1988—knowing that Deukmejian could help bring home California's huge trove of electoral votes and thus help ensure Bush's election—but Deukmejian turned Bush down. He was afraid to turn control of the state over to Leo McCarthy. A Democrat, McCarthy was the lieutenant governor who would have succeeded Deukmejian if he were elected.

Even Schwarzenegger is said to harbor national ambitions despite the legal barrier. During his first year in office, for instance, there were rumblings about trying to amend the U.S. Constitution to allow the European-born governor to run for president. Although the notion received a polite nod from Republicans who control the Congress in Washington, no effort was made to elevate the idea beyond the status of cocktail party chit chat.

This history is relevant for understanding how important and desirable being governor of California is in American politics. Short of running for the presidency itself, which usually requires a multi-year marathon of human endurance and a mastery of modern media politics, running for governor of California is probably the next hardest campaign to wage. It requires the steely discipline to raise prodigious amounts of campaign money—the 2002 campaign between Democratic Governor Gray Davis and Republican challenger Bill Simon saw the two candidates spend more than $100 million—and successfully navigate the state's many media markets via television advertising, and events designed to produce "free media" or newspaper, radio, and television coverage.

In a state where it is impossible to meet more than a relative handful of residents one-on-one, those who succeed must be able to fashion various campaign themes into a memorable "message" that drives campaign coverage and enables even the most inattentive voters to figure out fairly quickly who a candidate is, why that candidate is running for governor, and what he or she would do if elected. Indeed, Republican incumbent Pete Wilson's success over Democratic challenger Kathleen Brown in 1994 was due in large part to his ability to seize the agenda from the beginning and frame his campaign message around two big and harshly polarizing themes: crime, for which he supported a popular "three strikes" initiative to put repeat felons away for long periods, and illegal immigration, which translated into support for Proposition 187, another popular ballot measure that would deny health and education benefits to illegal immigrants. Brown was unable to frame a coherent message or rationale for her candidacy or drive Wilson off his message. Consequently, he overcame a 24-point deficit in the polls and defeated her by 14 points.

Although Wilson could not subsequently translate these formidable political skills into a successful presidential run the following year, those who succeed in California political wars often have a leg up on candidates from smaller states whose paths to power are less rigorous. California is so geographically and sociologically diverse—from conservative farm communities to upscale environmentalist coastal enclaves, from multi-ethnic inner-city neighborhoods, barrios, and "Little Saigons" to prosperous largely white suburbs, from rural mountain towns to prickly working-class reservoirs of rage and resentment—that fashioning a majority here is good preparation for a national campaign. Because of the great distances and diversity, television advertising—and the money to buy it—is by far the most important component of any successful statewide campaign. As Democratic political consultant Robert Shrum once said, "A political rally in California is three people gathered around a television set."

More than any one thing, the governor's office is what the occupant makes of it. The most successful modern-age governors understand the limitations of the office—a permanent bureaucracy that is slow to move; a state budget, much of which is driven by successful ballot initiatives and beyond a governor's ability to influence; an often hostile legislature with its own priorities—and still manage to achieve their goals. Effective governors like Wilson, Reagan, or Pat Brown—Jerry and Kathleen Brown's father—figured out what others wanted and wove those desires together with what they wanted, often through hard bargaining and legislative compromise. In doing so, they satisfied the constituencies that put them in office. Less effective governors such as Jerry Brown, Deukmejian, and Davis rarely engaged in what is often down and dirty bargaining, or took the time to understand how to maneuver interest groups and other political forces into seeing things their way, let alone give them something in return. These governors had little interest in anybody else's agenda. While they achieved some of their policy goals early in their first terms, they could not sustain success over eight years.

Davis, in fact, was recalled less than a year into his second term, and part of the reason was his failure to build effective bridges to Democratic lawmakers and other power centers that may have rallied to him once the recall movement gained momentum during the spring and summer of 2003.

Terms and Structures of the Governor's Office

The governor of California is elected every four years in even-numbered "nonpresidential" years. Nominees are selected in expensive and often hotly contested Democratic and Republican primaries earlier in the year, usually in June. Smaller political parties have primaries at the same time, but no third-party candidate for governor has achieved any significant portion of the vote in many years. Until 1990, governors could serve an unlimited number of terms, although Earl Warren was the only governor ever elected three times (Governor Pat Brown sought a third term in 1966 but was defeated by Ronald Reagan). With

the passage of Proposition 140 in 1990, which imposed term limits on state constitutional officers and state legislators, governors can serve no more than two
terms.

Republican Goodwin Knight, who as lieutenant governor became governor
when Warren was named chief justice of the U.S. Supreme Court in 1953,
served out the remainder of Warren's term and was elected on his own in 1954.
He might have been re-elected to a third term in 1958, but fellow Republican
William F. Knowland, a powerful U.S. senator and publisher of the *Oakland
Tribune*, decided he wanted to use the governorship as a stepping-stone to the
presidency. Knowland had enough muscle to force Knight into a controversial
job swap, but voters rejected both men. Since Knight's ill-fated move and with
the exception of the current incumbent, every governor of California—Edmund
"Pat" Brown, Ronald Reagan, Jerry Brown, George Deukmejian, Pete Wilson,
and Gray Davis—has been elected to a second term. Davis, of course, was recalled a year into that term and his successor, Arnold Schwarzenegger, must run
for a second term in 2006.

A candidate for governor must be 18 years old, a U.S. citizen, and a resident
of California for five years immediately preceding the election. Of the state's
recent governors, only Pat Brown and Jerry Brown are native-born (Wilson and
Reagan are from Illinois, Deukmejian and Davis from New York, and Schwarzenegger from Austria). The governor, whose annual salary is $175,000, is the
commander-in-chief of the state's militia and the sole official organ of communication between the government of California, other states, and the federal government. The governor can appoint someone to fill a vacancy in any of the
state's other constitutional offices—lieutenant governor, secretary of state, attorney general, treasurer, controller, superintendent of public instruction, and
state board of equalization—subject to confirmation by a majority in both
houses of the legislature. If there is a vacancy in the office of governor, the state
constitution requires that it be filled by the lieutenant governor, who serves as
acting governor when the governor leaves the state, is temporarily disabled, or is
impeached. Eight lieutenant governors have moved up to become governor, the
most recent being Davis, who was elected lieutenant governor in 1994 and governor in 1998. His ascension ended a 45-year drought for lieutenant governors,
because not since Knight in 1953 had number two been elevated to the top job.

Davis also was the first governor in 20 years to have a lieutenant governor
from the same party when Democrat Cruz Bustamante—a former Assembly
speaker—was elected to the second spot in 1998. The Davis-Bustamante "team"
ended two decades of split partisanship at the top—a run that began in 1978
when Republican Mike Curb was elected to the lesser office while Jerry Brown
was re-elected governor. Because Brown spent so much time out of state campaigning for president, Curb was often acting governor. On several occasions,
Curb appointed Republican judges in Brown's absence and made other decisions
that Brown quickly countermanded on his return. Curb was heavily criticized for
his childish behavior, which likely contributed to Deukmejian's victory over
him in the 1982 gubernatorial primary.

Deukmejian had to share his gubernatorial stage with a Democratic lieutenant governor, Leo McCarthy, who served three terms and whose presence, as noted, made Deukmejian reluctant to accept any offer from George H. W. Bush to be his running mate. McCarthy's successor was Davis, who found himself in the same position in 1995 that Curb had been in 1979–80. Governor Wilson was busy campaigning for president out of state, leaving Davis as acting governor. Indeed, Wilson's failure to keep his promise to serve a full term as governor if re-elected in 1994, and the certainty that Democrat Davis would succeed Wilson as governor if he won, angered many Californians. His broken pledge severely damaged Wilson's fundraising efforts and ultimately his campaign.

Ironically, Davis had been Jerry Brown's chief of staff while Curb was lieutenant governor. Having seen first hand how Curb's antics blew up in his face and probably cost him his political career, Davis was careful to pull no such stunts, even though Wilson administration officials often treated him with contempt. At one point, the Wilsonites tried to force Davis to vacate his own office in the state Capitol so that the governor's staff would have room to expand, and they often gave Davis no advance notice when Wilson left the state.

Not that his treatment by Wilson tempered Davis after he became governor. His relationship with Bustamante can best be described as "chilly," even though both were from the same party. By virtue of style and temperament, Davis kept his own counsel, mostly ignoring Bustamante on issues and matters of governance.

For all these reasons—and the accompanying tensions between governor and lieutenant governor—many reformers and advocates of constitutional revision recommend that the governor and lieutenant governor be required to run as a ticket, as the presidential and vice presidential candidates do. Having both candidates from the same party would simplify things if a governor decided to seek higher office or accept a presidential appointment, although—as the Davis-Bustamante relationship demonstrated—not necessarily create a framework for cooperation.

Every governor of the modern era has been a white male and most have been Republicans. Tom Bradley, the African-American mayor of Los Angeles, was nearly elected governor in 1982, but in the closest election of the 20th century, Deukmejian, the state's first Armenian-American governor, beat him by some six-tenths of one percent, less than three votes per precinct. Deukmejian easily defeated Bradley again in 1986. In 1990, former San Francisco Mayor Dianne Feinstein sought to become the state's first female (and Jewish) governor and led Wilson in polls for most of the spring and summer, but Wilson eventually prevailed and, as noted, defeated Kathleen Brown four years later. Pat Brown was only the second Democrat of the century to be elected governor in 1958 (the first, Culbert Olson, served one term from 1938–42). Jerry Brown was the third and Davis the fourth.

The Powers of the Governor

As the chief executive officer for the state, the governor sets policy and through executive orders, jawboning and, if possible, a loyal and competent team of political appointees, directs the state's bureaucracy to implement it. The state constitution requires that the governor submit a state budget within the first 12 days of each new year. By custom, the governor reports to the legislature in his annual "State of the State" address, usually in the first week of January. The governor also controls hundreds of appointments to top state jobs and thousands of judicial appointments.

Aside from developing the budget, his most important policy document, the governor signs or vetoes legislation approved by both the state Assembly and Senate. The "line item veto" allows a governor to delete or "blue pencil" specific spending items from larger bills. This gives him important leverage in crafting legislation more in keeping with his own policies and priorities. A governor cannot add money to a bill only subtract it. The legislature can override a governor's veto with a two-thirds vote of both houses. Such overrides tend to be rare. Governor Deukmejian reportedly made a deal with Assembly Republicans that he would veto any bill they disliked (they were in the minority), as long as they never voted with the Democrats to override him. They never did.

Democratic Governors Pat and Jerry Brown enjoyed Democratic legislative majorities in both the Assembly and Senate, which often made their jobs easier. But tensions can develop between members of the same party, as they did between Pat Brown and the legendary Speaker Jesse Unruh, who thought Brown had promised him an open shot for governor in 1966, only to discover that Brown was planning to run a third time. This dispute led to huge problems in the 1965–66 legislative session. A decade later, Jerry Brown spent so much time either running for president or ignoring fellow Democrats in the legislature that they had little use for him or his various agendas.

Davis, too, was often at odds with fellow Democrats who controlled both houses of the legislature. Although his secretive ways and tendency to micromanage every facet of his administration frustrated lawmakers, his overall relationship with them was soured early in his tenure by the governor's comment that the legislature's job was to "implement my vision."

None of the modern Republican governors—Reagan, Deukmejian, Wilson, or Schwarzenegger—ever governed with a Republican majority in both houses. Deukmejian and Wilson were saddled with an especially troublesome and skilled adversary in Democratic Assembly Speaker Willie Brown, the second most powerful elected official in the state. Brown, who set a record for longevity by keeping the speakership for 15 years, often did business with Deukmejian and Wilson but never without extracting major concessions for his party, for special interests who helped to finance his Assembly majority, or for his urban constituents in San Francisco.

Schwarzenegger, on the other hand, developed a love-hate relationship with the legislature during his first two years in office, cooperating with Democratic lawmakers in 2004 on such issues as workers compensation reform and bond measures designed to bailout a massive budget deficit. But that rapport soured in 2005 when Schwarzenegger sought to bypass the legislature altogether by calling a special November election and backing four ballot initiatives aimed at curtailing legislative power and shrinking the influence of the Democrats' labor allies. All four measures were defeated, and Schwarzenegger signaled a more conciliatory tone for 2006.

Even with a hostile legislature, governors are armed with enough carrots and sticks to get much of what they want. Legislators of both parties want their bills signed or friends appointed to various boards, commissions, or judgeships. Some, especially those facing term limits, would like appointments for themselves once their legislative careers are over or near their end. Governors are usually party leaders, a fact that makes legislators of the same party reluctant to cross them. If they do, they may find themselves having major problems with campaign contributors or other party elites. Many legislators want to socialize with the governor, be seen as a "friend" of the administration, or have the governor raise campaign money for them from his own political supporters or appear at a fundraiser in the member's district.

Despite these formal and informal powers, the governor's most important source of power is the bully pulpit, the platform the governor has to set the political and policy agenda for the state and to command attention from media, state legislators, and elites. Governor Wilson argued convincingly that the electronic media has become so disengaged from covering state politics and government that his job was harder than in the days of Ronald Reagan and Jerry Brown, when most Los Angeles and San Francisco television stations had permanent news bureaus in Sacramento. All Reagan or Brown had to do was call a press conference, and TV stations from the state's major media markets were on site to cover it. Davis also suffered from this kind of self-imposed blackout by TV stations. During the "dark years," television crews not based in Sacramento parachuted into the capital for "events," such as release of the annual budget. When Wilson or Davis had big news to break, they often traveled to Los Angeles and selected some scenic vista or dramatic backdrop in hopes that would be enough to draw TV cameras.

That ennui ended in 2003 when Arnold Schwarzenegger became governor—not because television suddenly regained its interest in state government but because Schwarzenegger's international celebrity focused a broad spotlight on Sacramento. Reporters representing European and Asian outlets joined a growing array of domestic journalists in covering the new governor, so much so that the standard briefing room (Capitol Room 1190) no longer could accommodate gubernatorial press conferences, which moved to an auditorium a block from the Capitol. Unlike Wilson or Davis, Schwarzenegger could command worldwide attention simply by showing up for a routine briefing.

As a result, TV returned to Sacramento on a more or less permanent basis as several stations from Los Angeles and the San Francisco Bay Area joined to form and staff a capital bureau, thus sharing the expense of covering the governor.

"The office has tremendous potential to achieve and concentrate power in the hands of a strong executive," said Joseph Shumate, a Republican political consultant who served as one of Governor Wilson's deputy chiefs of staff during his first term. "But you have to understand the process, you have to have an agenda, you have to have an administrative way of imposing your will and consistency of purpose. Otherwise you get lost."[1]

Added Dan Schnur, a former communications director for Wilson, "A good executive takes power until someone stops him. Like a president, a governor has prescribed constitutional powers. His real power comes from stature and position."[2]

Another source of extraordinary potential power—or peril—for a governor is how he handles disasters. A state such as California is constantly experiencing all sorts of natural or man-made disasters or emergencies, whether earthquakes, fires, floods, droughts, infestations, or riots. Gubernatorial candidate Ronald Reagan capitalized on two major social problems to hammer Governor Pat Brown's performance in handling student unrest at the University of California at Berkeley in the mid-1960s and the 1965 riots in Watts. Governor Jerry Brown's reluctance late in his second term to order the use of aerial spraying in residential neighborhoods of the pesticide malathion to combat the dreaded Mediterranean fruit fly—which posed a major risk to the state's $15 billion a year agricultural industry—angered many whose livelihoods depended on a vibrant farm economy. By the time Brown did order aerial spraying, much of the political damage had been done. His temporizing became an issue a few years later when Brown ran unsuccessfully for the U.S. Senate.

Wilson was able successfully to exploit a series of earthquakes and natural disasters in his uphill re-election effort. The Northridge earthquake in southern California early in 1994 gave Wilson the chance to show executive leadership and decision making and dominate the TV airwaves in Los Angeles for several weeks. Subsequent fires in Malibu and floods in the north allowed him to put his disaster jacket back on and display on television his "concern" for state residents. These events provided the impetus for his long climb back in the polls.

Ironically, Davis's finest moments as governor may have occurred after he was recalled. In the month between the October 2003 election and his leaving office in November, the state was wracked by a series of fires that devastated large portions of southern California. The soon-to-be-ex governor, graciously taking his successor along, helped supervise efforts to contain the blazes and lent comfort to victims and firefighters alike.

By executive order, governors can seize extraordinary powers to make things happen, whether public health quarantines or round-the-clock emergency freeway repairs to get major southern California freeways re-opened. When riots

---

[1] Interview with Joseph Shumate, August 30, 1996.
[2] Interview with Dan Schnur, August 31, 1996.

broke out in South Central Los Angeles after the first not-guilty verdicts in the Rodney King police beating case, Mayor Tom Bradley, a former L.A. police lieutenant, and Police Chief Darryl Gates despised each other so much that they were not even on speaking terms. Wilson used his office and the strength of his personality to force them to cooperate.

The Governor and the Budget

Nowhere does the governor exert more influence on policy than in his annual budget, prepared by his Department of Finance. The budget is released each January, and four months later an updated document, the "May Revise" adjusts the estimates of tax receipts and revenues available to spend. Aside from the chief of staff, the director of finance is the single most important appointment a governor makes. Usually, the choice is a respected and experienced professional whose knowledge of state government, ability to find and hide sources of revenue, and not delude himself or his boss about the true financial picture at any given time is far more important than any ideological predispositions. The director presides over a highly professional staff of about 300, primarily budget analysts who know government inside and out and who often have the institutional and historical memory a new administration lacks.

"The Department of Finance is the pocketbook of state government," said Roy Bell, a longtime veteran of finance who served as Jerry Brown's director and Reagan's assistant director. "The only way a governor could control everything in state government is through the pocketbook. Therefore, that's his best control of everybody. Finance doesn't work for anyone else. . . . So our loyalty goes entirely to the governor."[3]

After defeating Governor Pat Brown, Reagan got a quick lesson on how and why the Department of Finance mattered. When his transition staffers went to see Hale Champion, Brown's outgoing director, Reagan recalled, Champion told them, "We're spending a million dollars a day more than we're taking in. I've got a golf date. Good luck."[4] Reagan had promised a 10% across-the-board cut in state spending, and his new budget director, an outsider named James Dwight, quickly tried to implement it. Professionals Bell and Edwin Beach had to explain why that was not possible, despite Reagan's million-vote victory. They told Reagan he could cut the budget by 10%, but he would pay a terrible political price if he tried to cut every segment of state government by that amount. He

---

[3] Roy Bell, "Revenue Policies and Political Realities," an oral history conducted 1984 by Gabrielle Morris, in "California State Department of Finance and Governor Ronald Reagan," Regional Oral History Office, The Bancroft Library, University of California, Berkeley, 1986.

[4] Ronald Reagan, "On Becoming Governor," an oral history conducted 1979 by Sarah Sharp, in "Governor Reagan and his Cabinet: An Introduction," Regional Oral History Office, The Bancroft Library, University of California, Berkeley, 1986.

could not, for example, cut the number of prison guards by 10% or medical services to sick people by 10%. Reagan, Beach said, "understood this with some reluctance."[5]

When Deukmejian took office, he believed that the California Coastal Commission, which had been established by a 1972 ballot measure, had gone too far in blocking coastal development and had put too many "extreme environmental advocates" on its staff. His solution, as top aide Michael Franchetti recalled, was to "cut their staff, and there was nothing they could do about it." If the commission asked for 100 lawyers, Franchetti said, finance gave them enough funds for 50, and the legislature could not override that decision.[6] (For a more detailed description of the budget process, and the governor's role in that process, see chapter 2.)

The Governor's Appointments

In preparing for the 1958 governor's race, Fred Dutton, Pat Brown's campaign manager, made a tour of some of the eastern states with Democratic governors. In Pennsylvania, he found that the governor made between 17,000 and 18,000 appointments. It was similar in the other states he visited. When Brown set up his administration in California, he found, thanks to the good-government, civil-service reforms of predecessor Hiram Johnson (who served as governor from 1911 to 1917), that he had about 60 major appointment to make and several hundred minor ones. "You really do not have a disciplining or supportive network through the executive branch," Dutton concluded. "If it makes for better government, and that is arguable, it makes for poor politics."[7]

The number of top appointments a governor makes has grown since 1958, but it will never rival the appointments a governor of Illinois or New York or Pennsylvania can make. Still, California has the largest judiciary in the world. A governor appoints three times the number of state judges as there are federal judges in the entire country. Los Angeles County alone has more judges than England.[8]

A governor today has about a hundred senior staff appointments and about 550 full-time positions exempt from civil service rules out of a state bureaucracy

---

[5] Edwin W. Beach, "Some Technical and Political Aspects of State Budgeting," an oral history conducted 1984 by Gabrielle Morris, in "California State Department of Finance and Governor Ronald Reagan," Regional Oral History Office, The Bancroft Library, University of California, Berkeley, 1986, p. 31.

[6] Michael Franchetti, oral history transcript, California State Archives, Office of the Secretary of State, Sacramento, p. 247.

[7] Frederick G. Dutton, "Democratic Campaigns and Controversies, 1954–1966," an oral history conducted 1977–1978 by Amelia R. Fry, Regional Oral History Office, The Bancroft Library, University of California, Berkeley, 1981, p. 87.

[8] Anthony Kline, oral history transcript, California State Archives, Office of the Secretary of State, Sacramento.

of more than 270,000 employees. Senior staff includes top cabinet secretaries and undersecretaries and directors of departments such as water resources, corrections, health services, California Highway Patrol, transportation (Cal-Trans), motor vehicles, general services, office of emergency services, and of course finance, the most important. The governor gets another 300 or so appointments to major and minor boards and commissions, including the University of California Board of Regents, the California State University Trustees, the State Board of Education, the Unemployment Insurance Appeals Board, and many others. The governor also has several thousand minor, nonsalaried appointments, all the way down to county fair boards.

When Deukmejian was elected, he and chief of staff-to-be Steve Merksamer visited with outgoing Governor Brown, who said, "The worst decision I ever made was not focusing on my appointments. I was too cavalier. The best advice I have for you, George, is to spend a lot of time now, during the transition, on appointments."[9]

Differing Governing Styles

The Reagan Years

When Ronald Reagan, the "citizen politician," was first elected governor in 1966, he was determined to change state government, cut its funding, and make it run more like private business, with himself as chief executive officer and a strong chief of staff as chief operating officer. He had a council of about 80 to 90 people, including cabinet secretaries, that met monthly and a much smaller cabinet that met two or three times a week. This was where the important policy decisions of state government got made. Department heads would prepare memos for their respective cabinet secretaries who would meet with them in advance to organize and clarify issues. The secretary then would put these matters on the agenda for discussion with the governor.

"It was a very formal situation," recalled top Reagan advisor Gordon Luce.[10]

When Caspar Weinberger served as Reagan's finance director, all department heads had to present and defend their budgets to him, and word went out that they could not appeal directly to Reagan to restore budget cuts and hope to win.

"We operated in a different way than most governments had," Reagan recalled. "It was like a board of directors meeting. We had cabinet meetings about

---

[9] Interview with Steve Merksamer, May 1996.

[10] Gordon Luce, "A Banker's View of State Administration and Republican Politics," an oral history conducted 1981 and 1983 by Gabrielle Morris and Sarah Sharp, in "Governor Reagan and his Cabinet: An Introduction," Regional Oral History Office, The Bancroft Library, University of California, Berkeley, 1986.

three times a week, and all the issues would come before the cabinet. . . . At first, none of them were experienced in government, but still they heard enough to think that if a problem dealt with one cabinet officer, well, the others shouldn't interfere. That wasn't what I wanted. I finally got them convinced that what I wanted was like a board of directors, with only one difference, of course. They didn't vote. In other words, the decision had to be made by me."

Reagan described how he would sit at the head of the table, listening to the discussion after having done his own reading. "Finally, when I've really heard enough that I know what my decision is," he recalled, "I'd interrupt and say, 'Well, here's what we're going to do,' boom, and tell them."[11]

The Jerry Brown Years

Jerry Brown's style of governing was as different from Ronald Reagan's as it was possible to get. He was unconventional and unstructured and hated meetings. He was a creative thinker who often did not follow through, but he was often ahead of his time in identifying directions in which government should go, particularly in such then-visionary things as solar energy and recycling, mass transit and commuter freeway lanes, and equal opportunities for women and minorities. He was not hierarchical, as Reagan was, and wasn't terribly interested, as his legal affairs and appointments secretary Tony Kline recalled, in following somebody else's agenda or even discussing in meetings what was on somebody else's mind. Cabinet secretaries learned that if they wanted something done, they had to deal with Brown directly, outside of a meeting, either one-on-one or by telephone. This frustrated his chief of staff, Gray Davis, who was always trying to put order and structure around a chief executive who rebelled against it.

"Brown was also aware," Kline said, "of the way governors, including his father, were controlled by their advisors. I recall him pointing out to me once how much Reagan's system ensured the ability of those around him to control him. Reagan was presented, when he was governor, with decision memos. A decision memo outlined the facts, described the options and then asked the governor for a choice. Well, if you control the facts and you define the options, then you basically control the decision. I don't think Jerry Brown was about to permit that to happen to him."[12] For his part, Brown would immerse himself in an issue, ask for books, call up experts, and consult specialists in his administration on whatever topic.

Brown relished the idea of appointing to regulatory boards people who irritated the industries these boards regulated. He appointed nurses to the Board of Medical Quality Assurance, for example, which governs physicians. This outraged them. He appointed scholar/philosopher Gregory Bateson to what was

---

[11] Reagan oral history, p. 41.
[12] Kline oral history, p. 50–51.

otherwise a very corporate University of California Board of Regents dominated by wealthy, business-oriented appointees of Governor Reagan. Brown would show up at the regents' meetings in his role as *ex officio* member, and he and Bateson would debate Socrates, an exercise other regents found insufferable. Brown appointed Robert Treuhaft to the Board of Funeral Directors. Treuhaft, a longtime member of the Bay Area left and former Communist, was married to Jessica Mitford, whose muckraking exposé of the funeral industry, *The American Way of Death*, outraged funeral directors everywhere.

As Brown focused more and more on national politics and running for president again in 1980, the state legislature began making inroads into gubernatorial power, especially by creating new boards and commissions to which legislative leaders could make appointments. Brown didn't seem to care, which created problems for his successor, George Deukmejian.

The Deukmejian Years

After 16 years of high voltage, high visibility governors—Reagan and Jerry Brown—George Deukmejian came into office in January 1983 and promptly calmed things down. He had little interest in using the bully pulpit for anything other than his pet causes: building prisons and cutting taxes. A conservative Republican in Reagan's mold, though certainly without Reagan's engaging personality or star profile, Deukmejian set out to emulate Reagan's hierarchical system.

Deukmejian decided early on to reclaim from the legislature some of the power that Jerry Brown had ceded to it. This led to big problems the first year, including the legislature's vote to reject Deukmejian's first director of finance, Michael Franchetti. In a moment of pique, the legislature sold a newly constructed governor's mansion, in which Deukmejian and his family had been planning to live. The mansion was completed at the end of the Reagan administration. Jerry Brown had spurned it, preferring to sleep on a mattress on the floor of his apartment near the Capitol.

Merksamer said Governor Brown not only let the legislature encroach on gubernatorial appointments but also gave the legislature power to write much of the budget. "Jerry abdicated that process," Merksamer said, "so George Deukmejian came in and said, 'Look, I'm going to be the governor.'" It was like suddenly having a strict parent telling them to be in bed by nine, "and they rebelled," he said.[13] "Deukmejian comes in and says, 'This is our budget, this is what we're going to do,'" added Franchetti. "We made it stick, but it was a great price. Some senators would say, 'We'll share power,' and George would say, 'No, you're the legislature. I'm the governor. We're going to do it this way.'

---

[13] Steve Merksamer, oral history transcript, California State Archives, Office of the Secretary of State, Sacramento, p. 205.

They can approve it or not approve it, but we're not going to sit down with them and tell us what to do.' And that led to a big fight."[14]

Merksamer would have a daily meeting at nine a.m. with top staff to lay out the day and stay abreast of developments. He would meet with the governor at 10:30 and with the director of finance or deputy directors three or four times a week in the afternoon to discuss the budget. Every other week, the governor would meet with the cabinet only to sign off on policy. Deukmejian found that one excellent way of staying on top of his administration was to conduct regular press conferences, which he held about once every three weeks. Merksamer said he found them "a useful tool" to keep senior bureaucrats on their toes.

"There is nothing worse for a deputy director," Merksamer said, "than for a governor to be asked a question on which he has never been briefed, such as, 'Governor, why is the Department of Fish and Game not cleaning up that toxic spill on the south fork of the American River?'" Senior staff was required to report any problems, controversies, potential questions and answers. They went into a thick briefing book, which went to the press secretary, then to the chief of staff, and then to the governor 48 hours before the press conference. "For that snapshot in time," Merksamer said, "you are as thoroughly informed about your administration as it is possible to be."[15]

The Wilson Years

Pete Wilson was elected governor in November 1990 on what he called a "preventive agenda," which included health and mental health intervention in the public schools in the very early years to fix problems (and thus avoid costlier problems later on). He also urged programs and policies to give all pregnant women access to prenatal care, to preserve the coastline, to restore family planning funds cut by the Deukmejian administration and to be tough on crime.

Soon after the election, the worst economic downturn to hit California in 60 years froze Wilson's preventive agenda and forced him to scramble quickly to fill an unprecedented $14 billion budget shortfall. At the same time, Wilson lost his most trusted policy and communications advisor, 48-year-old Otto Bos, who had been with Wilson since his days as mayor of San Diego. Bos collapsed on a soccer field and died of a massive heart attack. Bos was more like a younger brother than an aide, and no one ever replaced him, though many tried.

The state's desperate fiscal condition placed a premium on adept management. Unlike Reagan and Deukmejian, Wilson was very much a hands-on governor, a policy enthusiast and workaholic who devoured memos, studies, state budgets, legislation, and news digests. Like Jerry Brown, Wilson was not satisfied with one-page summaries with boxes to check. "I have been in his office at bill-signing time," former deputy chief of staff Joe Shumate recalled, "and seen

---

[14] Franchetti oral history, p. 154.
[15] Merksamer interview.

him with 50 bills to sign and four hours to go before the deadline, suddenly bring everything to a stop on a relatively minor bill and send his staff out to get more information."[16]

Where Reagan and Deukmejian preferred a hierarchical order, with everyone reporting up the line to the chief of staff, who in turn reports to the governor, Wilson preferred a "spokes of the wheel" model, in which everything came to him. This satisfied his need to know as much as possible, but aides say it worked to his disadvantage at times. Bad decisions sometimes got made because not everyone who had an interest in a decision was consulted.

Wilson had a strong senior staff system and a strong cabinet secretary. He tended to appoint independent people for top agency or cabinet jobs and then install Wilson loyalists as their deputies to keep them focused on his policy agenda. Some critics said Wilson politicized the state bureaucracy far more than previous governors by placing highly paid aides, especially those adept in public relations and public affairs, in key agencies and departments all over state government. Wilson's chief of staff, longtime aide Bob White, was not much involved in policy, instead paying more attention to politics and personnel decisions. Wilson also instituted a practice of hiring deputy chiefs of staff and giving them no written job descriptions, which sometimes confused department heads when they mysteriously appeared at meetings, but it suited his style.

The Gray Davis Years

On paper, Gray Davis seemed the best-prepared governor in recent memory. During a public service career that began in 1975, Davis served nearly five years as a governor's chief of staff, four years in the state Assembly, eight years as state controller, and four more as lieutenant governor—an unbroken string of 23 years during which he held a variety of jobs that should have trained him for the governorship.

But Davis lacked two key ingredients that hampered his ability to work with the legislature and, in the end, proved fatal—courage and leadership skills. Although significant—in some cases, landmark—legislation was introduced during his tenure, most of those initiatives began in the legislature. Davis signed most of that agenda into law, but his relationship with lawmakers was tempestuous, starting almost from the get-go when he proclaimed that the legislature's job was to implement his vision. That comment did not sit well with lawmakers from his own Democratic Party, and Davis lacked the personal skills to smooth over the gaffe.

His tenure began well enough. Davis's election in 1998—a thumping defeat of Attorney General Dan Lungren—brought to a close 16 years of Republican rule and united the Democratic Party. For his part, Davis vowed at the outset to govern from the center, a pledge he was able to keep for the first two years of

---

[16] Shumate interview.

his administration. It was a time of plenty in California, a time when a booming economy filled state coffers with tax revenue and budget fights centered on how to spend money rather than cut programs.

Davis didn't so much have to lead as steer, which allowed him the time to indulge his tendencies to micro-manage his administration. He focused on education and took his political cues from then-President Bill Clinton. His popularity soared; in February 2000, for instance, the Field Poll revealed that the governor enjoyed a near-record 62% approval rating. His rating still stood at 60% in January 2001.

But the Davis administration was soon swamped with a pair of crises just as he headed into his 2002 re-election campaign—an economic and political crisis fueled by a failed energy deregulation program passed during the Wilson administration and the collapse of the high-tech sector, which had been a driving force for the state's booming economy. In this case, Davis's aptitude to micro-manage was less important than an ability to lead and to rally others to address the state's pressing problems.

"The energy crisis was really the beginning of Gray Davis's unraveling," Davis's chief political advisor Garry South told *California Journal* magazine. "There was a perception of the governor that developed in that crisis that bedeviled him from that point forward. It was toxic for him."

Part of that negative perception dealt with leadership; the electorate never believed that Davis could extract the state from its myriad problems. And that lack of faith had to do with his style and his priorities. Throughout his governorship, Davis displayed a mania for raising money from special interests that cast his entire administration as a "pay-to-play" enterprise.

The Davis Recall

Davis was a bundle of contradictions. As noted, he was the best-prepared chief executive in California history but lacked political courage and, most significant, leadership. His lack of charisma wasn't crucial, but his lack of command was. Davis's two immediate predecessors, Deukmejian and Wilson, certainly lacked charisma, but each knew how to be decisive.

The first signs of trouble for Davis began in May 2000 when electricity prices—deregulated at Wilson's urging by the legislature in 1994—skyrocketed in San Diego and prefaced a yearlong statewide energy crisis that Davis, for all his experience, proved ill equipped to handle. He was slow to react, and as the energy debacle deepened, the state was shaken again by a reversal of fortunes in high tech—a bust that saw many Internet-based companies evaporate, taking with them the tax revenues that had so enhanced the state's general fund. In 2002 the shrinking revenue base produced a state budget deficit estimated at $24 billion. As Republican and Democratic lawmakers engaged in deep philosophical and political combat over spending, Davis dithered, providing little guidance to a legislature locked in stalemate for 67 days past the constitutional deadline for enacting a budget.

Davis's lack of political courage was evident in the way the state went about raising the vehicle-license fee, which the legislature had lowered in times of plenty. A dip in fortune—as occurred in 2001 and 2002—was supposed to trigger an increase in fees, but Davis would not pull that trigger on the eve of his re-election even though it meant an additional $4 billion in much-needed revenue. He and lawmakers eventually worked out a plan by which the so-called VLF trigger was pulled by an undefined hand—with no one receiving either credit or blame.

In the midst of these various calamities, Davis won a second term by the slimmest of margins over an exceptionally weak Republican opponent—conservative businessman Bill Simon. A month after Davis was sworn in, an embryonic recall campaign took shape prompted by Republicans sensing a chance to reverse the election. The attempt to gather signatures for a recall sputtered through the late winter and spring until, on May 15, Darrell Issa, a wealthy Republican congressman from San Diego, seeded the effort with nearly half a million dollars. By July 23, the recall had qualified.

A gubernatorial recall asks two questions: (1) should the governor be bounced from office; and (2) who should replace the governor if he or she is recalled? Anyone interested in the job may file to run in the replacement phase, and there is no run off; the candidate with the most votes is elected governor should the recall succeed.

Under these circumstances, Davis's survival depended on two key factors—Democratic solidarity and the lack of a credible successor. He got neither. Bustamante shattered Democratic solidarity by entering the fray, as did Republican Arnold Schwarzenegger, who qualified as a "credible successor" because he captured voters' imagination and allowed them to dream of a plausible alternative. His announcement immediately transformed the recall, riveting world attention on what Davis and Democrats hoped would be an obscure exercise in electoral gymnastics and super-sizing what U.S. Senator Dianne Feinstein characterized as "a carnival."

Politically, the governor shed his centrist outer shell as he tried to shore up long-neglected Democratic roots. He backed a flurry of labor-related bills, as well as another that would haunt his effort to survive—legislation granting California driver's licenses to illegal immigrants.

Eventually, 247 candidates offered themselves up as successors to Davis, and 135 actually filed the necessary papers and paid the required fees to secure a place on the ballot. The five most notable were Schwarzenegger, Bustamante, GOP state Senator Tom McClintock, Green Party candidate Peter Camejo, and pundit Arianna Huffington. The iconoclastic McClintock caused some worry among Republicans that he might siphon enough votes away from Schwarzenegger to tip the election to Bustamante, but it was a needless bit of fretting.

Schwarzenegger's team—borrowed from Pete Wilson—ran the campaign as if it was promoting "Terminator Ultimate," complete with elaborate stunts, photo ops, and interviews from media softies such as Larry King and Oprah. The candidate was high energy all the time, hammering Davis on issues such as the drivers' license bill and the increased "car tax" or VLF. He promised to "blow up boxes" once he came to Sacramento and to end the gridlock that seemed to paralyze the way California government conducted its affairs, instituting a bipartisan approach and wrenching government out of the hands of "special interests"—whom he conveniently neglected to define. When votes were tallied, more than 55% of the electorate opted to recall Davis and nearly 49% had chosen Schwarzenegger to replace him.

The Schwarzenegger Years

Schwarzenegger came into office as governor of a state with financial problems of near mythical proportions. The centerpiece was a two-year budget gap between state revenues and spending that some estimated to be near $38 billion by the time he took the oath. Lurking along the periphery of the budget was a litany of festering problems such as high workers' compensation rates that lent credence to the notion that California was a rotten place to do business. The new governor exacerbated the fiscal problem on his first day in office when, only moments after taking the oath, he fulfilled his most prominent campaign promise—a rollback of the car tax. That action added $4 billion to the state debt.

But his first year in office was filled with accomplishments as he worked with the Democrat-controlled legislature to tackle some of the state's most immediate troubles. He persuaded voters to pass a $15 billion bond issue to refinance the state's debt, worked with Democrats to reform the troubled workers' compensation system, and cut side deals with educators, unions, and Native American tribes.

Politically, his administration reflected his mixed outlook. It was an eclectic group, including environmentalist Terry Tamminen as head of the state Environmental Protection Agency, farmer A. G. Kawamura as secretary of Food and Agriculture, moderate Sunne Wright McPeak to head the Business, Transportation and Housing Agency, and Bonnie Reiss, a Malibu liberal, as "senior advisor." But it also included those recruited from the business community, and from conservative ranks. He culled key aides from the state Chamber of Commerce, while a flock of former Wilson aides flooded the administration, including chief of staff Pat Cleary. Communications director Rob Stutzman once worked for former Attorney General Dan Lungren and conservative state Senator Rob Hurtt. Former Los Angeles Mayor Richard Riordan, a moderate Republican, became his education secretary.

Schwarzenegger was flamboyant and larger than life, breathing energy and panache into an office that had been occupied for 20 years by a trio of coma-inducing personalities. His poll numbers were staggering, his 65% approval rating higher than any governor of the past half a century, including Ronald Reagan. He developed a close working friendship with the most powerful Democrat in Sacramento—the acerbic, chronically grumpy leader of the state Senate, John Burton, an old-line lefty from San Francisco who also happened to be well connected in Hollywood. He tended relationships inside the Capitol, displaying a mastery of small gestures as well as big maneuvers. When Assembly Speaker Herb Wesson held an informal farewell buffet for Capitol reporters, for instance, Schwarzenegger dropped by for a few impromptu words of praise for the termed-out Democrat. It was a gesture no one could imagine from Davis.

As he cultivated majority Democrats, Schwarzenegger at times ignored the legislature's Republican minority, which went along because, as one GOP insider told *California Journal*, "we have no place else to go." But the governor did not neglect his party's delegation altogether, appearing at GOP fundraisers, including one that netted some $300,000 for the re-election kitty of his old recall foe, Tom McClintock. Schwarzenegger also went to the wall for the most significant Republican issue in that debt-riddled year: opposition to anything that smacked of a tax increase. Reagan and Wilson before him each had confronted similar budget shortfalls with a combination of spending cuts and tax increases, but Schwarzenegger would have none of it. Instead, he relied on the same short-term fixes that Davis applied to the fiscal problem: cuts, creative math, and borrowing, including a campaign to pass a measure—Proposition 57—designed to ease the state's fiscal morass by selling bonds to pay off debt.

At the same time, hints of another Schwarzenegger began to emerge, a combative and pugnacious governor more akin to the cutthroat bodybuilder who once belittled opponents to gain a competitive edge. When negotiations over the 2004 budget stalled, Schwarzenegger ridiculed legislators by referring to them as "girlie men" during a televised interview.

The combative Schwarzenegger emerged more forcefully during his second year in office. He was more truculent and confrontational, and there was a feeling among some of the administration's more conservative allies that the previous year's cooperation had gained the governor little in the way of true reform. He had patched over critical problems but had not gained structural changes he felt were necessary to correct the state's ongoing fiscal problems.

In his 2005 State of the State Address, Schwarzenegger challenged the Democratic-controlled legislature to enact his agenda of fiscal and political reform by a date certain, or he would take that agenda to the voters as initiatives in a special election. Politically, he moved to the right, his agenda increasingly shaped by the state's influential business community. When Democrats refused to move on that agenda, Schwarzenegger picked fights with their political allies. He engaged in verbal scuffles with teachers over tenure, merit pay and competency, with public employees over pension reform, with nurses over staffing ratios in hospitals. A pension proposal, introduced as legislation, was drafted so poorly that it would have denied survivor benefits to the families of slain police officers and firefighters. Nurses haunted his every public appearance. His political foes joined forces under the banner "Alliance for a Better California," and their continued pressure forced the governor to abandon efforts to impose merit pay on teachers and revamp public-pension programs.

When negotiations bogged down with Democrats over a variety of issues, Schwarzenegger carried through with his promise to call a special election for November 2005. Eight initiatives qualified for that ballot, including four of special importance to Schwarzenegger: removing redistricting from the legislature, increasing from two to five the years required to gain teacher tenure, preventing unions from spending on political campaigns without permission of their membership, and dramatically enhancing the governor's budgetary power in times of fiscal crisis. To finance the campaign, Schwarzenegger continued what had been a frenetic fundraising campaign, raising hundreds of millions of dollars from business and Republican sources all over the country.

The public responded to the gridlock and the election, but not the way Schwarzenegger and his allies might have hoped. His poll numbers plummeted, and in November, voters rejected all four of the governor's proposals—as well as four other measures on the same ballot. After the election, a chastened Schwarzenegger accepted full blame for the election disaster. He promised to cooperate with lawmakers in 2006, but his postelection *mea culpa* was greeted with skepticism by lawmakers, who wanted to see some cooperative action in addition to words.

Arnold Schwarzenegger came to office as a world celebrity, and his challenge was to comport himself in ways that would move his image away from that of a one-dimensional hulk and to wrap it in an aura of statesmanship and credibility. Thus far, he has stumbled, instead responding to criticism with stunts and ill-timed rhetoric. In his dealings with both the legislature and the public, Schwarzenegger has been inconsistent and difficult to predict. At times conciliatory, at times combative, his administration frequently plays good cop/bad cop with legislative Democrats and their allies. The governor, however, plays both roles, and it has become increasingly difficult to discover his real intent or to predict a course of action that might lead to meaningful negotiations with the legislature.

Suggested Sources

Cannon, Lou. 1969. *Ronnie and Jessie: A Political Odyssey*. Garden City, N.Y.: Doubleday.

_____. 1982. *Reagan*. New York: Putnam.

Governor's Budget. 1997/98. California Department of Finance.

Harris, Malcolm E. 1954. *California Governors*. Sacramento, Calif.: State Printing Plant.

Mills, James R. 1987. *A Disorderly House: The Brown-Unruh Years in Sacramento*. Berkeley, Calif.: Hayday Books.

Pack, Robert. 1978. *Jerry Brown: Philosopher-Prince*. New York: Stein and Day.

Quinn, Mildred. 1970. *California Governors, Past and Present*. Newport Beach: Franklin Publications

Samish, Arthur H., and Bob Thomas. 1971. *The Secret Boss of California, The Life and High Times of Art Samish*. New York: Crown Publishers.

Schell, Orville. 1978. *Brown*. New York: Random House.

Internet Sites

California Home Page: www.ca.gov/s/
Institute of Governmental Studies, UC Berkeley: www.igs.berkeley.edu

Chapter 5

The California Supreme Court

Preble Stolz, Gerald F. Uelmen, and Susan Rasky

The Business of the Courts

Many Americans, probably most, think they have a pretty good general understanding of what courts do and how they work. The source for this belief is what people saw of the Martha Stewart case, TV programs like Judge Judy and Boston Legal, and the oceans of ink spilled regularly in newspapers and magazines on crime and the courtroom antics of prominent people. Overlaid on top of this is an awareness of a very few high-profile decisions of the U.S. Supreme Court such as *Roe v. Wade*, which held that women had a constitutional right to an abortion during the first trimester of pregnancy.

In fact, that is a very misleading picture of the business of judges. Why? Because the vast bulk of the work of courts, even the U.S. Supreme Court, is of very little general interest.

Perhaps the best way to show this is to start, as it were, at the other end. Most people rarely get involved in a lawsuit; if they do it is most likely to be as a defendant in a minor traffic violation or as a party to a family law matter, most commonly divorce, now called a "dissolution" in California. If someone is more than routinely well off, a judge is likely to be involved in the distribution of the property after his or her death, a process known as the probating of an estate. A huge volume of these more or less routine matters is handled annually by the courts; in many ways this type of activity, often terribly important to the people involved—think, for example, of deciding which parent should have custody of the children in connection with a dissolution—is basically an administrative or bureaucratic function not essentially different from eligibility determinations made by the Social Security Administration or the Veteran's Administration.

Another major responsibility of judges is supervision of the administration of the criminal law, from relatively minor misdemeanors such as shoplifting or driving without a valid license to the most serious felonies, such as rape, murder, and the like. In California, as in most states, criminal law administration is largely in the hands of local government officials: city police and county sheriffs with both the district attorney and the public defender being county responsibilities. The district attorney is usually an elected official of the county. The county pays the cost of providing defense counsel to indigent criminal defendants, but the arrangement varies widely between counties. Some have a public defender, typically selected by the Board of Supervisors, with deputies who are county employees. Other counties contract with a lawyer to provide the defender service or rotate the work among panels of private lawyers.

If a defendant is to be sentenced to jail or prison, a judge must be involved because only a judge can perform that function. Jails are run at the county level by the sheriff. A defendant may not be sentenced to county jail for more than a year; sentences of more than a year are to prisons run by the state. A sentence of a year or less to county jail is by definition in California a sentence for a misdemeanor; a sentence of more than a year must be to state prison and can only be for commission of a felony. There is a parallel but somewhat different system for juvenile offenders. Most defendants charged with a crime are entitled to be released on bail pending trial. If a defendant is charged with a nonbailable offense or is unable to make bail, he or she will be held in jail pending trial. If such a person is convicted he or she will usually be given credit for time served pending trial; if acquitted, no compensation is given.

The overwhelming bulk of criminal cases is resolved without trial following a plea of guilty by the defendant. In the most recent year for which we have statistics (1997–98), 90.5% of the 150,695 criminal dispositions by the Superior Courts of California were on the basis of a guilty plea before trial.[1] An additional 3.7% were found guilty after trial. Five percent were dismissed before trial (most commonly on the motion of the district attorney), only 0.7% were acquitted after trial. (O. J. Simpson was, in short, a statistical freak.) Although criminal filings are only about 15% of the filings of the Superior Courts, they take up almost half of the judicial effort of those judges,[2] and that is true even though only about 4% of the criminal filings go to trial.[3] The whole system, civil as well as criminal, depends

---

[1] 1999 Annual Report of the Judicial Council of California, 55.

[2] This estimate is based on the "weighted filings" calculations of the Administrative Office of the California Courts. *1994 Annual Report* at 116. This figure is used chiefly to determine when legislation authorizing additional judgeships is needed.

[3] Much of the reason for this is that the process of determining the sentence takes judicial time whether it follows a plea of guilty or a jury determination of guilt.

upon over 90% of criminal defendants pleading guilty; if all criminal defendants or even a significantly larger number insisted upon a full dress trial, the whole edifice would be in danger of collapse.

The percentage of civil cases going to trial is also relatively small; statewide in 1997–98 only 3.2% of the general civil dispositions were decided after trial, all the rest were settled.[4]

The structure of California's court system in its essentials is like that of every other state and the federal courts. At the bottom are the Superior Courts. There used to be Justice Courts as well as Municipal Courts but a Justice Court judge (in the more distant past known as a Justice of the Peace) did not have to be a lawyer, and a typical Justice Court judge made most of his or her living selling insurance, running a grocery store or what have you. Being a Justice Court judge was not a full-time job for which legal training was required. By judicial decision in the '70s Justice Court judges were required to be lawyers, and in 1994 a constitutional amendment converted the few remaining Justice Courts into Municipal Courts.

The Municipal Courts were high volume courts with a jurisdiction limited to minor crimes (misdemeanors) and civil matters below $25,000. Because of those limits these courts were sometimes called courts of 'limited' jurisdiction as distinct from the Superior Courts, which were said to be courts of "general" jurisdiction, i.e., they had power to try all cases wherever another court did not have jurisdiction. On June 2, 1998, California voters approved Proposition 220, a constitutional amendment that permitted the judges in each county to decide whether to merge their Superior and Municipal Courts into a single unified Superior Court. Today, all of the 58 California counties have opted for unification, and former Municipal Court judges have become Superior Court judges. The cases formerly heard in the Municipal Court are now heard in the Superior Court, often in separate divisions. In any event, it is in the Superior Courts that evidence is taken, witnesses heard, documents introduced, etc. The "facts"—typically, who did what to whom and with what intent?—are found at the trial level, either by a jury or more commonly by the judge.[5] What might be described as the theatrical aspects of the law are almost entirely at the trial level; the examination and cross examination of witnesses is the meat of most television programs concerned with the law.

Above the trial courts are the appellate courts; in California the Supreme Court and the Courts of Appeal.[6] The Supreme Court sits at the top of the pyramid

---

[4] *1999 Annual Report* at 49. About 7% were dismissed for delay in prosecution; in substance that amounts to a settlement with plaintiff agreeing to abandon his claim. General Civil excludes chiefly Family Law and Probate; it includes about 26% of all civil filings.

[5] In fiscal year 1998 the Superior Courts heard 76,173 contested trials. A jury was employed in only 8,540 of those trials. *Calif. Judicial Council Annual Report* (1999), 41.

[6] The nomenclature of courts varies from place to place and seems to have been designed by someone determined to confuse the uninitiated. Thus in New York the highest court (comparable to the California Supreme Court) is called the Court of Appeals, whereas the trial court (comparable to the Superior Court in California) is called the Supreme Court. The trial court in the federal system is called the District Court, for many

with seven justices; beneath it are the Courts of Appeal. Today there are six geographic districts for the Courts of Appeal. These courts vary in size: that for the
Second District (Los Angeles) has 31 justices, whereas the Sixth (San Jose) has
only seven justices, but in all districts each case is heard by a panel of three justices. Only in the most extraordinary circumstances do these appellate courts make
any factual determinations; their role is restricted to the correction of errors of law
committed by the trial courts. That is an enormously important limitation because
most disputes are for the most part not about the law, but rather about what happened outside of the courtroom that provoked one of the parties to bring a lawsuit
(or, in criminal matters, the state to prosecute a defendant for the commission of a
crime). In some systems the reviewing court is empowered to hear additional evidence and set aside a trial court judgment on the ground that it was factually
wrong. In general that is not true in courts that trace their history back to the common law of England as is the case in virtually all states in the United States, including California.

Restricting appellate review to errors of law means that relatively few trial
court judgments will be reversed on appeal. Not only must the trial court have
been wrong on some point of law, but the error must have been of such a magnitude that it would likely have affected the overall result. Most rulings on eviden-
tiary points, for example, are not likely to be that crucial. So the judge allowed the
jury to hear some item of evidence that the judge should have ruled inadmissible.
Is that error likely to have been so important as to require a new trial? And some
judgments are nonappealable, e.g., if the defendant in a criminal case is acquitted,
the double jeopardy clause of the Constitution prohibits the state from appealing.

In general the losing party in the trial court has a right to appeal to the Court
of Appeal (with the big exception of the state in criminal cases). Having the right
to appeal does not mean that most losing parties do it. For one thing, it is expensive, and many cases are not worth the cost of preparing the record and having a
lawyer write an argument (known, often misleadingly, as a brief) in support of the
appeal.[7] But there is no right to appeal a decision of the Court of Appeal to the
Supreme Court. The losing party may file a Petition for Review with the Supreme
Court, and it is then up to the Supreme Court to decide whether or not to hear the
case. Most of the time it does not. Over 5,000 petitions were filed in 2001–02;

---

years the Courts of Appeal in California were known as the District Courts of Appeal and
many lawyers still refer to them as the DCA. For those who cherish idiotic points of detail, in California the intermediate appellate courts are properly called the Courts of Appeal; in the federal system they are called the Court of Appeals.

[7] In criminal cases if the accused is indigent the state, sometimes through the State
Public Defender's Office, will provide representation without charge. The convicted accused has very little to lose by filing an appeal and that no doubt explains the relatively
high percentage of appeals in criminal cases. (In civil cases about 25% of contested cases
are appealed; in criminal cases it is well over 100% because there are appeals from judgments based on a plea of guilty (not a contested case) involving issues having to do, for
example, with sentencing.

only 4% were granted, and over half of those did not result in any opinion by the Supreme Court.[8]

Death penalty cases are an important exception to the rule that the California Supreme Court decides for itself which cases it will hear. If the state prevails at trial and a sentence of death is imposed by the Superior Court, the case is automatically appealed to the Supreme Court without going through a preliminary review by a Court of Appeal. Over the past 50 years there has been a considerable variation in the number of death cases the California Supreme Court has had to consider, much of the variation caused by a notably opaque series of decisions by the United States Supreme Court in the '70s attempting to state the circumstances under which a penalty of death would not be "cruel and unusual punishment" under the federal Constitution.[9] Effectively the death penalty was suspended during most of the '70s; its resurrection since then has created a major problem for the California Supreme Court. Death penalty appeals now constitute a major portion of the Supreme Court's workload. Somewhere between 30 and 40 death penalty appeals were filed annually with the Court throughout the 1980s and 1990s. Currently, the annual number of new death penalty appeals ranges from 15–20. Since the Court files about 100 opinions a year, it is obvious that the Court is now forced to devote a very large percentage of its time to death penalty appeals. With 640 inmates on California's death row at the end of 2005, there is now a backlog of 270 death penalty appeals yet to be decided.

This attention to death cases exacerbates a problem that is already very serious. Over the past 50 years the very top of the judicial pyramid has remained fixed in size and capacity while the bottom grows and grows and grows. In 1940 there were 162 Superior Court judges; in 1990, 789.[10] In 1940 the Supreme Court was reviewing the work of 18 Courts of Appeal justices; by 2005 the number of Courts of Appeal justices had grown to 105. With that kind of volume it is self-evident that the Supreme Court cannot effectively monitor the work of the lower courts. The "correction of error" function, to the extent that it was ever part of the Supreme Court's responsibility, has devolved upon the Courts of Appeal (with, of

---

[8] *2003 Court Statistics Report,* 8. Not infrequently two cases presenting the same or nearly the same issue will come up from different Courts of Appeal at the same time. When that happens, the Supreme Court will grant a hearing in both, but write an opinion in only one and remand the other to the Court of Appeal to be decided in light of the Supreme Court's opinion in the first case. It mucks up the statistics but otherwise makes good sense.

[9] Justice Mosk in his concurring opinion in *People v. Frierson,* 25 C.3d 142, 188 (1979) discusses how the California legislature (and the people through the initiative process) attempted to comply with the U.S. Supreme Court's rulings. Justice Mosk in that case reluctantly concluded that he was obliged to sustain the constitutionality of the death penalty although it was personally repugnant to him. See also, G. F. Uelmen, "Review of Death Penalty Judgments by the Supreme Courts of California," 23 *Loy. L. A. L. Rev.* 237, 243–45 (1989) reviews the same history and brings it up to date.

[10] More recently, Superior Courts and Municipal Courts have been merged, making it impossible to compare the number of Superior Court judges to earlier decades.

course, the exception of death cases in which the Supreme Court continues to be responsible to correct trial court error because there is no other court that can).

A second function of the Supreme Court is to resolve open questions of law, for example, issues of constitutional or statutory interpretation and, to an ever lesser extent, issues of judge-made common law. If these issues are of California law, the California Supreme Court is the ultimate authoritative voice; if the question is one of federal law, the U.S. Supreme Court at least potentially has the final say. But the California Supreme Court has not been able to perform this function very well for many years simply because of the press of workload. In fact, the Courts of Appeal are now frequently the effective final voice, but, unfortunately, they sometimes speak, as it were, with forked tongue when two different panels of the Courts of Appeal come to different conclusions on substantially the same point of law. Ultimately, the California Supreme Court will resolve these sorts of conflicts, but it can take a long time and so long as the conflict (or even the potential of a conflict) exists, lawyers and trial court judges have to operate with an uneasy sense of insecurity as to what the law is.[11]

The Judges: Selection, Tenure, and Discipline

All appellate court judges—the justices of the Supreme Court and the Courts of Appeal—are selected initially by the governor. The nominee may not begin serving, however, until his or her selection has been confirmed by the Commission on Judicial Appointments. That body consists of the chief justice, the attorney general, and the senior presiding justice of the Courts of Appeal in the case of appointments to the Supreme Court or, if the appointment is to one of the Courts of Appeal, the senior presiding justice of that court. With only one exception, this confirmation process has been routine.[12] The appointment initially is for the remainder of the term of the justice who is being replaced. The full term of an appellate court justice is for 12 years. A newly appointed justice's name will appear on the ballot at the next gubernatorial election following the appointment but no opposition candidate can appear. The issue put to the

---

[11] The only reform proposal that would touch this problem is a suggestion made sometime ago by Justice Mosk to create a second Supreme Court with jurisdiction restricted to criminal cases. Because roughly half of the Court's workload is made up of criminal cases, adoption of this proposal would, in effect, just about double the capacity of the Supreme Court. The idea has been opposed on the basis that a Supreme Court of Criminal Appeals would be too apt to yield to pressure to be hard on crime. Many people believe it is useful to have the final voice on important issues of public law held by generalists. Certainly that has been the Anglo-American tradition. The generalist tradition could be continued by rotating the membership of the Criminal and Civil Supreme Courts periodically.

[12] Only one nomination has ever been rejected by the commission (of Professor Max Radin in 1940) although a very few nominations may have been withdrawn in anticipation of difficulty in confirmation.

voters (statewide for justices of the Supreme Court, districtwide for justices of the Courts of Appeal) is, shall Justice X be elected? With the exception of the election of 1986, when Chief Justice Rose Bird was defeated and carried down with her Associate Justices Joseph Grodin and Cruz Reynoso, no appellate justice has ever lost an election. A justice whose term is up who wishes to stay in office, files a notice to that effect with the secretary of state and that justice's name will then appear on the ballot at the next gubernatorial election. If not defeated, the term will be for 12 years.

Most trial court judges are also initially selected by the governor, but no commission confirms the governor's selection before the judge takes the oath of office. The term of trial judges is six years rather than the 12 for appellate court justices. Furthermore, when their name appears on the ballot any lawyer can file to challenge their election. Very few incumbent judges are challenged and even fewer are defeated, but from time to time a few challenges succeed. In large counties, such as Los Angeles, it is almost impossible to unseat an incumbent Superior Court judge because the cost of campaigning countywide is prohibitive. If a trial judge chooses to resign or retire at the end of his or her term, the position is filled not by gubernatorial appointment but by election from among any lawyers[13] who choose to file for the vacancy.

As this recital indicates, most judges owe their seat on the bench to a governor, and judgeships are probably the single most important block of patronage in the gift of a governor. If, as seems to be the case, the norm for a governor is two four-year terms, most governors by the time they leave office will have appointed well over half of the judges currently sitting in the state. As of 1990 that would be 750 judges. No governor knows that many lawyers very well; inevitably the governor comes to rely heavily on staff to generate candidates and to sift them down to a plausible few. For a position as a trial judge, trial experience is often thought useful. The effect of this is to tip the scales heavily in favor of lawyers experienced in the criminal law because overwhelmingly that is the main source of lawyers with significant trial experience. It is thus not surprising that the most common career path to the bench is through the district attorney's office, although there are also a fair number of judges with experience in a public defender's office. In sifting among qualified candidates, politics can be significant, and, especially since Governor Jerry Brown, generous representation of women, racial and ethnic minorities in judicial appointments is thought important.

For the appellate courts, prior judicial experience has come to be almost a prerequisite to appointment. In recent years nearly all justices of the Courts of Appeal were promoted from the trial bench, and most justices of the Supreme Court were elevated from the Court of Appeal bench.

---

[13] Technically a lawyer has to have been a member of the State Bar for five years to qualify for the Municipal Court bench; 10 years for the Superior Court.

There are three notable exceptions to the rule of prior judicial experience with respect to the Supreme Court: Chief Justice Phil S. Gibson,[14] Associate Justice Roger Traynor (both appointed in 1940 by Governor Culbert Olson—Traynor was made chief justice by Governor Pat Brown in 1964), and Chief Justice Rose Bird (appointed by Governor Jerry Brown in 1977[15]). Each of these chief justices deserves some discussion.

Chief Justice Phil Gibson was in many ways the architect of the modern California judicial system. He was an extraordinarily effective leader of some major structural reforms. He rationalized the lower courts of California, reducing what amounted to eight different types of trial courts with somewhat overlapping jurisdiction to a more orderly system of Superior and Municipal Courts.[16] He revitalized the Judicial Council, composed chiefly of judges from all levels of the system and persuaded the legislature to give the council power to issue rules, first for Appellate Procedure, later for family law and other subjects.

In response to Gibson's urging, the legislature increased the pay of judges at all levels so that it was, in general, competitive with the pay of a reasonably successful lawyer in at least a middle-sized city in California. The best paid lawyers in California are, of course, the senior partners in the big firms in the big cities, Los Angeles, San Francisco, etc. No judge's salary remotely approaches those amounts; on the other hand, the Superior Court judge in many counties is probably among the best paid lawyers in town. The obvious solution to this dilemma—pay judges in big cities more than their rural counterparts—has not been adopted in any jurisdiction. Gibson also persuaded the legislature to establish a generous retirement program for judges, but his retirement program had an ingenious kicker: In order for a judge to receive the maximum benefits, the judge had to retire when he or she reached the age of 70. No judge was required to retire at 70, but if the judge did not, the benefits would decline sharply. Effectively, only judges who were independently wealthy could afford the luxury of not retiring at 70.

In 1960 Gibson sponsored and, with some difficulty, persuaded the California Judges' Association not to oppose, a constitutional amendment creating a new body, the Commission on Judicial Performance, charged to discipline judges guilty of some form of misconduct. The commission, composed of judges, lawyers, and lay members, was given the power to censure judges, privately or pub-

---

[14] A quibbler might say that Gibson was not an exception since he had been appointed less than a year earlier to be an associate justice of the Supreme Court by Governor Olson.

[15] Justice Frank C. Newman was a professor of law when appointed by Governor Jerry Brown and had no prior judicial experience. Justices William Clark (Governor Reagan), Wiley Manuel (Governor Jerry Brown), Marvin Baxter (Governor Deukmejian), and Chief Justice Ron George and Kathryn Werdeger (Governor Wilson) all had meteoric careers on lower court or courts before their elevation to the Supreme Court.

[16] This reform was accomplished in 1950. At that time a county could be subdivided into judicial districts with a Municipal Court for districts with a population over 40,000; a Justice Court for districts with fewer people. Since then Justice Courts have been abolished, see n. 8 *supra.*

licly, as well as to recommend to the Supreme Court that a judge be removed from office. Up to that time the only mechanism for disciplining or removing a judge was impeachment, a process far too cumbersome to be of any use, especially in cases where the judge's failing was mainly due to age or the immoderate use of alcohol. Cleansing the bench, especially the trial courts, of judges who were senile or the victims of alcoholism was Gibson's chief goal. In general, the commission has been successful with a fair number of judges choosing to retire rather than go through the formal hearing process. This is not to say that the California judiciary is totally free of people with a drinking problem or that there are no California judges whose powers have slipped a bit because of age. But there are many fewer so afflicted than was true in the past. Unhappily, there remains untouched the problem of sustained judicial stupidity. The judge who is consistently wrong because he or she is dumb has done nothing censurable by the commission. The commission was unique when it was established in California in 1960; it has since been copied more or less by nearly every other state and the federal government. There has never been any suggestion that the commission's powers have been abused to get rid of a judge for political reasons.

Gibson was a masterful engineer of reform; he understood the importance of cultivating a favorable view of his reforms among the public; he willingly traveled up and down the state making speeches in support of his various reforms and gaining the support of important groups and individuals. In short, he was a superb politician who maintained excellent relations with all the governors and important legislators while he was chief justice (and he served for a very long time, almost 25 years). By the time he retired he seemed almost to personify professionalism and good government.

He was succeeded as chief justice in 1964 by Roger Traynor who was first appointed to the Court in 1940 to replace Gibson as an associate justice by Governor Olson. By the time Traynor became chief justice he had a towering reputation as a jurist, perhaps unique as a justice of a state court, on a level with his contemporary Learned Hand and some of the greats of the recent past such as Holmes and Cardozo. Traynor was a master craftsman of judicial opinions; he also wrote extensively in the law reviews about the role of judges and the function of courts in the evolution of the law. Traynor in a sense outlived his time. His chief interests were in torts, contracts, and other common law/statutory subjects rather than constitutional law, and it was the latter that was increasingly becoming the preoccupation of academic lawyers and judges. (Earl Warren was chief justice of the United States from 1953 to 1969; Traynor's judicial career started 13 years earlier but ended a year after Warren's.) As an administrator, Traynor carried forward the work started by Gibson and relied heavily on the staff of the Administrative Office of the Courts, an office created in Gibson's time and staffed by people selected by Gibson.

Donald Wright was appointed chief justice by Governor Reagan in 1970 when Traynor retired. Wright had gone through all the chairs. His judicial career began when he was appointed to the Municipal Court in Pasadena in 1953 by Governor Warren. He won an open seat on the Los Angeles Superior Court in

1961, and Reagan appointed him to the Court of Appeal in 1968. Wright was as apolitical a judge as it is possible to imagine; quiet, dignified, and undramatic in demeanor, he seemed to exude open-mindedness and fairness. His selection as chief justice was very popular among lawyers and especially with his fellow judges, but, in contrast especially with Gibson, he spent very little time cultivating alliances with legislators or in other sorts of political activity. Unlike Gibson and Traynor, Wright was loved as well as admired by other judges. He led the Judicial Council by gentle persuasion rather than by force of will or the powers of his office.

Traynor and Wright had some real administrative problems to deal with. The Courts of Appeal were in trouble; their workload was increasing very rapidly and the traditional solution—appoint more judges—was at least in part self-defeating since the more justices there were on the Courts of Appeal the more conflicts there would be for the Supreme Court to resolve. In Traynor's time, after considering some more radical proposals, the Judicial Council proposed to meet this increase in demand in significant part by increasing the staff of the Courts of Appeal as well adding some more justices. The result, accomplished for the most part in Wright's time, was a significant increase in the productivity of the Courts of Appeal.

The Supreme Court decided two very important cases early in Wright's tenure as chief justice. The first, *Serrano v. Priest*,[17] held that it was a violation of the Equal Protection Clause in the California Constitution for the state to support public schools by use of the property tax without taking account of the wealth of the community being taxed. The California Supreme Court was the first to confront this issue, ahead of the United States Supreme Court, which a few years later rejected the argument the California court had accepted, although, of course, the U.S. Supreme Court was construing the Equal Protection Clause of the U.S. Constitution.

Similarly, in *People v. Anderson*[18] in an opinion written by Wright the Supreme Court held that the death penalty was a violation of California's constitutional prohibition against cruel *or* unusual punishments. A majority of the U.S. Supreme Court not long thereafter found that the death penalty did not violate the federal prohibition on cruel *and* unusual punishments. Almost immediately the voters of California amended the California Constitution to conform it to the federal Constitution and to require that the California courts construe the same words the same way as the federal courts. No one can know for sure, of course, how Gibson or Traynor would have voted in *Serrano* or *Anderson*, but those cases were not their kind of judicial activism; what is certain, however, is that both decisions were profoundly divisive and unpopular among the public and especially among legislators.

When Wright retired early in 1977, the judicial branch of government had been running for the most part on inertia since Gibson's time, notwithstanding the

---

[17] 5 C.3d 584 (1971).
[18] 6 C.3d 584 (1973).

fact that there had been an amazing increase in the business of the courts. The appellate courts particularly were being buried under a crushing workload, and there was a luxuriant undergrowth of trial courts seemingly as prolific as a tropical rain forest. The California courts needed a new Gibson who could put together some fairly radical reform proposals and sell them to legislators and the public.

That is not what happened. Instead Governor Jerry Brown appointed Rose E. Bird as chief justice to replace Wright. What people noticed and commented on were the obvious: Bird was a woman (the first appointed to the Supreme Court), she was young (40, but she was no younger than Traynor had been when appointed), she had no judicial experience (but neither had Gibson or Traynor). Bird, not surprisingly, lacked Gibson's reputation as a reformer. She also lacked Traynor's talents as a judicial craftsman (California will be fortunate if it ever has another Traynor). But what was more important (although relatively hidden from view) was that Bird's temperament was almost the antithesis of Wright's. Where he was open, forthright, and candid almost to a fault, Bird was inclined to be reclusive, reticent about trusting others, and instinctively suspicious of the good faith of those who sought to advise and help her. Very shortly after her appointment Bird fired Ralph Kleps, the head of the Administrative Office of the Courts. Kleps, the first holder of that office, was selected by Gibson, worked well and easily with Traynor and Wright, and could have been enormously helpful to her in designing and implementing any reform program. Firing Kleps by itself was enough to make her fellow judges anxious.

But Bird was well positioned to be a judicial reformer because she was young and could plausibly look forward to a long career as chief justice. One of the main obstacles to significant reform since Gibson's time was the tradition of requiring prior judicial experience for appointment to the Supreme Court. Wright was a judge for 23 years, a judicial career almost identical in length to Gibson's, but Wright was chief justice for less than seven. That is much too short a time to accomplish much in the way of reform, especially if there is no professional consensus as to what is needed. In these terms, Bird was very well positioned to become a sorely needed reformer.

Unhappily her capacity to lead was almost immediately dissipated in controversy. Her name was on the ballot for confirmation in 1978 and her appointment became something of an issue in the re-election campaign of Governor Jerry Brown. On election day, the *Los Angeles Times* ran a story that Bird had delayed the release of a decision invalidating a popular anticrime measure until after the election, presumably to improve her chances for confirmation. As it was, she won by a very narrow majority (51.7%). The *Times* story and the denials that it triggered set off a small firestorm of controversy that ultimately resulted in an investigation and public hearings by the Commission on Judicial Performance.

In the end the commission determined not to file formal charges against Bird or any of the other justices, but in the process a great deal of unsavory material was made public, including a remarkable amount of personal hostility among the justices and their staffs and a startlingly archaic internal method of organizing the

Court's work that belonged to the age of carbon paper and white-out rather than electronic word processors.

During Gibson's tenure the pattern developed that each justice would have one or more "'research attorneys." These people worked in almost total anonymity[19] providing their employer-justice with everything from summarizing memoranda on routine matters to draft opinions, depending on how the justice for whom they worked wished to use them. As the workload increased, so did the size of the justice's staffs. Gibson recognized the importance of these people, saw to it that they were reasonably well compensated although they were not given any security of employment and worked "at the pleasure" of their justice. Gibson nonetheless made sure that when a justice retired, his staff continued to be employed if they wished. Traynor and Wright continued that tradition; Bird, in contrast, built a staff composed entirely of her own people brought in from the outside.

For most of Gibson's tenure it was not hard to protect staff when a justice retired. During most of Gibson's nearly 25 years as chief justice the membership of the Supreme Court was remarkably stable. Governors Warren and Knight during their combined 16 years made only two appointments to the Supreme Court. In contrast, Governor Pat Brown in his eight years, made nine appointments. That was followed by a period of relative stability during the tenures of Chief Justices Traynor and Wright (four appointments over 13 years, Governor Reagan made only three appointments). Ever since, there has been considerable turnover. Governor Jerry Brown made seven appointments in eight years, Governor Deukmejian eight in eight years (not including the elevation of Malcolm Lucas from associate justice to chief justice) and Governor Wilson two in the first four years of his governorship. In his second term Wilson elevated Associate Justice Ronald M. George to Chief Justice and appointed Ming W. Chin and Janice R. Brown as associate justices.

The rapid turnover of judicial personnel had some other unanticipated adverse consequences. The Supreme Court's headquarters are in San Francisco. The Court hears arguments in Los Angeles and Sacramento as well as San Francisco, but the staffs of the justices usually remain in San Francisco and at least through Traynor's time it was expected that when appointed a justice from southern California or elsewhere would move to the Bay Area. The tradition had the effect of giving a bit of northern California bias to the composition of the Supreme Court since some prospective appointees would be discouraged from accepting an ap-

---

[19] A very few broke through the curtain of anonymity to become public figures. One, the late Bernard Witkin, was actually working for the Supreme Court before Gibson's appointment. He became the official reporter for the Court and thereafter began a career of legal writing and publication that was enormously influential. Raymond Peters started his legal career as a research attorney to the Supreme Court and was appointed to the Court of Appeal in San Francisco by Governor Culbert Olson. He later was elevated to the Supreme Court by Governor Pat Brown. More recently, Kathryn Werdeger worked as a research attorney for the Supreme Court, was appointed to the Court of Appeal by Governor Pete Wilson, and after a few years was elevated in 1994 to the Supreme Court by Governor Wilson.

pointment because it meant severing a lifetime of family connections outside the Bay Area. That tradition ended when Justice Clark (from central California) and Justice Richardson (Sacramento) did not move (although Clark had a *pied-à-terre* in San Francisco that he used for two or three nights a week.) In truth, in an age of airplanes and electronic communications, there was less and less reason for a justice to move the family from a home out of the Bay Area to San Francisco just to have lunch with colleagues from time to time. That is, of course, especially true if the justice is old enough to expect to retire in four or five years. But something substantial is lost when justices see each other only when hearing arguments or at formal conferences.

Chief Justice Bird's name was next scheduled to appear on the ballot in 1986,[20] along with Justices Grodin and Reynoso. She had remained a figure of controversy, mostly because of her position on death penalty cases, even after the Commission on Judicial Performance's proceedings had fizzled to their somewhat inconclusive end in late 1979. Although the Court as a whole had affirmed the death penalty,[21] Bird in dissent never voted to sustain a death penalty judgment, and it was charged and believed by many that she was so committed to opposing the death penalty that she would never vote to affirm such a judgment. Republican candidates up and down the ballot knew full well that the death penalty was very popular, and they reminded voters that Bird was the appointee of a Democratic governor who could be replaced by an appointee of Governor Deukmejian if they would vote to reelect him and against Bird. When it became clear as the campaign was coming to its end that Bird was going to lose and Deukmejian win, the Republicans added Associate Justices Grodin and Reynoso (also on the ballot and also Jerry Brown appointees, but both had voted to affirm a death verdict) to their negative campaign.

"We need the death penalty. We don't need Rose Bird," Deukmejian told audiences as he campaigned for re-election in 1986. Voters agreed, handing him the opportunity to replace the three liberal jurists with conservatives. Deukmejian selected three Court of Appellate justices: John Arguelles, David Eagleson, and Marcus Kaufman, all three of whom stayed scarcely long enough to fatten their pensions. Deukmejian's appointment to replace Bird as chief justice was Malcolm Lucas whom he had earlier appointed as an associate justice. Lucas's career was unusual. He had been a United States District Judge before his appointment to the Supreme Court, and he is one of relatively few who resigned a seat on the federal bench to take a position on a state court. Earlier in his career he had been a law partner of Governor Deukmejian.

---

[20] Her first term was for the remainder of her predecessor's term. Had Bird won, she would have had a full 12-year term and thus would have appeared on the ballot next in 1998.

[21] Sixty-four death cases were considered by the California Supreme Court from 1979 through 1986, five or 7.8% were affirmed, but in every case Bird voted to overturn the judgment. G. F. Uelmen, "A Review of Death Penalty Judgments by the Supreme Court of California: A Tale of Two Courts," 23 *Loyola L. A. L. Rev.* 237 (1989).

Under Lucas, the court was friendlier to business and less likely to overturn voter initiatives (it upheld ballot measures on term limits, insurance rates, restricting criminal defendants' procedural rights, and limiting local tax authorities). In other matters, the court issued a 1993 opinion with widespread implications for California's political process, refusing to revive a voter-approved initiative intended to reform the financing of legislative campaigns. Lucas wrote the lead opinion that buried Proposition 68, arguing that a rival measure, Proposition 73, remained the law despite the fact that the courts had struck down the contribution limits it sought to establish. The court's dissenters argued that the action killed "the only real chance at reforming the link between money and politics that the voters of California have had in a generation." The court weighed in on another political issue in 1992, agreeing to draw new boundary lines for legislative and congressional districts after Wilson vetoed the Democratic legislature's versions. A six-member majority led by Lucas established new district boundaries that were applauded by Republicans as their chance to level the political playing field and undercut the Democrats' decade-long dominance.

Lucas was not a reformer like Gibson. And whether the Lucas legacy gave voters all that they asked for in 1986 is for historians to decide, but the court did make some significant changes. The most obvious occurred in death penalty cases, the focal point of the public's frustration with the Bird court, which had reversed 64 of the 68 death sentences it reviewed. The Lucas court reversed those numbers, upholding 85% of its death penalty cases. But behind those numbers lurk other less successful aspects of the court's death penalty administration. By the time Lucas stepped down in 1996, only five defendants in cases his court heard had been executed. Although the death penalty was reinstated in 1978, legal challenges prevented anyone from being executed until convicted double murderer Robert Alton Harris died in San Quentin's gas chamber on April 21, 1992. Sentenced to death for the 1978 murders of two San Diego teenagers, Harris was the first person executed by the state in 25 years. The last had been police killer Aaron Mitchell in 1967. In 1996, two death row inmates—William George Bonin, the murderer of 14 teenage boys, and multiple killer Keith Daniel Williams—were put to death by lethal injection, the first such executions in California. In early 2005, California had 640 inmates on death row, but only 11 had been executed since the death penalty was restored. During the same period, according to a *Los Angeles Times* review of the state's death row cases in 2005, 28 inmates died naturally, 12 committed suicide, and two were killed in incidents on the San Quentin exercise yard. As Chief Justice George observed, "The leading cause of death on death row is old age."

A lack of lawyers willing to handle death penalty cases has created a nagging backlog that has left defendants waiting years to have their cases heard. George said that 115 death row inmates still have not been appointed lawyers for the first direct appeal to the state Supreme Court, a right mandated by state law. Another 149 lack lawyers for state *habeas corpus* and executive clemency petitions, according to the *Times*.

The Court Today

Their individual opinions and dissents can be quite unpredictable, but the three women and four men who currently sit on the California Supreme Court seldom locate their majority too far from the political center. In that sense, and because by ethnicity as well as gender they are the most diverse court in the state's history, the current justices are probably a better reflection of California voters than any of their predecessors in the past two and a half decades. Since 1996, they have been led by Ronald George, who was elevated to chief justice by Governor Pete Wilson five years after Wilson first named him to the high court. Veteran legal reporter Bob Egelko calls George the most politically adroit chief justice in decades, noting that he has cultivated three different governors, the legislature, and the media while "tiptoeing with his colleagues through the minefields of abortion, civil rights, prisoner releases, and the (2003 gubernatorial) recall." In 2004, the court added same-sex marriage to that minefield, delivering a unanimous but narrow verdict striking down San Francisco's attempt to legalize same-sex marriage and letting the broader constitutional questions about the rights of same-sex couples percolate through the lower courts.

By no means a liberal, George nonetheless has moved the court toward a more centrist stance and is often the swing vote in close cases. Although his court remains a friendly place for prosecutors and manufacturers, he has been viewed favorably by many of the state's criminal defense attorneys, who supported his retention at the ballot. In that arena, George also proved himself adept at political maneuvering, helping engineer two changes in election law that may have improved his own chances at the polls. The first eliminated any reference on the ballot to the length of court terms, which has been found to suppress support for justices seeking full, 12-year terms. (Those appointed to fill the remaining term of a justice who has left the court must seek retention for that term at the first gubernatorial election following their appointment.) The other change added each justice's career history to the statewide ballot pamphlet—minus the politically perilous mention of the name of the appointing governor.

Through most of the 1990s, the court enjoyed a period of relative anonymity. Justices faced no opposition at election time, were routinely confirmed on the ballot, and were rarely mentioned by statewide officeholders in campaigns. That abruptly changed in 1998 when, for the first time in 12 years a pair of Supreme Court justices up for re-election came under attack. Anti-abortion foes, angered by the court's decision overturning parental consent laws on abortions for minors, took aim at George and Associate Justice Ming Chin, who had joined the court's 4–3 majority on the abortion ruling. Associate Justices Stanley Mosk and Janice Rogers Brown, who dissented on that ruling, ran without organized opposition.

Although unaccustomed to political campaigning, George and Chin did not sit idly by. They peppered the state with paid slate mailers, lined up endorsements from law enforcement, law firms, and business groups, and won editorial endorsements from newspapers throughout the state. Their message was consistent: We are solid, mainstream jurists under assault by single-issue extremists.

The opposition, meanwhile, was severely underfunded, raising only $40,000, compared to $700,000 each for George and Chin. Operating as Citizens for Judicial Integrity, the campaign had the support of conservative Christian groups; its spokesman was a vice president of the California ProLife Council, who viewed the court's abortion ruling as a further erosion of parents' rights. Hampered by its lack of funding, the anticourt campaign had no paid TV advertising and only one radio ad that ran sporadically around the state. There was a brief flicker of interest when a group of conservative legislators called for the state Republican Party to oppose Chin and George. But party leaders, mindful of abortion's political pitfalls and unwilling to gamble on creating vacancies that might be filled by a Democratic governor, chose to avoid the battle. The election results were stunning. George was confirmed with a 75% majority, 18 points ahead of his vote percentage just four years earlier. Chin captured 69%, 13 points higher than his previous ballot confirmation as an appellate justice. With Mosk and Brown winning 70 and 76%, respectively, the court received its strongest public support since 1974.

In 2001, the court lost its longest serving member, 88-year-old Stanley Mosk, an appointee of former Governor Edmund G. "Pat" Brown, and at the time the court's only Democrat. The legendary Mosk served 37 years on the state Supreme Court, writing landmark decisions on civil rights, free speech, and criminal justice. Smart, eloquent, and principled, Mosk was said by admirers to rank with Justices Matthew Tobriner and Roger Traynor as a giant of the country's judicial system whose trailblazing opinions at the state level often presaged by years those that the United States Supreme Court would adopt. Among the 1,688 rulings he authored was the *Bakke* case in 1976 that struck down racially based university admissions. Although viewed as a liberal, Mosk was often a force for consensus on the court, particularly in his later years. In his sole appointment to the state's high court Governor Gray Davis named Carlos Moreno, a Democrat, to replace Mosk.

In 2005, Justice Janice Rogers Brown left the court after winning a difficult U.S. Senate confirmation to the United States Court of Appeals for the District of Columbia. President George W. Bush first nominated her to the influential federal appeals bench in July 2003, but Senate Democrats filibustered to block her and other conservative Bush judicial nominees. When Bush renominated Brown two years later, both Senators Dianne Feinstein and Barbara Boxer vigorously opposed the appointment. She was eventually confirmed under a complex deal brokered by 14 moderate senators of both parties. A staunch, though not entirely predictable conservative, Brown has been a lightening rod for controversy since Governor Pete Wilson named her to the state's high court in 1996 over the objections of a state bar committee that rated her unqualified because she lacked experience and was thought to infuse her politics into her judicial decisions. In the years since, court watchers have come to regard her as a bold, decisive thinker despite some fiery solo opinions taking shots at the decisions of judicial colleagues on her own court, and on occasion, at fellow conservatives on the United States Supreme Court.

Chief Justice George's non-confrontational style is generally admired by legal scholars, although some critics of his approach believe he has gone too far in trying to please the lawmakers who control his budget. George is the first chief justice to secure a substantial increase in state funding for trial courts, a task he pursued while touring courts in all 58 counties shortly after he was named chief justice. Through the late 1990s, he worked to improve the court's frayed relations with legislators, who did not take kindly to the 1991 ruling upholding term limits in which the Lucas court decried what it called an "entrenched, dynastic legislative bureaucracy" in the Capitol. Thanks to term limits, all the legislators who might have chafed at that language were gone as of 2004. George has improved relationships with the press corps, becoming more accessible than either of his predecessors. In response to a discussion with a group of reporters, George changed the court's schedule for filing opinions, and he often returns reporters' phone calls, a practice unheard of under his immediate predecessors.

Chapter 6

Cities, Counties, and the State:
From Prop. 13 to 1A and the Future

Revan Tranter[1]

On June 6, 1978, three out of 10 adult Californians went to the polls and changed local government throughout the state for decades to come—maybe forever. They voted for Proposition 13. A minority they may have been, but since considerably fewer people voted against it, and many of their fellow citizens didn't vote, or weren't registered, Proposition 13 achieved a massive victory. As is often the case in life, the origins of this momentous change are clearer in retrospect.

Background

World War II greatly increased the federal government's role in California. Huge subsidies underpinned the state's aircraft, shipbuilding, and other defense-related industries, and later continued as the 40-year "cold war" period began. The economy boomed, wartime immigrants from other states remained or returned, more newcomers arrived, families grew, and by 1965 California's 1940 population

---

[1] The author is grateful for the valuable suggestions and insights provided by Michael Coleman, Kevin Duggan, Rod Gould, and particularly Michael Garvey.

of 6.9 million had nearly tripled, to 18.5 million. The state's government, under Republican and Democratic administrations alike, played a responsive and activist role. Bold plans were the order of the day, in Sacramento and in city halls and county courthouses across the state. Although a few, new, low-service cities managed to avoid it and rely on sales taxes and business license and other fees, the property tax was the principal source of income for most local governments. It gave local voters financial independence and control over the local services they wanted.

As the years went by strains began to appear. Increasing industrialization brought more air and water pollution, and multiplying subdivisions brought more mudslides and fires. Recreation facilities became more crowded, automobile registrations grew apace, and congestion became a frequent complaint. Life in the Golden State seemed a little tarnished. The expansion of social services and construction of new facilities, led from 1943 to 1966 by activist and fairly nonpartisan governors, Earl Warren, Goodwin Knight, and Edmund G. (Pat) Brown, Sr., were losing momentum. In 1966 Ronald Reagan was elected governor amid concerns over "big government," rising state expenditures and taxes, and "law and order."

Root Causes

It is possible now to see two principal roots that grew into the tall tree that became Proposition 13 and its branches. One was the conviction that the public sector was no longer fulfilling the promise of the early postwar years, when the bywords were optimism and expansion—it was becoming too big and too remote, and its solutions themselves seemed to be causing problems.

The other root was a feeling among homeowners that property taxes were increasing far too quickly. In 1965, the public started to notice that some county tax assessors seemed rather too often to find reasons to lower the assessments of business properties owned by campaign contributors. Trying to rectify matters, the legislature enacted AB 80 in 1967—with unintended consequences. Despite favored treatment given some businesses, most commercial properties were assessed at a higher ratio of market value than single-family homes. Instead of tax relief, the bill's required 25 percent of market value for *all* properties (as well as a more frequent reassessment schedule) brought a heavier tax burden to homeowners.

Not surprisingly, Sacramento's failure led to a ballot initiative the following year. Sponsored by the Los Angeles County assessor, Philip Watson, it would confine property tax revenues to "property-related" services (police, fire protection, public works, etc.), with the state taking over the cost of "people-related" services (health, welfare, and education). And—precursor of what was to come—taxes could not exceed one percent of current market value. Alarmed by something so radical, and fearing that sales and income taxes would have to be raised to pay for necessary state programs, the leadership of both political parties, including Governor Reagan, offered a milder form of tax relief that exempted the first $3,000 in assessed value of a single-family home. It succeeded with a 54 percent vote, the more radical alternative got only 38 percent.

In 1972, Proposition 14 was another attempt by Watson to reduce property taxes—while increasing the taxes on liquor, cigarettes, and corporate income, and placing a per-pupil limit on local school expenditures. Only the foolhardy would take on the alcohol and tobacco industries and the teachers' union at the same time. The electorate preferred the legislature's milder and safer SB 90, which increased the homeowner's exemption to $7,000 and placed limits on local tax rates.

As for Proposition 13's other root—the public sector's size and scope—Governor Reagan was becoming increasingly frustrated by his inability to halt the growth of state government. In 1973 he proposed a constitutional amendment (Proposition 1) to tie a permanent rope around its girth—by (among other things) requiring a two-thirds majority for state tax measures in the legislature, and confining the annual growth of state expenditures to the increase in state revenues. Deemed too radical, it won only 46 percent support. To Reagan's regret, taxes and expenditures continued to rise—partly because California was experiencing rapid growth, partly because some major programs were mandated by the federal government, and partly because the Democrats still controlled the legislature.

Galloping Inflation

Although in the Watergate atmosphere of 1974 the Republicans lost the governorship, there was a curious element of continuity about it, since the successful Democrat, Edmund G. (Jerry) Brown, Jr., considered himself a reformer and (like Reagan) something of an antipolitician. And like his predecessor, Brown found that national factors considerably limited what he wanted to do. Rising inflation was driving up state receipts, and the governor made the major mistake of allowing a massive, six billion dollar surplus (roughly 20 billion dollars in 2005 currency) to accumulate by the start of his re-election campaign. To be fair, he and the legislature were relying on regularly inaccurate projections by the state Department of Finance. But Brown was famously uninterested in the actual workings of government and the last person to try to get the accuracy problem corrected—as it has been today.

A good deal of legislative squabbling took place in 1977 over the most appropriate application of surplus funds for property tax relief. The governor, not known for his closeness to the legislators, was in no position to twist arms and achieve a compromise. At a time of rapid population growth, and a housing industry unable to keep pace with it, the value of both new and existing properties was climbing quickly. Homeowners' tax bills had begun to rise alarmingly. Legislative hearings were crowded with irate and even panic-stricken citizens expressing fear that, with no end in sight to these increases, they might be forced out of their homes.

Tax rates might be capped, but unless local governments and special districts cut their rates, double-digit inflation and soaring assessed values would greatly limit the effect of any cap. Local jurisdictions—faced with the effects of inflation on their own budgets—showed little inclination to cap rates, and people became steadily angrier. Michael Garvey, former president of the City Managers' Department of the League of California Cities, recalls a meeting of about 40 department heads and mid-level managers in the large city where he worked in 1976: "We were told there would be a surplus of about $500,000 [approaching $2 million in 2005 dollars] in the proposed budget, and asked what we would recommend be done with it. As we had one of the highest tax rates in the state at that time, when my turn came I recommended a tax cut. The room roared with laughter."

Jarvis and Gann

The legislature's failure to act in 1977 prompted two long-time conservative businessmen and political activists to circulate a property tax initiative petition to amend the state constitution. Different in temperament but alike in tenacity, Howard Jarvis and Paul Gann quickly secured enough signatures to place on the ballot in the June 1978 primary election a proposition given the number 13. It would:

- Cut *ad valorem* taxes on all property to one percent of assessed value—with 1975–76 as the base year.
- Require the proceeds of the one percent tax to be collected by the counties and apportioned among the various jurisdictions in each county.
- Permit no more than a 2% annual inflation allowance. Upon change of ownership, property would be assessed at its new market value.
- Extend to the approval of any new state taxes the two-thirds majority required in both houses of the legislature for the budget.
- Require a two-thirds majority for "special" local taxes.
- Allow no other property or sales taxes on real property, except transfer taxes.

Jarvis and Gann knew they had found a good target. A property owner's tax bill normally included payments to a wide variety of jurisdictions—city, county, school district, and special districts dealing with matters like parks, fire protection, flood control, mosquito abatement, etc. Typically, schools might get a little over half, the county a quarter to a third, the city an eighth (most city managers and council members have stories about some irate citizen who says, "Now, just a minute—I pay this city five thousand dollars a year," only to stare in disbelief when told it's only a few hundred), and special districts a sixteenth. All these bodies used to establish their tax rate annually to meet their budget, and then forward it to the county tax collector's office. It is fashionable nowadays to claim that, by contrast with today's Sacramento-dominated funding, the former system gave a sense of local control. In fact it was disjointed, uncoordinated, and not easily susceptible to popular control. Had it been, tax rates might well have been lowered as assessed values grew larger.

The Prop. 13 Campaign

Although the property tax made a good target, Jarvis and Gann took few chances. Rather than argue the merits of their confusingly worded proposal (and risk a prolonged debate on the merits of a rival proposal), they chose to attack "big government" and its supposed inherent wastefulness. Instead of discussing property taxes, Jarvis usually railed against runaway congressional salaries, long black limousines, lazy bureaucrats, welfare queens, forced school busing, and courts that let criminals go free. The success of this approach was evident a few days before the election, when 92% of those responding to Mervin Field's California Poll said that state and local government income could be slashed by 20%, with no reduction in services. Indeed, 38% thought this cutback could even be doubled to 40% without any adverse effect. By now public awareness of the huge state surplus had grown, with popular discourse frequently using the term "obscene surplus." Legislative Analyst Bill Hamm suggested sardonically that the digital clocks frequently seen on banks might add, to their constantly changing record of time and temperature, the size of the surplus.

A chastened legislature, meanwhile, finally managed to put together a tax-relief measure, in time to appear on the June 1978 ballot as Proposition 8. It would cut taxes for homeowners by approximately 20%—about half that of Proposition 13—largely by taxing commercial and residential property at different rates (the "split roll"). It gained establishment support in Sacramento and among local officials throughout the state—as well as two future Republican governors, George Deukmejian and Pete Wilson. The leaders of the state's major businesses were on board, along with the AFL-CIO. Despite being attacked by Howard Jarvis as a "cruel hoax," the California Poll showed Proposition 8 pulling ahead by April—boosted no doubt by the increasing frequency of doomsday forecasts by Proposition 13 opponents.

On May 16, a bombshell was thrown into the campaign. Information was leaked to the news media in Los Angeles that in the past year the city's total assessed value had risen by 17.5%. With only one in three properties reassessed each year, the average increase would presumably be about 50%. Moreover, the practice of using the recent sale price of nearby properties as a yardstick meant that some homeowners might receive a bill double that of the previous year. This tax on an unrealized gain caused widespread fear among people whose incomes had increased at nothing like that rate, especially elderly taxpayers on fixed incomes, who feared being forced out of their homes. All hell broke loose.

The Aftermath

On June 6, Proposition 13 was overwhelmingly approved. It took effect as Article XIIIA of the state constitution, and local government income fell by 22% (property tax receipts by a dramatic 57%). Almost half of the approximately seven billion dollar reduction went to business, just over a third to homeowners, and not quite one-fifth to landlords of rental properties. An unintended side-effect was a windfall tax gain to the federal and state governments from reduced income-tax deductions for property owners. In fact, 22% ($1.6 billion) of the property tax cut went to Washington, D.C.

The day of reckoning had arrived. Or rather, it had been due to arrive on July 1, but was diverted by the governor and the legislature. Alarmed by public opinion polls, just before primary election day, that showed him likely to lose in November to Attorney General Evelle Younger, the enigmatic Brown experienced a miraculous conversion. He would be Proposition 13's guiding light and implement it "in the most humane, sensitive way that I can." With the aid of the two massive Democratic legislative majorities, he transformed the unpopular state surplus into a welcome bailout of local government. Essential services would continue largely intact (and the voters would apparently not suffer the consequences of their recent action).

In the three weeks between Proposition 13's passage and its taking effect, the legislature enacted Senate Bill 154, a massive emergency "bailout" for local governments. It made available $4.4 billion to offset partially the $7 billion revenue loss. It based the future allocation of property tax revenues to local jurisdictions upon the pattern of the previous three years, shifted the funding of various health and welfare programs from the counties to the state; and provided block grants to the counties, cities, and school and special districts.

By the beginning of 1979, it was evident that in the long run SB 154's bailout solution was not going to be viable. State surpluses for block grants might be available in future years—or they might not. Thoughtful budget planning by local governments would be next to impossible. Moreover, the allocation formula paid no attention to the special needs of those counties and cities experiencing rapid growth and development.

The bailout bill was superseded by the "long-range solution," Assembly Bill 8. It adopted many of SB 154's provisions with several key modifications. Block grants for counties, cities, and special districts were eliminated. They were replaced by shifting to these jurisdictions a substantial portion of the property tax that SB 154 had allocated to schools. In turn, the schools received increased state funding, gaining about a billion dollars in the process. The state takeover of costs for MediCal, and programs for the elderly, blind, and disabled, was made permanent. In future years, property taxes were to be allocated along the new SB 154 lines, but with revenue increases attributable to growth in assessed value going only to the jurisdiction where the growth had occurred. A "deflator" clause was added, automatically reducing (or "deflating") revenues to local governments and school districts if state revenues fell below certain specified levels.

In 1979, not yet satisfied that government had been reined in sufficiently, Gann returned with Proposition 4. Known as "the Spirit of 13" initiative, it was a direct descendant of Reagan's failed 1973 effort and took aim at expenditures rather than income. Its intent was to limit state and local expenditures to the levels of 1978–79, through a complicated formula tied to population growth and the cost of living. Proposition 4 won with 74% of the vote, but its provisions were sufficiently flexible, and state and local governments sufficiently astute, that it never became the straitjacket opponents feared.

Not one to be left in the dark by his rival, Jarvis once again launched an attack on government income as the only way to reduce the public sector. Proposition 9 ("Jarvis II," as it was inevitably known), on the June 1980 ballot, proposed to cut state income tax roughly in half. This time, Governor Brown led a strong opposition, arguing that, so soon after Proposition 13, the state would suffer lasting damage, and Jarvis's knockabout tactics had started to pale. Proposition 9 got only a 39% vote. Two years later, voters showed the tax revolt was still alive, enacting at the June primary a measure that wiped out inheritance taxes and permanently indexed income tax brackets to account for inflation.

A State and Federal "Perfect Storm"

Bailout funds helped to keep local jurisdictions in business until the recession of 1981–82 when state revenues fell below the "deflator" provisions of AB 8. The legislature suspended their implementation for two years. But it was felt necessary to make selective reductions in state aid. To cushion the blow, local governments were given greater flexibility to levy various fees and user charges. The cities' and counties' travail was heightened by the steadily increasing pull-back of the federal government from the direct local assistance that had been a hallmark of the Nixon and particularly the Johnson administrations. For many jurisdictions, federal programs had been a major source of revenue. Within a decade, they were cut by two-thirds. There were, as Dean Misczynski, Director of the California Research Bureau, put it, "no more fairy godgovernments."

Raising Fees and Charges

Cities found themselves in a dilemma. As Peter Detwiler, principal consultant to the Senate Housing and Land Use Committee, commented, "When Proposition 13 passed, [the voters] didn't say 'no parks,' they said, 'You don't get the money.'"

Service and staffing reductions were inevitable. Initially they were mainly in parks, recreation, libraries, cultural programs, street cleaning, and capital improvements. Financially more independent than counties, cities soon introduced or increased user fees or taxes on such services as utilities, trash collection, golf courses, and hotel rooms.

Before Proposition 13, fees for things like dog licenses, animal shelters, document copying, building permits, plan checking, refuse collection, and recreation, were to a varying extent subsidized from ample property tax revenue. Nowadays the "user pays" philosophy has taken root, as local governments aim to recover the full costs of what they provide. As far as any new taxes are concerned, a 2004 survey by the Public Policy Institute of California found that city officials were most likely to favor them to maintain spending for public safety and streets and roads, rather than social services, culture and leisure, or general government.

The most notable increase in fees has been those levied on developers, who in turn pass on most costs to buyers or tenants. New homes, shopping centers, offices, and manufacturing plants depend on the provision of public facilities. Schools, police and fire stations, streets and sidewalks, freeway connections, sewer lines, treatment plants—any number of these may be necessary. In the golden days before the federal and state governments began to disengage from local financing, they paid much of the cost of the more expensive facilities. In essence, local population and economic growth were substantially subsidized by other levels of government. The shortfall was made up by general local taxation and modest developer contributions.

Developers face subdivision exactions, impact fees, benefit assessments, or other financing arrangements. Exactions may oblige a major subdivider to provide all necessary public facilities, along with sewer and water trunk lines, and perhaps arterial street connections and interim school facilities. Typical impact fees might be for hooking up each dwelling unit to an existing water or sewer system. Benefit assessment districts that affect every parcel of land within a defined area have multiplied in recent years. They may encompass even a whole city, and have been used to finance (for example) streets, lighting, and parks. Since their assessments are on a per-parcel basis, rather than *ad valorem*, the courts found that only a simple majority approval was needed, rather than the two-thirds required by Article XIII. Other financing arrangements have included tax-exempt borrowing under the Mello-Roos Community Facilities Act (1982), by which a local government and a developer might create a district that (with approval by two-thirds of its voters) could levy taxes and issue bonds to be paid off by those taxes. Mello-Roos revenues could be used quite broadly—for example, for schools, libraries, jails, streets, water and sewerage facilities, parks, and police and fire protection.

The growing creativity of cities in finding alternative income, and the generally liberal interpretation of the law by the judiciary, greatly angered those who had led the fight for Proposition 13, and in November 1996 they succeeded in achieving passage of Proposition 218 (see below), a constitutional amendment that severely changes the law regarding local taxes, assessments, fees, and charges.

Fiscalization of Land Use

What became known as "the fiscalization of land use" has gradually become familiar in recent years—city councils or county boards of supervisors judge the suitability of a development proposal less by its intrinsic need or value than by who is going to pay for the necessary infrastructure, and by what means. One of Proposition 13's lasting legacies is an increased preoccupation with how much a proposed development will contribute to a city's or county's treasury. Under the so-called *situs* rule, the state collects a 1% tax as part of its overall 7.5% tax on retail sales and refunds it to the jurisdiction where the sale took place. As of January 2006, 0.75% is for general operations, and 0.25% for county transportation funds, with further increases if local voters approve. With property tax revenues reduced and the sales tax more prominent, land-use decisions are nowadays more likely to be guided by enhancements to the city or county treasury than by improvements to the local and areawide economy. A small manufacturing plant with full-time jobs at $25 per hour and good benefits is likely to prove less appealing than a "big-box" retailer with part-time jobs paying $10 an hour and few or no benefits. A statewide survey of city managers by the Public Policy Institute of California in 1998 showed the following desirability ratings for new development and redevelopment. See Table 1.

Not surprisingly, this situation does no favors for the housing market in a rapidly-growing state where every year housing demand exceeds production, not least with regard to affordable housing.

ERAF: The Big Hit

The decade of the eighties was a hard one for California's cities and counties, but the nineties proved no easier. In 1988, the electorate had enacted Proposition 98, which dedicated 40% of California's general fund to K-14 education with no regard for any of the state's other responsibilities. Unsurprisingly, there was no appetite in Sacramento for raising state income or sales taxes to fund this obligation In 1992, in a difficult period of state-local relations, the state hit local governments (counties, cities, special districts and redevelopment agencies) with a compulsory annual property tax shift to a so-called Educational Revenue Augmentation Fund (ERAF), established within each county and earmarked for K-14 education. In 1992–93, $1.2 billion was transferred.

County and city elected officials and employee unions twice demonstrated vociferously in front of the state capitol and harangued their representatives. But despite the rhetoric of their STOP ("Stop Taking Our Property Taxes") campaign, highlighting the plight of the poor and the disabled, and predicting danger from reduced police and fire protection, theirs was a parade with many leaders but not enough followers. The general public—perhaps disgusted by yet another year of legislative brawling, and no doubt skeptical of doomsday forecasts they'd heard

Table 1. Desirability Score of Various Land Uses for Development and Redevelopment Projects, as Rated by California City Managers on a Scale of 1 to 7

	New Development	Redevelopment
Retail	6.2	6.4
Office	5.6	5.6
Mixed Use	5.5	5.6
Light Industrial	5.5	5.0
Single-Family Residential	3.6	3.8
Multifamily Residential	3.6	3.8
Heavy Industrial	3.5	3.3

Source: PPIC City Manager Survey, 1998.

before—stayed away. The League of California Cities, the California State Association of Counties and all their individual members (even the five Los Angeles County supervisors, each representing nearly two million people) were no match for the real winners—the well-heeled and campaign-contributing teachers' and prison guards' unions.

The governor and the legislature did, however, betray some nervousness about the ERAF consequences for police and fire protection. In 1993, they successfully submitted to the voters Proposition 172, which replaced a half-cent sales tax for earthquake insurance by a permanent one to help fund sheriffs, police and fire services, district attorneys and corrections. Consequently there was no increase in tax collections. Most of the money was intended for services performed by counties, who have received 94% of Prop. 172 funds.

Despite the Prop. 172 mitigation, massive sums of money have been transferred to the state, with angry local officials frequently referring to them as "stolen." Michael Coleman, principal fiscal advisor to the League of California Cities, has estimated that in 2005–06 the ERAF tax-shift will cost California's local governments about $4.56 billion in net revenue ($7.20 billion, less $2.64 billion in Prop. 172 mitigation funds). The cumulative total since 1992–93 is $32.19 billion ($58.46 billion less $26.27 billion). That huge sum of money would normally have been devoted to public safety, parks and recreation, libraries, street repairs, garbage pickup, and other essential public services. Just as significantly, it would also have led to less reliance on debt financing, and on deferred infrastructure maintenance (and its built-in future liabilities). See Table 2.

Jarvis and Gann: Beyond the Grave

The cities' and counties' burdens were increased not only by live politicians, but by dead populists. Although Howard Jarvis died in 1986, and

Table 2. Impacts of ERAF and Proposition 172 ($ in millions)

ERAF	1992-93	1993-94	1994-95	1995-96	1996-97
Cities	-216	-483	-525	-523	-518
Counties	-544	-2,374	-2,583	-2,567	-2,540
Spec Districts	-212	-252	-281	-285	-279
Redev't Agencies	-200	-65	-65	0	0
	-1,173	**-3,175**	**-3,454**	**-3,374**	**-3,337**

Proposition 172	1992-93	1993-94	1994-95	1995-96	1996-97
Cities	--	84	88	92	91
Counties	--	1,301	1,400	1,510	1,595
Spec Districts	--	0	0	0	0
	0	**1,385**	**1,488**	**1,602**	**1,686**

ERAF net of Prop. 172	1992-93	1993-94	1994-95	1995-96	1996-97
Cities	-216	-399	-437	-431	-426
Counties	-544	-1,073	-1,183	-1,057	-945
Spec Districts	-212	-252	-281	-285	-279
Redev't Agencies	-200	-65	-65	0	0
	-1,173	**-1,789**	**-1,966**	**-1,772**	**-1,651**

Sources: PSAF (Prop 172) actuals through 2000–01 from state controller. ERAF and PSAF actuals by agency from California State Association of Counties survey of county auditors. FY05–06 is estimated. Updated May 05. Data compiled by Michael Coleman, CaliforniaCityFinance.com.

Paul Gann in 1989, their influence continued, and indeed is still felt today. Increasingly offended and frustrated by what they perceived as local elected officials and bureaucrats piercing holes in barriers carefully erected by the people, the Howard Jarvis Taxpayers Association—supported by Paul Gann's Citizens Committee and other groups—placed on the November 1996 ballot Proposition 218, the "Right to Vote on Taxes Act." Eased out of the limelight by more glamorous measures on affirmative action, health care, campaign finances, securities fraud, and marijuana for medical treatment, it passed handily, with 56% support. By adding Article XIII C (dealing with taxes) and XIII D (assessments and fees) to the state constitution, Proposition 218 affects three sources of local revenue: taxes, property assessments, and property-related fees and charges.

Table 2. continued.

ERAF	1997-98	1998-99	1999-00	2000-01	2001-02
Cities	-511	-574	-606	-652	-704
Counties	-2,665	-2,787	-2,934	-3,181	-3,447
Spec Districts	-271	-316	-339	-339	-364
Redev't Agencies	0	0	0	0	0
	-3,447	**-3,677**	**-3,879**	**-4,171**	**-4,515**

Proposition 172	1997-98	1998-99	1999-00	2000-01	2001-02
Cities	104	109	123	131	134
Counties	1,682	1,757	1,974	2,153	2,096
Spec Districts	0	0	0	0	0
	1,786	**1,877**	**2,119**	**2,283**	**2,218**

ERAF net of Prop. 172	1997-98	1998-99	1999-00	2000-01	2001-02
Cities	-407	-465	-483	-520	-570
Counties	-983	-1,030	-960	-1,028	-1,351
Spec Districts	-271	-316	-339	-339	-364
Redev't Agencies	0	0	0	0	0
	-1,662	**-1,812**	**-1,782**	**-1,887**	**-2,285**

Taxes

General taxes provide revenue for overall operation of government and may be used for anything lawful on which the governing body wishes to spend them. In 1986, California's voters had approved Proposition 62, a statutory amendment requiring local governments to obtain majority approval from their voters in order to levy a general tax. During the next few years, the appellate courts found this requirement to be unconstitutional, but in *Santa Clara County Transportation Authority v. Guardino*, in 1995, the California Supreme Court upheld it. One might have thought that the Jarvis/Gann forces would be well satisfied that local elected representatives would need voters' approval for all new, extended, or increased general taxes. But the antitax hawks were troubled by a remaining ambiguity: whether the 89 charter cities (mostly the larger ones among the state's 470 cities) would have to comply, since the California constitution permitted them control over their own "municipal affairs." Proposition 218 has now "constitutionalized" Proposition 62, closing the charter cities' escape hatch. It also introduced a troublesome attribute—retroactivity—by stipulating that any local taxes established after December 31, 1994, had to

Table 2. continued.

ERAF	2002-03	2003-04	2004-05	2005-06e	SumTotal
Cities	-760	-807	-1,223	-1,275	-9,377
Counties	-3,688	-3,930	-4,597	-4,852	-42,690
Spec Districts	-384	-409	-797	-824	-5,352
Redev't Agencies	-75	-135	-250	-250	-1,040
	-4,906	**-5,281**	**-6,867**	**-7,201**	**-58,459**

Proposition 172	2002-03	2003-04	2004-05	2005-06e	SumTotal
Cities	130	139	145	152	1,523
Counties	2,143	2,274	2,373	2,492	24,750
Spec Districts	0	0	0	0	0
	2,273	**2,413**	**2,518**	**2,644**	**26,273**

ERAF net of Prop. 172	2002-03	2003-04	2004-05	2005-06e	SumTotal
Cities	-630	-688	-1,078	-1,123	-7,854
Counties	-1,544	-1,656	-2,224	-2,360	-17,940
Spec Districts	-384	-409	-797	-824	-5,352
Redev't Agencies	-75	-135	-250	-250	-1,040
	-2,633	**-2,868**	**-4,349**	**-4,557**	**-32,186**

be submitted for majority voter approval within two years of Prop. 218's passage.

Special taxes, which may be used only for a particular purpose (*e.g.*, a county sales tax for highway construction), require a two-thirds vote of the electorate, and are not affected by Proposition 218. However, it makes clear that "special districts or agencies, including school districts, shall have no power to levy general taxes." In other words, all their taxes are special ones, demanding two-thirds support of the voters.

Property Assessments

A benefit assessment may be imposed on a property owner to cover the costs of a local improvement or service, such as parks or street lighting. Usually appearing on property tax bills, it cannot be based on a property's value, but may be a flat amount per parcel or based on a measure such as square footage. Proposition 218 gave local governments until July 1, 1997, to obtain majority approval from property owners for all existing assessments, except those exclusively for sidewalks, streets, sewers, water, flood control, drainage, and vector control. After that date, all assessment impositions, extensions, or increases are subject to extensive requirements.

Under the old system, a majority of property owners (who might number in the thousands) would have to be sufficiently organized to protest in writing if they were to derail a proposed assessment (and even then could be overridden by a two-thirds vote of the governing body). By contrast, Article XIII D obliges local governments to hold a mail-in election, with ballots weighted according to the proposed assessment of each property, and a weighted majority necessary for an assessment to take effect. The vote of a corporation (even headquartered outside the state, or indeed the United States) may thus outweigh those of many homeowners. Moreover, section 4, with the clear intent to discourage assessment districts as much as possible, establishes onerous and costly procedures, including determination of each parcel's proportionate special benefit and preparation by a registered engineer of a detailed report. Agencies must be prepared to prove that a property will receive a special benefit over and above those conferred on the public at large.

Property-Related Fees and Charges

Unlike assessments, property-related fees and charges may also apply to renters, the most common being for utility services. Article XIII D, as it did with assessments, replaced existing law on procedures for setting fees and charges with far more detailed and onerous provisions—including a majority vote of affected property owners or a two-thirds vote by electors within the affected area. For reasons hard to discern, fees or charges for sewer, water, and refuse collection services are exempt from majority vote approval. By contrast, specifically disallowed are fees or charges for a general service, such as police, fire, ambulance, or libraries, where the service "is available to the public at large in substantially the same manner as it is to property owners."

Prop. 218's Consequences

There were differing opinions in 1996 as to how severe the consequences would be for local governments from the passage of Prop. 218. Certainly the Jarvis/Gann forces were playing for keeps, insisting not only on (a) retroactivity, but (b) reversal of laws and traditions, to place all burdens of proof on the local agencies, and (c)—most tellingly—the ability to reduce or repeal through the initiative process any local tax, assessment, fee, or charge. After nearly a decade's experience, in both good and bad economic times, it remains hard to say with precision what the effect has been, because cities, counties, and special districts are affected by so many laws and circumstances, such as the severe ERAF shifts mentioned earlier, and marked variations in the national and state economic cycles.

It seems fair, however, to observe that the most dire predictions have not come about, and that local jurisdictions up and down the state have been able to gain support for a variety of measures, though usually not without great effort, often communitywide. It helps greatly if a city or county has taken clearly visible steps to cut back (e.g., in staffing, salaries, or services) and yet is still unable to provide one or more services at an acceptable or expected level. General purpose tax increases, requiring only a simple majority, are easier to achieve than those dedicated to a particular purpose (such as libraries, parks, or emergency medical services), which need a 2/3 majority vote, and often end up disappointing their backers. Transportation measures tend to gain more support than others, presumably because voters see them as offering something more tangible and often (in a fast-growing state) overdue. In keeping with the old adage, "Don't tax you, don't tax me, tax the fellow behind that tree," transient occupancy (hotel/motel) tax increases tend to be a good bet. In 2003, cities and counties were granted a further measure of flexibility by SB 566, which allows them to levy a sales tax of 1/4 or 1/2% subject to a 2/3 vote of the governing body and the provisions of Prop. 218—a simple majority for a general purpose, and 2/3 for a dedicated use.

The fact that Prop. 218 has brought merely difficulty, rather than disaster, to California's local governments, should not obscure a key reality. It has seriously weakened the decision-making capacity of local elected leaders, and it represents a substantial leap in the continuing move from representative to direct democracy.

City-County Relations

In the 20th century's last two decades, the increasing financial pressures on counties and cities led to deteriorating relationships between the two groups, at both the state and the local level. Counties became angered by (for example) cities' prolific use of redevelopment districts. Authorized by the California Community Redevelopment Act of 1945, these were originally intended to revive economically depressed and socially deprived areas through tax increment financing (the issuance of bonds repaid by increased property tax receipts from within the revived area), with the use, if desired, of eminent domain (the power to purchase land compulsorily). Property tax revenues to overlapping jurisdictions, such as the county or a school district, are frozen, and the increased revenues from economic growth and inflation accrue solely to the city. The state has to reimburse the school district's loss—in effect subsidizing the city's development—but does not make up the county's loss.

By law there must be a finding that "blight" exists—the criteria for which (although tightened somewhat in recent years) are far from stringent. Blight has been deemed to exist in places as unlikely as the extremely affluent desert resort community of Indian Wells, near Palm Springs—as a result of which the city built and owns two top-flight public golf courses. Although by no means all of California's approximately 400 redevelopment districts involve abuse of the law's original intent, it is easy to see, in the dog-eat-dog world of post-Prop. 13 local finances, how city-county relations might deteriorate.

Similarly, cities were annoyed by new or substantially increased county charges for a variety of activities, ranging from animal control and crime laboratories, to booking fees for offenders arrested by city police and taken to the county jail.

Mutual irritation grew over the years, tempered in most cases by the professional relationship between county administrator and city manager. Yet even here, awkwardness could arise when, for example, at a monthly meeting of a county's city manager and the administrator, the city members of the group might want toward the end of the meeting to excuse their county colleague so they could discuss political, legal, or administrative actions against the county.

Gradually, however, signs of improvement began to occur, as it became increasingly apparent that the state, with its growing structural budget deficit, would continue to use local governments and special districts as virtual ATMs, from which money could go on being extracted to cover Sacramento's inability to handle its finances prudently. Cooperation was in everyone's interest: counties, cities and special districts.

Proposition 1A

The previous edition of this chapter, published eight years earlier, suggested that "at some time in the future, when the economic cycle again takes California into a tailspin, and the governor and the legislature again send local governments an undue share of cutbacks, people will say, like the Peter Finch character in the movie *Network*, 'We're mad as hell and we're not going to take it any more.' It may be that some group—perhaps led by mayors and council members—will draft a constitutional amendment to build a wall around local revenues, impervious to indifference or interference from the Capitol."

By late 2001, after the economic cycle had once again turned south, local governments decided not to take it any more. What galled them, even more than the state's use, in hard times, of local revenues as a kind of piggy bank, was that it had continued to do so when its coffers were flush, during the now-ended technology boom. Leaders of the League of California Cities, the California State Association of Counties, and the California Special Districts Association began meeting to discuss drafting a ballot initiative. By the spring of 2002, they had decided to try a different strategy, attempting instead to achieve change through the legislature. To do so, they formed LOCAL (Leave Our Community Assets Local), a statewide coalition of over 300 agencies and groups representing health care, law enforcement, fire and emergency services, park districts, utility districts, labor, chambers of commerce, and civic and community groups. But by

September 2003, unconvinced that the legislature would depart from its habit of raiding local funds, LOCAL resumed the initiative drive.

Two months later, cities, counties, and special districts received a rude shock. Battered by the state's substantial financial loss in the energy crisis of 2001 and its resulting annual costs for ratepayers and his decision to triple vehicle license fees (VLF), Governor Gray Davis had been recalled the previous month. He had negotiated a deal with local governments by which they would receive the proceeds of the restored VLF tax in exchange for giving up one quarter's revenue—about $1.3 billion. His successor, Arnold Schwarzenegger, had promised, as a candidate, that he would cancel the VLF increase—funds that cities and counties typically use toward the cost of police, fire and paramedic programs, and health and welfare services. The new governor immediately made good on his campaign pledge and did not seem seriously interested in making up the loss. City and county officials were stunned in December when checks arrived from Sacramento short by hundreds of thousands of dollars (millions for larger jurisdictions). Then they learned they might still get no VLF funds at all for the first quarter of 2004 (so refunds could be sent to motorists who had already paid at the higher rate).

No more incentives were needed for city, county, and special district representatives to push as hard as they could for their initiative. In the spring of 2004, it qualified for the November election as Proposition 65, and if enacted by the voters, would immediately and retroactively block the state from carrying out its so-called ERAF III transfer of $1.3 billion in property taxes proposed in the 2004–05 budget and again in 2005–06. Thereafter, anything of this sort, including reduction of local receipts from sales taxes and VLF fees, would need statewide voter approval. In addition, a particular *bête noire* of California cities, and especially its counties—unfunded mandates—would be slain. In future, if the state did not fully reimburse local governments for complying with a state requirement, they would be free to ignore it, or carry it out and obligate the state for the future.

For the first time, local government leaders started to raise the millions of dollars hitherto seen only in the coffers of big business and major unions. Their obvious determination and common interests, cutting across left-right political boundaries, and uniting employers and employees, labor and business, succeeded in getting Sacramento's attention. The governor and legislative leaders and their staffs finally began to realize that the coalition might well succeed in its attempt to amend the constitution. Serious negotiations began, becoming increasingly con-tentious as the LOCAL coalition, the Republican governor and the Democratic leadership each struggled to attain their key demands. Because of the financial matters involved, the bargaining behind closed doors was inescapably tied to the brutal annual struggle to achieve a state budget requiring a two-thirds majority in each house of the legislature.

Faced with the prospect of an enormous gap between income and expenditures in the coming fiscal year (July 1 to June 30) and the year after, there was no way the governor and legislative leaders could agree to local governments' proposals. The state needed money, and it needed it now. In May, the governor and LOCAL leaders reached an agreement, in which essentially local governments would yield to the state's immediate needs in return for a guarantee of future security for local finances. Still further bargaining with the Democratic leadership (concerned by, among other things, the need to protect K-14 education) proved critical, and it was not until mid-July that enough support was ensured for a senate constitutional amendment (SCA 4) that would appear on the November 2004 ballot as Proposition 1A. It was apparently in competition with Prop. 65, but as part of the deal, local leaders agreed to suspend support of their own proposition, and the governor agreed to join with them in campaigning for Prop. 1A.

The state would get its extra $1.3 billion in 2004–05, and again the following year. Among other provisions, it would be allowed to borrow up to 8% of total property tax revenues, if (a) the governor proclaimed a "severe fiscal hardship"; (b) the legislature, by a 2/3 vote of each house, enacted an urgency measure; and (c) legislation was enacted to provide full repayment, plus interest, within three years. Such a temporary property tax shift could not take place more than twice in any 10-year period, and only if all previous borrowing had been repaid. Voter approval would not be required. As in Prop. 65, unfunded mandates could not be forced on local governments, although under Prop. 1A, if they chose to carry it out anyway, the state would be let off the hook. In November 2004, Proposition 1A passed by a greater margin than any of the other 15 measures on the ballot, gaining support from a remarkable 84% of those voting. The state had once again postponed its financial day of reckoning, and local governments had exchanged short-term pain for long-term gain.

The Future

Proposition 1A has repaired some of the damage done to California local governments and special districts over the past three decades. But one of the reasons offered by legislators and others who opposed the compromise leading to its enactment was that it would lock into place a seriously flawed system. That would be a valid criticism even in a state, such as Ohio or Pennsylvania, with a relatively stable population. But in California, where the Department of Finance projects approximately 11 million more people between 2005 and 2030, it is of much greater importance. In that period, California will probably add virtually the equivalent of another Ohio. To do that, with a financing system that encourages local elected bodies to favor (and compete with neighbors for) big-box retail stores and auto malls, rather than housing and job-creating production facilities, is to promise—especially in the Central Valley and the Inland Empire, where growth will continue at a dizzying pace—a future more flawed than it needs to be.

One thing still with us, of course, is the dubious property assessment system that came with Prop. 13. By now, it is not uncommon to find a homeowner paying an annual property tax five or six times that of a neighbor in a similar house across the street. How long that will continue is anyone's guess. It has often been said that Prop. 13 is the third rail of California politics, and yet it has been altered—

albeit gently—since its 1978 enactment. As a result, school bonds can now be issued with only 55% (rather than two-thirds) of the vote. One can see the possibility of a similarly reduced requirement being introduced for school parcel taxes, and eventually perhaps for other local financing methods. It is possible that eventually there might be a return to the "split roll" of pre-Prop. 13 days, by which commercial and industrial properties (which change ownership far less often than residential ones) would be assessed at a higher rate.

An unavoidable challenge to local governments, and the state too, will come from powerful economic, technological and societal changes that have been taking place across the country and around the world. The information highway, electronic commerce, and virtual businesses are starting to have a major impact on trade, marketing, and sales—and therefore on taxes that fund everyday services. With a sales tax on tangible goods, derived from an earlier agricultural and industrial society, severe financial problems lie ahead if there is no adaptation to the fastest-growing sector—services—and to a society in which anyone with a computer can conduct business not just in California but around the world. Action is already overdue in Congress, and in many of our states.

It seems likely that changes will be made in the state's redevelopment laws. As described above, recent decades of financial stress have led to practices and outcomes not envisaged originally, and which a growing number of critics have deemed to be abusive. The 2005 U.S. Supreme Court decision in *Kelso v. City of New London*, a case from Connecticut on the use of eminent domain to take private property for ultimate transfer to another private owner, has stirred animated debate, crossing the usual political boundaries. It will no doubt find its way into legislative and public discussions on improvements to California's redevelopment system, with regard both to the definition of "blight" and the question of public use (e.g., building a highway) as opposed to public benefit (e.g., replacing a small group of old stores with a modern shopping center).

Another problem for local governments will be pension plan funding, especially for public safety employees. Over the years, substantial political (and financial) pressure on governors and legislators in Sacramento has led to a situation in which both state and local public safety workers, such as police officers, firefighters, and prison guards, can bargain for retirement formulas as high as 3% of their highest annual salary, for each year of service, at age 50; and other employees can seek formulas as high as 2.7% at 55 or 3% at 60. Because of recent and forthcoming decisions by GASB (the Governmental Accounting Standards Board), state and local governments will increasingly have to emulate the private sector and account for future liability for retirement costs (and for the value of current infrastructure). As human longevity continues to increase, public employee retirement costs will rise to a level politically unsupportable among an electorate for whom such pensions are virtually unknown in the private sector, and changes are inevitable. As the burden mounts, they are likely to occur more than once—by legislative action, ballot initiative, or both.

The two forces likeliest to lead to major changes in governmental policy are the "mad-as-hell-and-not going-to-take-it-any more" feeling (of which both Prop.

13 and Prop. 1A are products) and some cataclysmic event like that of September 11, 2001. It is possible, as California residents are well aware, that one day the state could be struck by an earthquake savage enough to dwarf that of 1906, cause damage it would take years to repair, ruin countless lives, and for a period of time leave state and local government financing systems shattered. Absent either of those forces, we may assume that our somewhat dysfunctional system will continue, structurally and financially.

The force least likely nowadays to bring about fundamental change is the concerns of "good government" advocates. In 1993, enough concern was expressed about California's confusing, overlapping, and inefficient array of almost 7,000 local governments and school and special districts, and the manner in which they relate to the state government, that the legislature established a Constitution Revision Commission, charged with recommending how the constitution might be revised to increase governmental accountability, get rid of roadblocks preventing effective allocation of state and local responsibilities, reduce duplication, and increase productivity in local service delivery. After two years' diligent work, including thousands of hours of hearings and meetings, the commission completed its report to the legislature, which could then place on the November 1996 ballot as much or as little as it wished. But, as many commentators had predicted, most legislators were too preoccupied with re-election campaigns and fundraising to treat the report seriously. In the Senate, a watered-down version of the commission's proposals gained nine votes in favor, and 17 against (with 14 members not even voting), while in the Assembly the proposals never even got to the floor. A similar fate was in store for the Speaker's Commission on Regionalism (2001–03), formed to seek improvements to California's weak and sometimes confusing system of handling regional land use, transportation, and environmental problems.

Perhaps all this should not surprise us, because, among all the deficiencies in state-local relations, one is overarching. In a state that is home to one in every eight Americans, and set to add many more millions, it is the complete absence of an integrated plan for California's current and future growth. By contrast, local governments must develop and adopt a general plan that includes provisions for land use, traffic, the environment, public safety, and so on. Two improvements come to mind. First, it is high time to restore California's Commission on Intergovernmental Relations (abolished in 1974), once again bringing regions, counties, cities, and school and special districts—as well as influential state officials—together on a regular and continuing basis. Second, California's governor is its chief executive and by definition should be its chief visualizer and planner for the years and decades ahead. After World War II, in the gubernatorial years of Earl Warren, Goodwin Knight and Edmund G. Brown, Sr.—until the arrival of Ronald Reagan in 1967—that is what they were, and the benefits can be seen to this day. For more than a generation, that is not what governors have been. Now, more than ever, they need to be.

This chapter need not end on a somber note. A key reform did take place. Hopefully, Propositions 13 and 1A, separated by 26 years, can be seen as virtual bookends to a series, now over, of damaging and dispiriting publications. Considering the blows that have struck it, California local government is in better shape than it ought to be, and it is even something of a miracle that several rural counties have managed to remain solvent. Much of the credit for the overall situation belongs to the superb standards of professional leadership prevalent throughout the state—perhaps the best in the nation—as well as the dedicated efforts of countless elected officials. Ingenuity and innovation are encouraged and widespread, a somewhat Rube Goldberg system is made to look good, and examples are set daily of which the state would do well to take note.

Suggested Sources

Associated Press. 1997. "Counties Hand-to-Mouth from Prop. 13 to Prop. 218." *Oakland Tribune* (January 13).

Barber, Mary Beth. 1993. "Local Government Hits The Wall." *California Journal,* Vol. XXIV, No. 8 (August).

Cain, Bruce E., and Roger G. Noll (eds.). 1995. *Constitutional Reform in California.* Berkeley: IGS Press, University of California.

California Constitution Revision Commission. 1996. "Recommendations to the Governor and the Legislature." *CCRC News* (May).

Chapman, Jeffrey I. 1998. *Proposition 13: Some Unintended Consequences.* San Francisco: Public Policy Institute of California.

Citrin, Jack, and Donald Philip Green. 1985. "Policy and Opinion in California after Proposition 13." *National Tax Journal,* Vol. 38, No. 1 (March).

Coleman, Michael. 2005. "A Primer on California City Finance." *Western City,* Vol. LXXXI, No. 3 (March)

Coleman, Michael, and Michael G. Colantuono. 2003. "Local Fiscal Authority and Stability: Control and Risk in California City Revenues." *Western City,* Vol. LXXIX, No. 8 (August).

_____ 2003. "The Origin and Devolution of Local Revenue Authority." *Western City,* Vol. LXXIX, No. 6 (June).

Dardia, Michael. 1998. *Subsidizing Redevelopment in California.* San Francisco: Public Policy Institute of California.

Dresch, Marla, and Steven M. Sheffrin. 1997. *Who Pays for Development Fees and Exactions?* San Francisco: Public Policy Institute of California.

Ellwood, John, Michael A. Shires, and Mary Sprague. 1998. "Has Proposition 13 Delivered? The Changing Tax Burden in California." San Francisco: Public Policy Institute of California.

Field, Mervin. 1978. "How Voters Would Cut Government Spending" [The California Poll]. *San Francisco Chronicle* (June 16).

Hyink, Bernard L., and David H. Provost. 2004. *Politics and Government in California,* 16th ed. New York Pearson Longman.

Jacobs, John. 1995. "A Job Well Done" [Constitution Revision Commission]. *Western City,* Vol. LXXI, No. 9 (September).

Los Angeles Times. 1996. "Reform Issue Passes to Legislature; Constitutional Change Must Not Die in that Bitterly Partisan Arena." [editorial] May 30.

Lucas, Greg. 1994. "Credit Raters Say Prop. 13 At Root of State's Woes." *San Francisco Chronicle* (July 20).

Lyon, David W. (Ed.). 2000. "From Fiscal Rule to Home Rule: Taking a Measure of Local Government Finance in California." San Francisco: Public Policy Institute of California.

Misczynski, Dean. 1986. "The Fiscalization of Land Use." *California Policy Choices,* Vol. 3, Chapter 5 (John J. Kirlin and Donald R. Winkler, eds.). Sacramento: University of Southern California School of Public Administration.

O'Sullivan, Arthur, Terri A. Sexton, and Steven M. Sheffrin. 1993. *The Future of Proposition 13 in California.* Berkeley: California Policy Seminar.

_____. 1995. *Property Taxes and Tax Revolts: The Legacy of Proposition 13.* Cambridge, U.K., and New York: Cambridge University Press, 1995.

Raymond, Valerie. 1988. *Surviving Proposition 13: Fiscal Crisis in California Counties.* Berkeley: Institute of Governmental Studies, UC Berkeley.

Saxton, Gregory D., Christopher W Hoene, and Stephen P. Erie. 2002. "Fiscal Constraints and the Loss of Home Rule: The Long-Term Impacts of California's Post-Proposition 13 Fiscal Regime." *American Review of Public Administration,* Vol. 32, No. 4 (December).

Schrag, Peter. 2004. "Coming on Nov. 2 ballot: A lot more of the same." *Sacramento Bee.* September 29.

_____. 1998. *Paradise Lost: California's Experience, America's Future.* New York: The New Press.

Sears, David O., and Jack Citrin. 1985 (enlarged edition). *Tax Revolt: Something for Nothing in California.* Cambridge, Mass.: Harvard University Press.

Silva, Fred. 2000. "Local Governance and Finance Reform: Déjà Vu All over Again." *Western City,* Vol. LXXVI, No. 11. November.

Smith, Eric, and Jack Citrin. 1979. *The Building of a Majority for Tax Limitation in California: 1968–1978.* Berkeley: State Data Program, University of California.

Speers, Joanne. 1996. "Whither (Or Is It Wither?) Home Rule." *Western City,* Vol. LXXII, No. 1 (January).

Strain, Stephen A. 2004. *Proposition 1A: Protection of Local Government Revenues."* Unpublished paper. Sacramento: McGeorge School of Law, University of the Pacific.

Walters, Dan. 2004. "Locals need to remember real purpose of redevelopment." *Sacramento Bee* (June 15).

_____. 2004. "Ten little words generate another state-local budget confrontation." *Sacramento Bee* (January 14).

Internet Sites

The website of U.C. Berkeley's Institute of Governmental Studies is a valuable gateway to the references in this chapter, and many more beyond: www.igs.berkeley.edu/library/gallery-ca.html

I.   Part II: Politics

Chapter 7

The Initiative Boom:
An Excess of Democracy

Eugene C. Lee[1]

The Vision

Nearly a century ago, Governor Hiram Johnson, elected in a popular revolt against the Southern Pacific Railroad's infamous political machine, delivered his inaugural address:

> The electorate has rendered its decision.... Successful and permanent government must rest primarily on recognition of ... the absolute sovereignty of the people.... The first duty that is mine to perform is to eliminate every private interest from the government and to make the public service of the state responsive solely to the people.

> How best can we arm the people to protect themselves hereafter? . . . the INITIATIVE, the REFERENDUM and the RECALL [will] give to the electorate the

---

[1] The author is grateful for the valuable assistance provided by IGS graduate students Kristin Egan and Mike Salamone in preparing this chapter.

power of action when desired, and . . . place in the hands of the people the means by which they may protect themselves.[2]

The initiative, passed by the legislature in 1911 and approved in a special election that same year, established the right of citizens by petition to place constitutional amendments and statutes directly on the ballot for voter consideration. (These appear together with a generally much larger number of proposals submitted by the legislature.) Since 1911 and through 2005, some 309 initiatives have appeared on the ballot; 104 have been approved. (See Table 1.) Many of these constitutional amendments and statutes have dealt with minor details of state government and are known only to a specialized few. Others have involved major public policies, impacting the lives of millions of Californians.

The Initiative Process

Any citizen seeking to amend the state constitution or to add a new statute to California law may start the initiative process. Most serious sponsors seek the assistance of attorneys and policy specialists in drafting their measures. Scores of other proposals appear "home-made" and rarely qualify, for example, one in 1994 to "refound" the nation by repealing all constitutional amendments except the Bill of Rights, or a proposed constitutional amendment in 1991 guaranteeing all workers a four-to-six-week annual vacation.

Regardless of source, a draft of the proposed measure must be submitted to the attorney general, accompanied by a payment of $200. That office prepares a title and 100-word summary of the proposed measure, which must appear on each petition to be circulated to the voters. When this official summary is complete, the signature race commences. Sponsors have 150 days to seek and file the necessary petitions. To qualify for the ballot, these must include the signatures of 5% (for a statute) or 8% (for a constitutional amendment) of the number of registered voters participating in the last gubernatorial election.[3]

In 24 other, mostly western, states, citizens are similarly empowered; most of these states permit both statutory and constitutional initiatives. California is one of only two states that do not allow legislative amendment or repeal of statutory initiatives. This has led to the creation of a quasi-constitutional body of law, subject to change only by a vote of the people unless the measure itself authorizes legisla-

---

[2] Governor Hiram W. Johnson, "Inaugural Address," before the Senate and Assembly of the State of California in Joint Assembly, Sacramento, January 3, 1911.

[3] For a thorough review of the processes governing California initiative campaigns see Jim Shultz, *The Initiative Cookbook* (San Francisco: The Democracy Center, 1996); for a broader national description see Caroline J. Tolbert et al., "Election Law and Rules for Using Initiatives," in *Citizens as Legislators: Direct Democracy in the United States,* ed. Shaun Bowler, Todd Donovan, and Caroline J. Tolbert (Columbus: Ohio State University Press, 1998).

Table 1. California Initiatives on the Ballot and Adopted, by Decade, 1912–2004

Decade	Qualified for Ballot	Adopted	
	Number[a]	Number	Percent of qualified
1912–19	30	8	27
1920–29	33	10	30
1930–39	37	10	27
1940–49	20	6	30
1950–59	12	2	17
1960–69	10	3	30
1970–79	24	7	29
1980–89	44[b]	21	48
1990–99	61	25	41
2000–05	38[c]	12	32
Total	309	104	34

[a]Includes four "indirect" initiatives submitted to the legislature, one each in 1936 and 1942 and two in 1952. Only the 1936 measure was approved by the legislature.

[b]Excludes two measures removed from the ballot by the Supreme Court.

[c]Excludes one measure removed from the ballot by the Supreme Court.

tive action. And with respect to constitutional amendments, "By any standard, California puts the fewest restrictions of all states on what can be decided by initiative, and, as a consequence, Californians use the [initiative constitutional amendment] process often and in many varied ways."[4]

The Reality

Today, how fares the initiative? Who are "the people" that Hiram Johnson declared to be sovereign in contrast to the "private interests" that he vowed to eliminate? How does "direct democracy," adopted in a state with 3.5 million people, work in a state 10 times that size? Indeed, more people vote on more issues in California than anywhere else in the world. What has happened?

---

[4] Bruce E. Cain, et al., "Constitutional Change: Is It Too Easy to Amend our State Constitution?" in *Constitutional Reform in California*, ed. Bruce E. Cain and Roger G. Noll (Berkeley: Institute of Governmental Studies Press, 1995), 265.

Richard Coke Lower, a student of the Johnson era, offers an answer: "[while] Johnson and his progressive allies did indeed strip power from boss-ruled parties, the corrupt legislature, and the dread corporations, they did not effectively relocate it elsewhere."[5] Whatever the case in 1911, by the mid-1930s Johnson's vision of a "people's" initiative and the end of "private interests" had disappeared. Instead, Key and Crouch reported in 1939, "the groups using the initiative have not differed from the organizations lobbying before the legislature . . . organizations representing interests—commercial, industrial, financial, reform, religious, political."[6]

Carey McWilliams updated the scene in 1949: "Interests, not people, are represented in Sacramento . . . the marketplace of California where grape growers and sardine fishermen, morticians and osteopaths bid for allotments of state power."[7]

The Initiative in the 21st Century

By the 1990s and into the 21st century, many of the interest groups had changed, but the overall trend was one of an increasing intrusiveness of state government into societal and economic affairs. This is not peculiar to California, of course, but the existence of the initiative has provided a powerful incentive for a wide variety of groups to become directly involved in McWilliams' "marketplace." In recent years, for example, voters have been asked to consider such diverse issues as AIDS, legislative districting, campaign finance, automobile insurance, term limits, pesticides, timber harvesting, terminal illness, illegal aliens, stem cell research, casino gambling, gay marriage, open primaries, and tort reform. Volunteer grassroots organizations, single-interest economic groups, political parties and elected officials, farmers, organized labor, environmentalists, doctors, and lawyers—all have been a part of the contemporary initiative scene.

Indian gambling on tribal land is one recent example of a major issue spearheaded by an interest group.Two initiatives aimed at increasing gambling in the state were on the 2004 ballot: Proposition 68, sponsored by the racetracks and card rooms, asked tribes to pay 25% of their winnings to the state, and Proposition 70, sponsored by some of the wealthiest Indian tribes in the state, aimed at undercutting a deal Governor Schwarzenegger had signed with smaller tribes earlier in the year. Backers of the two initiatives spent millions on their campaigns, although both propositions ultimately failed.

The frequency with which interest groups, like the Indian tribes, have utilized the initiative has varied over the decades. Although widely used in the first half of the century, the initiative was little employed in the 1950s and 1960s; just 22 initiatives qualified for the ballot in this 20-year period, and only five were approved

---

[5] "The Man Who Invented California," *The Atlantic Monthly* (November 1993).

[6] V. O. Key, Jr., and Winston W. Crouch, *The Initiative and Referendum in California* (Berkeley: University of California Press, 1938), 487.

[7] Carey McWilliams, *California, The Great Exception* (New York: Current Books, 1949), 213.

by the voters. However, as indicated in Table 1, the past 25 years have seen 143 initiatives qualify for the ballot, and more than half of all initiatives ever to be approved by voters have passed in this period. In 1988 alone, a record-breaking 18 initiatives qualified for the ballot, and this was repeated in 1990.

The increasing use of the initiative process involves far more than the role of state government in societal and economic affairs. For many observers, much of the explanation rests in increased partisanship and ideological polarization in the legislature, leading to deadlock and frustration. Divided party control of the legislative and executive branches is another reason. In a context of fragmented political power, the initiative has been used, not just by groups to bypass the legislature and the governor—the original intent of Hiram Johnson—but by legislators unable to pass their bills. Lobbyists, too, have been giving increasing attention to initiatives—time previously spent lobbying for or against specific bills. Instead, they work with clients and political leaders to shape the language and strategy of ballot measures or to head off the threat of one.

Jim Shultz reports that "[Many] initiatives have been either sponsored or very closely affiliated with candidates for statewide office or other politicians, usually as a clear tool of their personal campaign."[8] Peter King of the *Los Angeles Times* agrees: "Both parties now routinely plant initiatives on the ballot—to drive wedges through the populace, coax blocs of friendly voters to the polls, tie up special interest money that might otherwise be spent on opponents' campaigns, force adversaries to make unpopular public positions, and so on."[9]

Governor Arnold Schwarzenegger has increased gubernatorial involvement in the initiative process to a new level. In what columnist George F. Will terms an "all-out assault on the political system,"[10] the governor took the lead in 2005, ordering a special election to deal with several initiatives outlined in his State of the State speech to the legislature:

> If we here in this chamber don't work to reform government, the people will rise up and reform it themselves. And I will join them.[11]

In 1996, presidential politics even became a factor in California's initiative wars with candidates Robert Dole and Bill Clinton publicly taking opposing positions on Proposition 209, the "civil rights" initiative.

---

[8] Shultz, *ibid.*, 85.

[9] Peter H. King, "The Curtain Pulled Back, For a Moment," *Los Angeles Times*, September 11, 1996.

[10] *Washington Post*, February 10, 2005.

[11] *The Press Democrat*, January 10, 2005.

The Initiative Industry

Elected officials, lobbyists, and interest groups have not been acting on their own. While elements of the process are as old as the initiative itself, more recent developments have led to the creation of an "industry" of political consultants, lawyers, pollsters, media specialists, and signature gatherers, all lured by the prospect of expensive campaigns.[12] Law firms alone billed more than $1 million for their work on ballot-measure campaigns in 1996, "among the most lucrative election years in history for the initiative legal industry."[13]

The initiative industry is in an enviable position. It profits regardless of the success or failure of the ballot measure. John Balzar of the *Los Angeles Times*, observed that "California's biennial orgy of ballot initiatives is tops in the consulting world. . . . Here is a chance to get rich and do battle over driving issues of the day, all without the distraction of a candidate."[14] Dick Woodward, a political consultant, adds, "I've never met a ballot measure with a drinking problem."[15]

A Typology of Initiatives

Bowler et al., describe two types of groups that engage in initiative contests: "broad-based" (e.g., environmental organizations, political reform advocates) and "narrow" (e.g., trial lawyers, insurance companies). Most initiatives, they suggest, involve contests between such groups, for example, between competing economic interests, or between loosely organized popular groups and business interests.[16]

Initiatives come in all sizes, colors, and flavors. Berkeley political scientist Jack Citrin has categorized measures according to their sponsors and strategic purposes:[17]

Grassroots: The category that Hiram Johnson might well have had in mind— campaigns mounted by activists and financed by small donations: Proposition

---

[12] In 1991 the California Green Book listed 161 campaign consultants, 14 polling firms, 3 petition management companies, 22 fundraising firms, and 15 firms offering legal and accounting services to campaigns. California Green Book (Winter 1991), 260. Dutra Communications, Sacramento, California.

See also, Shaun Bowler, Todd Donovan, and Kim Fernandez, "The Growth of the Political Marketing Industry and the California Initiative Process," *European Journal of Politics*, Vol. 30, Number 10/11(1996): 173–85.

[13] Tom Dressler, "Hitting Ballot-Box Paydirt," *San Francisco Daily Journal,* October 18, 1996.

[14] John Balzar, *Los Angeles Times*, June 12, 1989.

[15] *Sacramento Bee*, February 12, 1990.

[16] Shaun Bowler, Todd Donovan, Caroline Tolbert, eds., *Citizens as Legislators: Direct Democracy in the American States* (Columbus: Ohio State University Press, 1998).

[17] Jack Citrin, "Who's the Boss?: Direct Democracy and Popular Control," 1994, unpublished ms.

13—and property-tax reform (1978); Proposition 103—a roll-back of auto insurance rates (1988); Proposition 117—Save the Mountain Lion (1990).

Program Protection: The creation of preferential funding mechanisms to protect budget allocations, as in Proposition 98—the K-12 budget measure, backed by the California Teachers Association.

Partisan Conflict: Republican attempts in 1984 and 1990 to forestall legislative districting by the Democratic majority in the legislature.[18]

Self-Promotion: Building individual campaigns for public office around initiatives, as did gubernatorial candidate John Van de Kamp in 1990 in endorsing measures dealing with the environment ("Big Green"), campaign reform, and crime and drug prevention; or Governor Wilson in 1994 with Proposition 184, the "three strikes" anticrime measure, and Proposition 187 concerning illegal immigration.

Self-Defense: Attempts of specific industries and professions to control government regulation over, for example, rent control, smoking, and medical malpractice.

Others have categorized initiatives in terms of their origins and underlying political motivation. Examples include:

The Trojan Horse: A measure with a hidden agenda, of which Proposition 36 in 1984 is the clear champion—the state lottery measure designed ostensibly to aid public education but with all campaign expenses paid for by Scientific Games, the nation's leading supplier of lottery tickets. (The first three contracts totaled $62 million.)

The Park Barrel or Christmas Tree: A measure giving organizations a specified benefit (e.g., a park or program listed in a bond initiative) in return for their campaign contribution or signatures.

Log Rolling or Horse-Trading: Closely related to "park barreling," a measure inviting participation in drafting in return for a campaign contribution. In 1990, those willing to contribute $250,000 or more to signature gathering were allowed to include items in Proposition 128 ("Big Green") in which they were most interested.

The Poison Pill or Counter-Initiative: Peter Schrag suggests that "Some measures, indeed, go on the ballot for no other purpose than to confuse voters and/or divert support from competing propositions, and thus preserve the status quo."[19] In November 1990, there were four sets of competing measures—two each on alcohol taxes, pesticides, timber harvesting, and legislative term limits. Dual measures concerning campaign finance, health care, and rules for lawyers and lawsuits faced voters in November 1996, and two competing measures (Proposi-

---

[18] In 2001, legislative and congressional leaders crossed party lines to pass a bipartisan districting plan favoring incumbents. In 2005, Governor Schwarzenegger sponsored an initiative (Proposition 77) to have district lines drawn by a judicial panel. The measure failed.

[19] Peter Schrag, *Paradise Lost* (New York: The New Press, 1998) 198.

tions 78 and 79) concerning drug discounts appeared on the November 2005 ballot.

Shootouts: Attempts by one special interest to weaken another, as illustrated by the three business-sponsored tort reform measures in March 1996, designed to undercut the role of trial lawyers.

The Campaign Against a Campaign: The very threat of a counter-initiative may forestall the pursuit of another. In 1993, Ralph Nader indicated that an initiative would be drafted to repeal tort reforms previously won by business and doctors unless a proposed initiative to limit trial lawyers' contingency fees was dropped. It was. In 1991, an alliance of health insurers and small business groups engaged in a $300,000 lobbying effort—including the threat of a counter-initiative—whose sole purpose was to intimidate the California Medical Association from putting a universal health insurance initiative on the November 1992 ballot.[20] The CMA abandoned its plans.

The Preemptive Strike: A measure designed to eliminate existing regulations, such as the measure sponsored by Philip Morris in 1994 to overturn local control of smoking.

The "Neverendum": Repeated measures (as recently as 1996) to amend a previously successful initiative, such as Proposition 13, passed in 1978.

The Hiram Johnson Memorial Initiative: A rail bond measure in 1990, supported by the Southern Pacific Railroad, Hiram Johnson's *bête noire*, which included construction that would aid the company. The initiative was defeated.

Qualification for the Ballot

With few exceptions in recent years, obtaining signatures with only unpaid volunteers has not proved successful; the number of signatures required—from a half-million to a million—is simply too large. Instead, at the heart of the initiative industry is the paid petition-gatherer.

> "Hey, this is a good one. Stop political corruption. Sign right here." Dan Jansen, 28, is going to repeat this 1,000 times in the next 10 hours as he stands in front of a Santa Rosa supermarket behind two ironing boards and eight clipboards. Jansen is one of a few people with the robotic persistence to make a good living circulating initiative petitions. Ten hours a day, six days a week, he gathers signatures that he sells for an average of 40 cents apiece. Jansen brings in 300 to 400 signatures a day, clearing about $600 a week. "The average person burns out after about a week and a half," Jansen says.
>
> The secret of volume, Jansen says, is not only to keep the message short and simple but to project conviction.... Other rules Jansen has formulated over the years: One out of three will sign. Never argue or explain. Look clean-cut but wear

---

[20] Bill Ainsworth, "Derailing Initiatives before They Reach the Ballot," *California Journal* (January 1992): 47.

a crazy hat and an interesting button. If there are two exits from a supermarket, always set up next to the merry-go-round.[21]

Although over 30 California signature-gathering firms have been identified, Andy Furillo of the *Sacramento Bee* reports that the petition "industry" is largely controlled by about a half-dozen professional firms.[22] These work through a few-dozen coordinators who, in turn, employ crew-chiefs who—like Dan Jansen—actually do the signature gathering. These large firms often assist volunteer efforts and process signatures to assess their validity.[23] Specialists in the laws and regulations that govern the content and timing of the petition process, these and similar firms virtually guarantee qualification of the initiative.[24]

The Dan Jansens of the world are independent contractors, who move from campaign to campaign—and from firm to firm—depending on timing and who is paying the most per signature. As the petition season heats up and time grows short, they may bid up the price for their services.

> A crew chief says, "I'll give you 35 cents per signature," and a solicitor says "I want 45 cents, or I won't do it." . . . Kelly Kimball [a leader in petition management] notes, "If you're slow in getting signatures, you've got to raise the price for the solicitors. It's a stock market out there. Some circulators will delay turning in their signatures on one of the petitions they are carrying. . . . We raise the price [per signature], and suddenly thousands of signatures come in. They bought low and sold high."[25]

And if there are competing initiatives—as in the "insurance war" of 1988 involving five measures—petition firms may increase the price per signature and attempt to lure the opposition's forces into their own camp.

The petition phase of an initiative campaign is often the most expensive. Andy Furillo reports that 2004 was a record year, in which petition campaigns spent $24.2 million and that during the workmen's compensation signature gathering effort, circulators were making as much as $4.50 a name "at crunch time." The big firms also benefited, with fees varying from 10% to 40% of the per-signature cost.[26] The high cost of qualification, combined with the successful record of the large petition firms—"anyone willing to put up the funds can buy a place on the ballot"—has led two leading scholars to propose that sponsors pay a substantial

---

[21] Dan Jansen, "Petition Drive," *California* (February 1990): 13.

[22] Andy Furillo, *Sacramento Bee*, March 21, 2005.

[23] In 2005, controversy arose over out-sourcing of signature verification to an Oregon firm—TechSpeed—which in turn had the work done in India. David Lazarus, *San Francisco Chronicle*, March 8, 2005.

[24] Ernest Tollerson, "In 90's Ritual, Hired Hands Carry Democracy's Petitions," *New York Times*, June 10, 1996.

[25] Price, "Signing for Fun and Profit," *California Journal* (November 1992): 547.

[26] Furillo, *op. cit.*

fee in lieu of signatures: "a useless exercise would be avoided, and a modicum of relief would be provided to beleaguered state treasuries."[27]

Two alternatives remain: Direct mail, while expensive, is often beneficial in developing lists of supporters for the sponsoring organization, as well as gaining campaign contributions. Whatever the case—volunteer, paid petition circulator, or direct mail—the petition campaign remains a huge hurdle for the "people" to whom Hiram Johnson wished to give power.

It can also be a controversial hurdle. In 1992, members of the California Teachers Association (CTA) appeared at the tables of supporters of a school voucher initiative to urge prospective petition signers not to sign. Michael Arno, head of American Petition Consultants, hired to gather signatures, cried "foul" and complained of intimidation. The CTA antivoucher supporters revealed that they had hired Arno's major competitor, Kimball Petition Management, to advise them as to where the signature gatherers were likely to be. "It's been very useful to us in knowing how to discourage potential signers," a CTA spokesman said. The proposition failed to qualify. A new dimension had been added to initiative campaigns.[28]

Another alternative is the internet, suggested to help groups that cannot afford to pay high priced consultants qualify for the ballot. Advocates of internet signature gathering say it will substantially lower the cost of qualifying for the ballot and therefore reduce the influence of organized and well-financed groups. Opponents of this strategy, however, have many concerns about on-line signature gathering: limited access to the internet for certain demographic groups, the security of the internet, and the cost of implementing a state system.[29]

The Campaign and the Voter

Once qualified to appear on the ballot, the target is the voter, but often in an unfamiliar role.

> Voting on ballot propositions places voters in a distinctive decision-making role [requiring] more information and involvement than does voter decision-making in a candidate contest . . . candidate appeal is irrelevant, partisanship is less impor-

---

[27] Daniel H. Lowenstein and Robert M. Stern, "The First Amendment and Paid Initiative Petition Circulators: A Dissenting View and a Proposal," *Hastings Constitutional Law Quarterly* 17 (Fall 1989): 200, n.116.

[28] *Los Angeles Times*, February 21, 1992.

[29] Walter Baer, "Signing Initiative Petitions Online: Possiblities, Problems, and Prospects." The Speaker's Commission on the California Initiative Process. January 22, 2001.

tant, and public opinion on current public-policy issues assumes greater significance.[30]

But voter awareness of most initiatives is often lacking. On the eve of the November 2004 election, for example, *The Field Poll* reported that only 40% of likely voters were aware of Proposition 64, the tort reform initiative.[31] Low   levels of public awareness and occasional confusion about the meaning of a "Yes" or "No" vote are typical of most initiatives. In marked contrast, 83% of likely voters had heard about the "hot button" stem-cell research proposition in late October 2004.[32]

Successful or not, initiative campaigns increasingly involve television and radio commercials. Thirty-second spots are typically the product, with the emphasis on a quick or emotional message for or against the measure in question. These spots are aimed at a more general audience. In contrast, direct mail targets those citizens most likely to be sympathetic to the particular cause. Computerized listings indicating party registration, gender, age, voting frequency, and home-owner vs. renter status provide information, not only with respect to voting but to fundraising potential as well.

Paid political advertising is not unique to initiatives. The ballot pamphlet is. Sent at state expense to every registered voter, the pamphlet contains the complete wording of every initiative and measure submitted by the legislature, the attorney general's ballot title and summary, a brief review by the legislative analyst, and arguments submitted by proponents and opponents of each of the measures.

Before publication, there is a brief period for public review. Any voter may seek a writ of mandate requiring that any ballot materials be amended or deleted. Litigation over ballot titles and summaries occurs frequently, and the attorney general's office is often in court over titles and summaries long before any measures are even adopted. The court's role is critical.[33]

---

[30] David B. Magleby, "Opinion Formation and Opinion Change in Ballot Propositions," in *Manipulating Public Opinion*, ed. Michael Margolis and Gary Mauser (Pacific Grove, Calif.: Brooks-Cole, 1989), 98.

[31] The Field Poll, October 30, 2004.

[32] The Field Poll, October 31, 2004.

[33] For example, opponents of Proposition 209, the "civil rights" initiative, argued that the attorney general's ballot title and summary were false and misleading because they failed to state that the measure would prohibit affirmative action by state and local government. The trial court agreed, but on appeal its decision was overturned, and the attorney general's language was upheld. In the case of Proposition 198, the "open primary" initiative, opponents charged that the measure was really a "blanket primary." They requested the court to order that all references in the ballot title, summary, and arguments be changed from "open" to "blanket." The judge denied the request, and the admittedly more politically positive "open" wording continued. The measure passed. Examples of court actions in 2005 concerned both substantive and procedural questions involving initiatives dealing with energy, redistricting, and parental notification of abortions on minors.

This does not rest solely on the importance of the ballot pamphlet to voters. In fact, in contrast to "The World's Greatest Voter," described in the Appendix to this chapter by the late Chronicle columnist Art Hoppe, most voters do not read the pamphlet or use it as a source of information. The reason is clear. To understand the pamphlet, citizens must have a reading level of a third-year college student; more than two-thirds of those who receive the document cannot meaningfully read it.[34]

But judges can. Despite evidence to the contrary, the state Supreme Court has held the ballot pamphlet to be "an important aid in determining the intent of the voters in adopting a constitutional amendment or a statute."[35] Attorneys who represent initiative sponsors say they are increasingly being asked to review ballot arguments in advance in anticipation of legal challenges, with respect to both court review of the pamphlet and, as discussed below, postelection litigation involving successful initiatives.

Television and radio, direct mail, ballot pamphlet—all are aimed at encouraging the citizen to vote. But in the 2004 general election, only 57% of eligible citizens voted. Stated another way, the election preferences of millions of qualified citizens were not recorded. The primary figure was even lower, 31%.

Equally important is the fact that voting Californians differ markedly in demographic characteristics from those adult citizens who do not vote. Voters are older, have more formal education, more income, and include more homeowners. Voters include proportionately more white/Anglos, and fewer Latinos, African Americans, and Asians. In short, the vote on initiatives reflects the popular will of only a portion of the citizenry.

Further complicating the picture, the partisan makeup of the primary election turnout is critically affected by whether there are statewide contests for president, governor, or senator in one or the other party. For example, in 1990 with no contest for the Republican gubernatorial race, voting on the propositions reflected the stronger influence of the more liberal Democratic vote. In 1996, in a hotly contested GOP presidential primary race and an uncontested Democratic primary, the pattern was reversed. The low turnout and arbitrary impact of primary politics on initiative outcomes has led to a proposal to restrict ballot measures to the November general election, the policy prior to 1970.

Primary or general election, most initiatives fail. Since 1911, only one-third have won the approval of voters. As suggested in the *California Journal*, "the 'yes' side has to prove its case, all the 'no' side has to do is create doubt."[36] Jim Shultz concludes that initiative campaigns are a "lousy time" to try to change public opinion and that successful measures almost always tap already popular initial support.[37] Mark DiCamillo of the Field Institute agrees: "If [the measure] starts out

---

[34] David B. Magleby, *Direct Legislation: Voting on Ballot Propositions in the United States* (Baltimore: The Johns Hopkins University Press, 1984), 138.

[35] Lungren v. Deukmejian, 45 C.3d 729 (1988).

[36] Steve Scott, "Ballot Bulge," *California Journal*, July 1996, 19.

[37] Shultz, *ibid.*, 6.

with any kind of hesitancy, if it isn't widely embraced by the public from the beginning, its chances are nil."[38] In the over 150 statewide propositions contests measured by The Field Poll since 1978, in just three cases was a proposition that started out behind in the poll's initial measure ultimately approved by the voters.

Voting by Mail

Roughly one-third of Californians voted by mail ballot in 2004. Increasingly, voters are being encouraged to vote from their homes, well in advance of election day. Advocates for state or national voting by mail policies argue that participation would increase, long lines at polling places would be eliminated, money spent on election officials would be saved, and there would be a permanent paper trail of votes. But, as noted above, two-thirds and more of the citizenry do not become familiar with most ballot measures until a few days before the election, necessitating a heavy emphasis on last-minute inducements to support or oppose an initiative. The paradox of seeking the vote of "pre-informed" citizens or of persons who have already voted is only now being fully recognized. Political strategists will increasingly have to deal, not only with traditional election-day get-out-the-vote campaigns, but with a voting period extending over several weeks.[39]

Campaign Finance

Low turnout or not, millions of citizens still go to the polls, each of whom must be persuaded to go far down the ballot to vote on initiatives and to vote the way the initiative sponsor or opponent wishes. In a world of information overload, this is a large order, and millions of dollars are required to fill it. And the United States Supreme Court has ruled that, in contrast to candidate elections, limits on contributions to initiative campaigns are unconstitutional, in violation of the First Amendment.

As a partial result, the 1992 report of the California Commission on Campaign Financing indicates that "money often dominates the initiative process even more than it does the legislative process. . . . In both 1988 and 1990 more dollars were spent to persuade voters in ballot measure contests than to lobby California state legislators."[40]

---

[38] As quoted in Sam Stanton, "Taking the Initiative," *Sacramento Bee*, August 4, 1996.

[39] See J. Eric Oliver, "The Effects of Eligibility Restrictions and Party Activity on Absentee Voting and Overall Turnout," *American Journal of Political Science* (May 1996): 498-513.

[40] California Commission on Campaign Financing, *Democracy by Initiative: Shaping California's Fourth Branch of Government* (1992), 263.

The bulk of campaign expenditures is borne by economic interests, generally in opposition to measures affecting a particular industry, but also in support of counter-initiatives. "The fact is you have to contribute to these things," said Kirk West, president of the California Chamber of Commerce. "It's part of the cost of doing business in California."[41] Proponents and opponents of the five automobile insurance measures in 1988 spent a combined total of $80 million. A political consultant commented, "It was the most money in the history of the world."[42]

The level of money spent is not always an indication of the outcome. Specifically, one-sided negative spending is generally effective in defeating a measure, but one-sided "Yes" spending often fails. This is exemplified by the tobacco industry's ill-fated Proposition 188, despite a campaign expenditure of nearly $20 million, nearly 14 times the opponents' $1.4 million. Elisabeth Gerber concludes: "it is a mistake to equate money with influence in the context of direct legislation. . . . To pass initiatives referendums, interest groups must be able to mobilize an electoral majority. As wealthy interests such as the insurance industry, trial lawyer associations have recently learned after expensive defeats at the ballot box, if voters do not like what initiatives proponents are selling, not even vast amounts of campaign spending can get them to vote for a new policy."[43]

Judicial Review and Implementation

The product of initiatives, presumably the most "popular" of political institutions, often requires interpretation by the courts, the least "popular." The end of the line for many initiatives is not the election, nor legislative implementation, but the Supreme Court of California. In recent years, many initiatives have either been totally overturned by the Court as violative of either the state or U.S. Constitution, or invalidated in part or so narrowly construed as to defeat at least part of what the proponents intended. A key example in 1999 involved a Supreme Court ruling that Proposition 5, the casino gambling measure approved by 63% of voters in 1998,

---

[41] Nina Munk, "Lobbyists New Toy" (California's Ballot Initiative), *Forbes* (November 21, 1994): 62.

[42] California Commission, 285. In 2005, with an eye on Proposition 77, the redistricting measure, even more money was made available when the Federal Elections Commission ruled that members of Congress could raise unlimited sums to support or oppose ballot measures. In a separate proceeding, an appellate court struck down a regulation of the state Fair Political Practices Commission that limited contributions by politicians to ballot measure campaigns.

[43] Elisabeth R. Gerber, *The Populist Paradox* (Princeton: Princeton University Press, 1999), 6.

violated a provision of the state constitution.[44] (Casino gambling was later allowed by a state constitutional amendment put on the ballot by the legislature.)[45]

Former Supreme Court Justice Joseph Grodin describes the difficult position in which the Court finds itself: "It is one thing for a court to tell a legislature that a statute it has adopted is unconstitutional; to tell that to the people of a state who have indicated their direct support for the measure through the ballot is another." And Grodin suggests that justices are well aware of the potential impact of an unpopular decision on a forthcoming confirmation election to determine whether a justice should continue in office.[46] At issue are such questions as whether parts of an initiative can stand, even though other parts are found to be unconstitutional; or whether an initiative improperly includes more than a single subject.

Julian Eule has expressed concern that while initiatives demand the most careful judicial scrutiny, "it is precisely the examination of voter action that puts elected judges at greatest risk."[47] One wonders whether the ballot pamphlet, that little-read document, will continue to be used by the Court as the basis for determining the intent of the voters.

The judicial arena often includes the federal courts as well. For example, Proposition 198, the "open primary" initiative, passed in 1996, was ultimately overturned by the United States Supreme Court.[48] Proposition 208, also passed in 1996, which limits campaign contributions, has been similarly blocked by federal court action.[49]

Whether in state or federal court, the office of California's attorney general is charged with defending the constitutionality of initiative measures. Personal opinions regarding the merits of the individual measures are irrelevant to the deputies in the office assigned to defend the state. Often joining the suits are private attorneys representing proponents of the measures or amici on either side of the lawsuit, thus adding another measure of complexity to the already complicated initiative process.[50]

One hurdle remains—or perhaps a series of hurdles: implementation of the measure by government. *Stealing the Initiative* examines the conditions under

---

[44] Harriet Chiang, "Indian Casino Proposition Ruled Illegal; State Supreme Court rules Prop. 5 violates constitution," *San Francisco Chronicle*, August 24, 1999.

[45] *San Francisco Chronicle*, "Yes on Proposition 1A—Gambling on Indian Lands," February 16, 2000.

[46] Joseph R. Grodin, *In Pursuit of Justice: Reflections of a State Supreme Court Justice* (Berkeley: University of California Press, 1989), 105.

[47] Julian N. Eule, "Judicial Review of Direct Democracy," *The Yale Law Journal* (May 1990): 1525, 1580–84.

[48] John Wildermuth, "Search Starts Over for Voter-Friendly Primary," *San Francisco Chronicle*, June 27, 2000.

[49] Denny Walsh, "Edict dooms election-ad reporting rule Judge strikes down most of Prop. 208's remaining strictures," *Sacramento Bee*, October 28, 2004.

[50] Correspondence with Linda A. Cabatic, Supervising Deputy Attorney General, April 29, 1997.

which government does (and does not) comply with winning initiatives. The authors conclude: "Winning initiatives neither implement nor enforce themselves.... For a winning initiative to effect public policy, government actors must choose to comply with its instructions. . . . As a result, all initiatives grant some discretion over how to comply with what the proponents write down in their initiative . . .government actors regularly reinterpret, and sometimes reverse, electoral outcomes . . . full compliance is the exception rather than the rule."[51]

Conclusion

In 1911, the initiative was a natural institutional response to the dominance of California political life by a single monopoly—the Southern Pacific Railroad. The threat to representative government was real; the public's reaction was rational.

Today, representative government is again under challenge, not by a private monopoly, but by the initiative process itself. Instead of a safety-valve, it has become an uncontrolled political force of its own. It is a force that has produced occasional benefits but at an extraordinary cost—an erosion of responsibility in the executive and legislative branches of state government, a simultaneous overload in the judiciary, and an excessively amended state constitution alongside a body of inflexible quasi-constitutional statutory law. At a time when the ultimate in statecraft is required to achieve even a minimum of coordinated public policies, the initiative offers the politics of simplification.

Peter Schrag puts it this way: "In effect, Californians, pursuing visions of governmental perfection have made it increasingly difficult for elected officials to make any rational policy decisions . . . and nearly impossible for even well-informed people to know who's accountable for what."[52] Much of the public agrees. Surveys report strong criticism of the legislature for failing to deal with many of the issues that voters are asked to decide. Voters believe that many measures are too complicated to be decided at the polls. Some 77% of California residents think that the ballot wording for citizen's initiatives is often too complicated and confusing for voters to clearly understand what would happen if the measures pass.[53] Yet, despite these concerns, the great majority of Californians believe in the initiative process—that they should be able to vote directly on important issues. Leading up to the 2005 special election, 74% of California residents thought that initiatives bring up important, unaddressed policy issues that the governor and the

---

[51] Elisabeth R. Gerber, et al., *Stealing the Initiative* (New Jersey: Prentice Hall, 2001), vii, 4, 15, 209.

[52] Peter Schrag, "California's Elected Anarchy," *Harper's Magazine*, November 1994, 52.

[53] "Special Survey on California and the Initiative Process." *Public Policy Institute of California*, September 2005.

state legislature have not addressed.[54] A paradox, to be sure, but one not likely to change.

To be critical of the initiative is not to ignore the failings of the legislature, the weaknesses of the executive branch, or the excesses of the electoral process. It is to suggest, rather, that instead of being a positive response to these shortcomings, the initiative contributes to them. The initiative is part of the problem. As Bruce Cain and Roger Noll conclude, as it is practiced in California, the initiative involves "a shift from deliberative to nondeliberative mechanisms, substantial inflexibility in dealing with changing circumstances and crises, and, ironically, even higher barriers to policy change . . . added to the already formidable requirements for changing policy in a highly dispersed political power structure."[55] And, Cain adds, important policy gains won by ethnic and racial minorities in legislative arenas are often threatened by the majoritarian bias of the initiative process.[56]

Turned on its head, "direct democracy" is no longer democratic. Important aspects of the state's political agenda are being set, not by its elected leaders, but by unaccountable, single-interest groups operating in a fragmented, uncoordinated, and frequently contradictory manner. It is not just successful initiatives that preoccupy the elected branches of state government. It is the impact of all those that appear on the ballot, forcing attention, time, and energy onto those few measures that have attracted signatures (for a price) and providing an excuse for legislators and governors to abdicate their leadership roles in deference to a questionable "voice of the people." In direct contradiction to Hiram Johnson's rhetoric, if not his politics, that voice generally reflects a special interest that often develops its proposal in private and, with uncontrolled spending, seeks its qualification and approval.

It is also a "voice of the people" to which the courts have paid homage, with little regard to its authenticity. Instead, it is a voice dominated by million-dollar campaigns and 30-second television spots and represents a declining electorate. The initiative process adds special gravity to Mervin Field's concern that "the more that nonvoters become different than voters in color, in class, in attitudes toward life, we create and build threatening pressures which could easily explode and alter for the worse the future course of our precious democracy."[57]

If the initiative is to play a constructive role in California in the 21st century, it is increasingly clear that the process should be changed. In the early 1990s, at least four major reports, including that of the California Constitution Revision Commission, suggested the route to be taken to restore the balance between repre-

---

[54] *Ibid.*

[55] Bruce E. Cain and Roger G. Noll, "Principles of State Constitutional Design," in *Constitutional Reform in California*, ed. Cain and Noll, 21.

[56] Bruce E. Cain, "Voting Rights and Democratic Theory: Toward a Color-Blind Society," in *Controversies in Minority Voting*, ed. Bernard Grofman and Chandler Davidson, eds. (Washington, D.C.: The Brookings Institution, 1992), 273–75.

[57] As quoted in *The New York Times*, June 12, 1990.

sentative and direct democracy.[58] These reports contain many recommendations of value. Two proposals go to the heart of the problem:

- After qualification, all proposed initiatives would go before the legislature (and governor in the case of statutes) for review and possible action. Sponsors would be able to amend their proposals accordingly. Measures could still go on the ballot if the sponsors were not satisfied with the legislature's proposal.
- As is true in virtually all other initiative states, the legislature and governor would be empowered to amend and repeal statutory initiatives after a specified period and/or by an extraordinary majority.

Elisabeth Gerber suggests that these changes would bring California into line with other states where "the initiative has been used to enhance, rather than undermine the legislative process."[59] In addition, with respect to initiative constitutional amendments, Cain and his colleagues suggest that measures involving institutional change—those that would alter the organization, powers, or structures of branches of the state government—should have to pass by a two-thirds or three-fifths vote and/or in two successive November elections. These requirements "would at least ensure that large stable majorities approve of changes before they are implemented."[60]

The people of California face one of the most dramatic and challenging political futures in world history—a state in which no racial or ethnic group constitutes a majority, an economy of staggering complexity but enormous potential, an environment of unparalleled beauty under siege from the pressures of unprecedented growth, a society of rich cultural differences trying to forge a common destiny. Citizens look to their representative political institutions to address these challenges, to their political leaders to try to develop consensus out of diversity.

These challenges confront an initiative process that freezes into the constitution or law some special program or benefit with little regard for its impact on the larger society. As in 1911, it is time for Californians to reshape their government and their future.

---

[58] California Commission on Campaign Financing, *ibid.* Philip L. Dubois and Floyd F. Feeney, *Improving the California Initiative Process: Options for Change*, (Berkeley: University of California, California Policy Seminar, 1992). Citizen's Commission on Ballot Initiatives, *Report and Recommendations on the Statewide Initiative Process* (January 1994). California Constitutional Revision Commission, "CCRC Report to the Governor and the Legislature." (May 1996).

The Constitutional Revision Commission proposed three changes:

- All initiative *constitutional* amendments should be placed on the November ballot.
- The legislature and governor should be empowered to amend *statutory* initiatives after they have been effective for six years.
- The legislature should have the power to amend a qualified initiative, with the consent of the proponents before the measure was placed on the ballot.

[59] Elisabeth R. Gerber, "Reforming the California Initiative Process: A Proposal to Increase Flexibility and Legislative Accountability," in *Constitutional Reform in California*, ed. Cain and Noll, 292.

[60] Bruce E. Cain, et al., *ibid.*, 283.

Appendix

THE WORLD'S GREATEST VOTER

by Arthur Hoppe

San Francisco Chronicle, November 7, 1988

Hats off today to Milo Trueheart, The World's Greatest Voter. Milo, as you may know is the man who read all 350 pages of the current Ballot Pamphlets.

Milo has been reading Ballot Pamphlets for the past 23 years, but the hefty tomes this time proved his greatest challenge. When they arrived in the mail two weeks ago last Tuesday, his eyes lit up, and he carried them reverently into his study.

"Don't disturb me, Genefreen," he said to his devoted wife. "I must do my duty as a citizen."

"Milo!" she gasped. "Why on earth do you want to read all 350 pages?"

A noble expression lifted Milo's brow. "Because," he said serenely, "they are there."

Locking the door and determinedly sharpening his pencils, he began with the State Propositions, reading each Official Title and Summary prepared by the Attorney General, studying each Analysis by the Legislative Analyst, weighing the Arguments in Favor, the Rebuttals to the Arguments in Favor, the Arguments Against, the Rebuttals to the Arguments Against and, finally, poring over each Text of the Proposed Law.

The first proposition took him well into Wednesday morning. "Only 54 more to go," said Milo happily. With the caution of a veteran Ballot Pamphlet reader, Milo moved slowly onward, his heart beating ever faster. He knew he must avoid being panicked by scare tactics, misdirected by devious ploys, suffocated by noxious rhetoric, or drowned in treacherous pools of turgid prose.

On Friday, Milo's boss called to find out where he'd been all week. "At the moment," said Milo, "I am trying to determine whether I favor the homogeneity of loss experience or the extent of competition in the line, subline or class of insurance in each affected territory."

"You mean you've spent four days trying to decide how to vote?" demanded his boss. "There's no room for the likes of you here at our olive sorting plant. You're fired!"

On Monday Genefreen rapped on his study door. "Please be quiet," said Milo. "I'm trying to determine whether 'historical losses per exposure and the basis for any duration of the estimated future losses per past experience' means what it says."

"Democracy has outlived its attraction, Milo," said Genefreen, "and so have you. I am running off with a monarchist I met at the 7-Eleven."

But Milo persevered. On Tuesday, he emerged from his study for one brief moment and his dog bit him. "Yes," he said thoughtfully, as he applied iodine to the wound, "I agree with the Argument Against Proposition V: Police horses *should* wear diapers."

By now, the end was in sight. It came as Milo, for the 36th time, went over the Paid Arguments Against Proposition Z—The Hetch Hetchy Power Contracts.

"But why," he muttered as his eyes glazed over, "should enforcing the Raker Act lead to increased drug addiction?"

They found him curled up on the floor in a fetal position, mumbling something about "pursuant to applicable base year jurisdiction notwithstanding, implementation there under shall not be prorated proportionately."

"Poor man," said the Judge sympathetically "why couldn't he be satisfied with making reasonable guesses like other good citizens?"

And so Milo Trueheart was committed to The Daffodil Deli Home for the Serene—another victim of too much democracy in action.

Suggested Sources

Bowler, Shaun, et al. 1998. "Election Law and Rules for Using Initiatives." In *Citizens as Legislators: Direct Democracy in the United States,* ed. Todd Donovan and Caroline J. Tobert. Columbus: Ohio State University Press.

Cain, Bruce E., and Roger G. Noll, eds. 1995. *Constitutional Reform in California.* Berkeley: Institute of Governmental Studies Press.

California Commission on Campaign Financing. 1992. *Democracy by Initiative: Shaping California's Fourth Branch of Government.* Los Angeles: Center for Responsive Government.

Cronin, Thomas E. 1989. *Direct Democracy: The Politics of Initiative, Referendum, and Recall.* Cambridge, Mass.: Harvard University Press.

Dubois, Philip L., and Floyd F. Feeney. 1992. *Improving the California Initiative Process: Options for Change.* Berkeley: University of California, California Policy Seminar.

Eule, Julian N. 1990. "Judicial Review of Direct Democracy." *The Yale Law Journal* 99 (May).

Gerber, Elisabeth R. 1999. *The Populist Paradox: Interest Group Influence and the Promise of Direct Legislation.* Princeton, NJ: Princeton University Press.

Gerber, Elisabeth R., et al. 2001. *Stealing the Initiative: How State Government Responds to Direct Democracy.* New Jersey: Prentice Hall.

Lowenstein, Daniel H. 1982. "Campaign Spending and Ballot Propositions: Recent Experience, Public Choice Theory, and the First Amendment." *UCLA Law Review* 29 (February).

Magleby, David B. 1994. "Direct Legislation in the American States." In *Referendums Around the World: The Growing Use of Direct Democracy,* ed. David Butler and Austin Ranney. Washington, D.C.: American Enterprise Institute Press.

Schrag, Peter. 1998. *Paradise Lost: California's Experience, America's Future.* New York: The New Press.

Shultz, Jim. 1996. *The Initiative Cookbook.* San Francisco: The Democracy Center.

Chapter 8

Redistricting:
California 1971–2001

J. Morgan Kousser

The struggle for control over redistricting has been at the core of California politics since 1970, sparking extremely bitter partisan strife and ultimately under-mining both the legitimacy and the institutional capacities of the legislature and the state Supreme Court. The outcomes of these reapportionment wars have been profoundly ironic in three ways: First, while redistricting has markedly increased the representation of ethnic minority groups, which until recently has been a largely uncontroversial enterprise, it has had a much more modest effect on the partisan composition of the legislative and congressional delegations, which has been the principal focus of conflict. Second, while Democrats in general and Afri-can-American and Latino Democrats in particular won nearly every reapportion-ment battle, Republicans were able to turn their own persistent defeats into a seemingly permanent ability to block public policy that they oppose, including redistricting itself. Third, while voters presumably supported limits on legislators' terms partly to minimize partisan squabbling, their action has, in fact, ensured that partisanship will become ever nastier in the legislature, especially in the millennial redistricting.

1971: Targeting Your Opponents

The last chance for compromise over redistricting between California's parties may have been blown away by a volley of rifle shots in 1971. Like any good California story, this one starts with a flashback. Despite a pro-Democratic redistricting in 1965, when the state faced up to the strict equal population standards that federal courts had imposed after *Baker v. Carr,* Republicans gained a slight majority in the lower house, the Assembly, in the 1968 election. Assuming that his party would retain control in 1970, and would therefore be able to design a partisan reapportionment, Rep. Jerry Lewis of the Elections and Constitutional Amendments Committee drafted an internal memo outlining Republican plans. "In my judgment," he proclaimed,

> our number one criteria [*sic*] should be a program designed to establish districts in California that will elect the highest possible number of Republicans to the State Legislature and the House of Representatives. A second item for consideration is to include in the plan Democrat [*sic*] districts with sizable majority [*sic*] for those who are measured to be the "least effective members" of the minority party. . . . I believe we have an unusually good opportunity to develop a "balanced and representative plan" which in reality is totally designed for partisan purposes.

Unfortunately for the GOP, the party lost its Assembly majority in the 1970 elections, and Democrats retained a slim majority in the state Senate. To add mortification to defeat, Lewis's revealing memo was left in the committee files when the Democrats took over. When Lewis gave an especially sanctimonious speech on the floor denouncing the Democrats for engaging in what he termed partisan gerrymandering, Democratic Speaker Bob Moretti whipped out the memo, quoting the pertinent passages, no doubt to Democratic guffaws and Republican chagrin. In fact, both parties viewed reapportionment as primarily a partisan battle— the Democrats were just a bit more open about it.

With Ronald Reagan in the governor's chair and thin Democratic majorities in both houses of the legislature and in the congressional delegation, the 1971 redistricting should have been a compromise, an incumbent gerrymander that did not overly advantage or disadvantage either party. It nearly happened that way. In late 1971, Governor Reagan, the Democratic state legislative majority, and the 38 incumbent members of Congress from both parties had agreed on boundaries for the congressional and state Senate seats and had just settled on a redistricting of the state Assembly when a millionaire Anglo Republican upset a Latino Democrat in a special election. Attracting state and national attention in his effort to become the third Latino in the Assembly, Richard Alatorre was a solid favorite to carry a heavily Democratic, ethnically and culturally diverse district in Los Angeles. Alatorre was derailed, Democrats charged, by a series of "dirty tricks" in a West Coast Watergate campaign managed by the future Los Angeles county chairman of the "Committee to Reelect the President"—i.e., President Richard Nixon. Anglo Democratic voters received mail from nonexistent "Democratic committees" at vacant-lot addresses alleging ties between Alatorre and violent Latino gangs, a radical Chicano political party ran a suspiciously well-funded campaign openly aimed at defeating Alatorre, and on the night before the election, someone fired rifle shots through a window of the house of the campaign manager of Alatorre's Republican opponent—an event that received widespread newspaper and television coverage throughout election day. As the Republican's chief political consultant later remarked about his efforts to defeat Alatorre, "I called the shots."

Having won the district, Republicans demanded that it be redrawn to favor the Republican victor. Outraged Democrats balked, and a potential deal collapsed when Gov. Reagan refused to pledge to endorse agreements negotiated by Republicans in the legislature. After a stormy confrontation between Reagan and the Republican legislative caucus, Democrats passed their own redistricting bill for the Assembly and the bipartisan bills for the other two bodies on Dec. 20, 1971, Reagan immediately vetoed all of them, and power passed to the State Supreme Court. Thus, the 20-year partisan battle over reapportionment in California was set off when an attempt by Democrats to increase ethnic minority representation was blocked by Republicans. Partisan and ethnic factors in California reapportionment are inseparably intertwined.

Brushing aside Republican arguments that their proposed districts were more competitive than those of the Democrats, as well as the Democratic answer that the competition in the Republican plan was between Democratic leaders whose districts had been scrambled so that nearly all of them would have to run against each other, Chief Justice Donald Wright in effect postponed the controversy until after the 1972 elections. Despite the fact that the Assembly and Senate districts were no longer equal in population, the state Supreme Court temporarily kept them as they were, adopted the congressional lines (including five new congressional seats) that both parties had agreed upon, and gave the 1973 legislature a chance to compromise, threatening to have Special Masters draw up a plan if the legislators could not come to an agreement. After Democrats won solid majorities in all three bodies in 1972, incumbents from both parties hammered out a new agreement, but Reagan again vetoed it.

The state Supreme Court appointed three retired Anglo Appeals Court judges, two Democrats and one Republican, and they, in turn, relied on law professor Paul McKaskle and political scientist Gordon Baker to draw the actual redistricting plans. Placing 29 members of the Assembly and 18 senators in districts with at least one other incumbent, the McKaskle-Baker plan, which the Supreme Court approved, appeared likely to decimate the ranks of sitting politicians of both parties. It also substantially increased the possibilities for minorities in Congress, drawing one more majority-black seat than the incumbent-oriented compromise had provided for, and in the state Senate, where McKaskle returned, in effect, to a Democratic plan that Reagan had vetoed. (See Figure 1.) Not subject to the pressures of satisfying the governor and majorities of both houses of the legislature, McKaskle was free to draw squarish districts that looked quite regular on a flat, featureless map, which is how they were typically presented to the public. They were also politically disadvantageous to the Democrats, at least if the conditions of

Figure 1. Ethnic Minority California
Legislators, 1970-1994

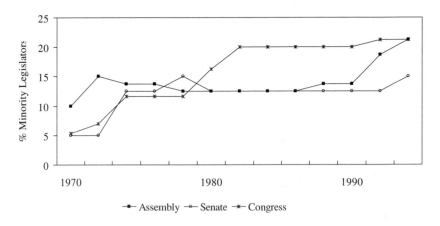

-■- Assembly -○- Senate -*- Congress

the 1972 elections had continued throughout the decade. Using methods detailed in papers published elsewhere,[1] I estimate that Assembly Democrats would have won only 42 Assembly seats, instead of the 51 that they actually carried, if the 1972 elections had been held using the boundaries drawn by the Masters.

By the time of the 1974 elections, however, the first oil price shock, the 1973–74 recession, the Watergate hearings and resignations, and the pardoning of Richard Nixon had taken place, the electorate had shifted massively away from the GOP, and many districts that McKaskle may have rated as marginally Republican[2] became solidly Democratic. As a result, Democrats gained their largest majority in the Assembly since 1877 and won 28 of the 43 congressional seats. (See Figure 2.) The Democratic landslide was not the result of the McKaskle plans. If the 1974 elections had been held within the 1972 boundaries, instead of those of 1974, I estimate that Democrats would have won one more congressional and three more Assembly seats than they actually did in 1974. Other methods of estimation show the Democrats perhaps gaining a congressional seat as a result of the court-ordered plans. In any event, their successes in the 1970s under districting arrangements

---

[1] "Estimating the Partisan Consequences of Redistricting Plans—Simply," Caltech Social Science Working Paper #929 (June 1995); "Reapportionment Wars: Party, Race, and Redistricting in California, 1971-92," Caltech Social Science Working Paper #930 (August 1995).

[2] The Masters' Papers in the IGS Library indicate that they computed party registration figures from 1970 for their proposed districts in each legislative body, and that they tallied the winners the 1970 gubernatorial and U.S. Senate campaigns for each of their own districts. Surviving papers do not make clear exactly what analysis the Masters or their staff performed on the basis of these figures.

Figure 2. Partisanship of California
Legislators, 1970-94

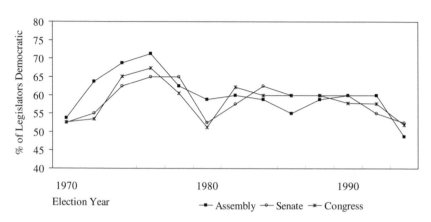

drawn for the judiciary primarily by McKaskle inclined Democrats to trust that courts and Special Masters, especially if advised by former poverty lawyer McKaskle, would not be terribly unfair to them in reapportionment. This expectation was to become an important consideration in the 1990s redistricting battles.

The 1980s: Protracted War over Redistricting

As the 1980s round of redistricting approached, the political situation in California had changed considerably. Six percent fewer voters registered with one of the two major parties in 1980 than in 1972, and the volatility of voters and their tendency to split tickets rose with the amount of political independence. Although Democrat Jerry Brown had replaced Republican Ronald Reagan as governor and the Democrats still held the edge in both houses of the legislature and the state's congressional delegation, their majorities had been much reduced by the reverberations of the Proposition 13 (property tax reduction) campaign in 1978 and the electoral thunder of Ronald Reagan's presidential campaign in 1980. After the 1976 election, the numbers of Democratic seats in the Assembly, Senate, and Congress, respectively, were 57, 26, and 29; after the 1980 election, 49, 21, and 22. While Republicans wished to lock in or improve on their recent gains with favorable district lines—they asserted a right to between six-tenths and two-thirds of the congressional seats—Democrats wanted to reclaim several close districts that they had previously controlled. The Democratic majority on the state Supreme Court was more solid, six to one, but Republicans had already backed an almost-successful campaign against the state's first female chief justice, Rose Bird, three of the Jerry Brown-appointed justices were subject to voter rejection on the 1982 ballot, and Republicans hoped that threatened judges would veto any partisan Democratic reapportionment. If all else failed, Republicans believed that they might be able to cut a deal with the Democrats. It was this last belief that so inflamed the fight for the Assembly Speakership in 1980.

Since Jess Unruh modernized the California legislature during the 1960s, the Speaker has been the state's second most powerful official, centrally coordinating fundraising and campaign planning, controlling the agenda and appointing all committee chairs in the Assembly, doling out or denying perquisites, and using these powers to foster or blight legislation and careers. Because the Speaker is elected by the members of the Assembly and can theoretically be replaced at any time, she must be particularly concerned with redistricting. In 1980, Republicans were frantic over the prospect that Howard Berman might become Speaker and his brother Michael, a reapportionment staffer in 1971, might be put in charge of reapportionment. In another ironic twist, Republicans defeated the Bermans by throwing their support to Willie Brown, later their *bête noire* in every sense of the word. All they received from Brown was veto power over Republican committee assignments and a vague promise of partisan fairness in redistricting. More tangibly, the Republicans got corporate allies to finance a computerized redistricting operation at the Rose Institute of Claremont McKenna College, staffed by veterans of the 1971 Republican redistricting effort, and threatened lawsuits and referenda if the Democratic plans did not meet with Republican approval.

They did not, especially the congressional plan drawn by San Francisco Congressman Phil Burton—without a computer, but with the help of a mechanical adding machine and, more importantly, of Michael Berman. Together, Burton and Berman drew safe districts for their friends and relatives, paid back a few old enemies, and, without much pressure from the Voting Rights Act, tripled the number of congressional seats that Latinos could expect to win. Latino and black support for the Democrats also guaranteed fair treatment for ethnic minorities in Assembly and Senate redistricting. In the Assembly, which he had managed to enter in the Watergate landslide election, Richard Alatorre became chairman of the Elections and Reapportionment Committee and, with his chief consultant, Bruce Cain, substantially increased the number of Assembly districts in which Latinos could strongly influence the outcome. Along with Speaker Brown, an African American, Alatorre also made sure that state Senate and congressional lines were fair to blacks, Latinos, and Asian Americans. In no reapportionment in the state's history have members of ethnic minorities had more power than in 1981—a sharp contrast to the all-Anglo Masters' redistrictings of 1973 and 1991.

Republicans exploded, one likening the Democratic plans to the Nazi Holocaust, another comparing Speaker Brown (unfavorably) to the contemporary Iranian theocrat, the Ayatollah Khomeini, while a third, speaking in the understated manner so characteristic of attorneys, called the Burton plan "the most egregious partisan gerrymander, not only of this decade but any other decade as well." Charging that the Democratic lines would cost them from six to 10 seats in Congress, Republicans qualified the first referendum ever held on specific reapportionment plans in the history of the state for the June 1982 primary ballot, and they petitioned a federal district court and the state Supreme Court to enjoin operation of the redistricting of all three legislative bodies until the voters had had a chance to overturn them. They insisted that the judges ignore the facts that, unlike the 1971 and 1972 plans, the 1981 statutes had passed both houses of the legislature and been signed by the governor, and that, if an injunction were granted, completely new primaries would have to be held in either the pre-1981 districts or in new ones devised by the courts.

As in 1971, the state Supreme Court unanimously decided to put the new congressional districts into effect immediately, because otherwise, the two additional members of Congress would have to be selected at-large, which was illegal under a 1967 federal law. But unlike the case decided a decade earlier, the Court also ruled that the 1982 elections for the Assembly and the Senate should be held in the districts created by the legislature. For a four-three majority, Chief Justice Rose Bird wrote that to use the old, by now severely malapportioned districts would violate the equal population requirement that courts had ruled to be implicit in the federal and state constitutions. Republicans responded by threatening to join an ongoing effort to defeat the four Jerry Brown-appointed members of the Court, and the party did oppose three of them in the November election. In the federal court, Republican moves for a temporary injunction against the plans on the grounds that they favored the Democratic party, that they had not yet been pre-cleared by the U.S. Department of Justice, and that shifts in Senate lines would prevent some voters from selecting senators for six years were unceremoniously rejected. The GOP was more successful in the June referendum, as voters objected to each of the Democratic plans by margins of 62–65%, setting the stage for a November 1982 vote on a redistricting commission.

Written by Republican activist and attorney Vigo Nielsen, Jr., backed by the good government group Common Cause, and bankrolled by $400,000 from the state Republican party, the complicated 10-person commission plan appeared, on the surface at least, so carefully balanced between the two major political parties that it was likely to result in a bipartisan gerrymander. (Proponents of the plan, numbered Proposition 14 on the November ballot, did not stress this implication of their handiwork.) Six members were to be representatives of the two major parties selected by partisan caucuses in the Assembly and Senate and by the state party chairpersons. Four "independent" members who were, in the words of the initiative, to "bring ethnic, social, and geographic diversity to the commission" were to be chosen by a two-thirds vote of the seven most senior justices on the State Court of Appeals. Since it took seven votes to adopt a plan in the commission, at least one partisan from each side would have to approve any redistricting. If the commission deadlocked, the state Supreme Court had 60 days to draw up a proposal, probably using the commission and its staff as Special Masters.

While the commission was directed to encourage electoral competition, there was no mention of protection of the rights of ethnic minorities as a goal of its plans—an omission that Democrats and representatives of minority groups pounced upon. Proposition 14 got lost in the cacophony of elections for state officers and a U.S. senator, and showier propositions on handgun and nuclear arms control. In any event, after November but before Republican governor George Deukmejian could be sworn in, Democrats drew compromise redistricting plans that appealed to enough Republican legislators to obtain two-thirds majorities (which precluded another referendum), and lame-duck governor Jerry Brown signed them. By this time, most agreed with Senate Minority Leader Bill Campbell's remark: "I'm sick and tired of reapportionment."

Two groups, however, were not: extreme right-wing Republicans, who had no desire to see incumbents of either party solidified in control, and Republican political consultants, whose livelihood depended on the expectation of close elections. They united in early 1983 behind plans drawn at the Rose Institute and initially financed by state Assemblyman and wine company heir Don Sebastiani. Responding to the rightward pressure, the Republican State Committee pledged $300,000 for the Sebastiani Initiative, a statute consisting largely of maps of regularly shaped districts, which were actually designed to decimate Democrats, particularly those from minority groups. Privately, Democrats quipped that Sebastiani had jammed so many African Americans into one Los Angeles Assembly district that it contained more blacks "than any district this side of Lagos, Nigeria." Governor Deukmejian set a special election for December 13, 1983, a date whose proximity to religious holidays guaranteed a low turnout.

This time, Democrats went to court, stressing not only Sebastiani's minority vote dilution, but also the state constitutional provision mandating a reapportionment every decade, which had been interpreted by a previous state Supreme Court decision to set both a minimum and a maximum of one rearrangement of lines every 10 years. In a 6-1, party-line vote, Chief Justice Bird and the state Supreme Court ignored the federal minority vote dilution point, but agreed with the Democrats on the once-a-decade provision, dismissing the Republican argument that since no election had been held under the lame-duck lines, the redistricting had not actually become final yet. The justices therefore enjoined the proposed December election.

Although Common Cause next proposed a reapportionment commission that would go into effect only in 1991 and Sebastiani floated an initiative that renamed his maps a constitutional amendment in order to sidestep the Bird Court, Gov. Deukmejian and the Republican leadership rejected both in favor of a new commission, set up by state constitutional amendment, that would draw lines that would take effect in 1986. Rejecting the partisan balance of the defeated Proposition 14, the governor proposed to draw the commission from among the justices of the State Courts of Appeals. When the State Judicial Council objected that the task was too political for sitting judges to be involved in, Deukmejian substituted retired Appeals Court justices. Both the second proposal and the judges' reaction to the first provided the very well-funded Democratic campaign against the commission with lines of attack. The commission would inevitably tarnish the judicial ermine, Democrats announced in simplistic television commercials, billboards, and targeted mail, because judges would be picked with an eye to their future partisan loyalties. And retired judges, 34 of the 38 of whom in 1984 were Anglo males, many having resumed lucrative law practices, were hardly representative of minorities and women and might have clients who would benefit from a reapportionment biased in a particular direction. Republicans countered with advertising that treated Democratic politicians as if they had recently invented gerrymandering, bringing a previously pristine process into disrepute, and they announced that the Democrats' boundaries were so biased that Republicans would seriously contest only a few marginal seats, devoting their millions instead to the commission fight. In practical terms, this meant that Republicans conceded seats to the Democrats in their potentially strongest election of the decade, allowing Democrats to solidify their positions with the electorate. Voters responded to this unedifying spectacle, which only served to blacken the reputations of all politicians further, by rejecting Deukmejian's commission by a 55-45% margin on the same day in November 1984 that they overwhelmingly elected Ronald Reagan to a second term as president.

After this loss, Sebastiani tried again to interest Republican party leaders in his initiative, but they preferred to continue their federal lawsuit challenging the redistricting as unconstitutionally partisan, a suit that gained credibility in 1986, when the U.S. Supreme Court, in an Indiana case, ruled partisan gerrymandering justiciable. In 1989, however, the Supreme Court summarily affirmed a three-judge district court's decision that the Burton plan was not sufficiently partisan to be unconstitutional.

Republicans then proposed two reapportionment initiatives in 1990. The first, Proposition 118, aimed at forcing a bipartisan or perhaps pro-Republican plan by requiring that any redistricting scheme be passed by two-thirds of both houses of the legislature, signed by the governor, and ratified by the voters. The second, Proposition 119, established a judge-appointed commission of five Democrats, five Republicans, and two independents. Although both propositions set out guidelines about following geographic and city-county boundaries and requiring "competitive" districts, neither mentioned protection of ethnic voters, leaving the propositions open to charges by Democrats that "both measures are designed to aid Republicans by concentrating ethnic minorities into a few districts." Environmentalists joined ethnic minorities and labor unions in opposing both measures, while major corporations and the Republican National Committee poured money into the pro-118/119 campaigns. Although each side spent about three million dollars, the Democratic campaign, masterminded by Michael Berman and his partner Carl D'Agostino, proved more skillful, as voters turned down both propositions by two-to-one margins.

In three other elections with direct connections with reapportionment, however, the Republicans were more successful, setting the stage for their strategy in 1991 and beyond. First, they spearheaded an unprecedented nine million dollar campaign in 1986 to replace Chief Justice Bird, another liberal Anglo justice, and the first Latino liberal associate justice with a Republican majority on the state Supreme Court. Believing that begging for money, running commercials, and making campaign speeches were improper for jurists, Bird and her colleagues could not or would not respond to the virulent assaults on them. All three lost and were supplanted by Deukmejian appointees, most prominently the governor's former law partner, Malcolm Lucas, Central Casting's image of a chief justice, under whose aegis the California Court led the nation in affirming death penalties and voiding consumer protections. Thus, Republicans eagerly politicized the judiciary, as the Democrats' campaign against Deukmejian's commission proposal in 1984 had warned of, because of an underlying desire to control redistricting. Second, after bashing Speaker Willie Brown for a decade, often placing a picture of Brown next to that of their Democratic opponents in Assembly contests in heavily Anglo districts, Republicans found a way to retire him: a limit of three two-year terms for every member of the Assembly and two four-year terms for the Senate. This November 1990 initiative, heavily backed by the state GOP, also ensured that no incumbent in 1991 would have much of an incentive to compromise on a reapportionment plan, since she could enjoy her seat for at most two more terms, and that no veteran legislator, except perhaps some who switched houses, would be around for the redistricting of 2001. Even if Democrats retained their majorities in the legislature in 1990, then, it would be harder to find Republicans who would compromise with them in return for safer seats. Third, Republicans fought especially hard to win the governorship in 1990, which Republican National Committee Chairman Lee Atwater called his committee's "No. 1 national goal," because, as Atwater put it, "the governorship of California has more than any other single thing to do with the national reapportionment." After spending much of the decade and many millions of dollars condemning the Democratic redistricting of 1981–82 and seeking to overturn it, Republicans gained a second veto over the state's redistricting in 1991 (the first was control of the state Supreme Court) with Pete Wilson's hard-fought victory over Dianne Feinstein in the gubernatorial race.

But was the Republican party's wrath of the 1980s exaggerated, its funds seemingly spent irrationally? Did Phil Burton singlehandedly reverse the "Reagan Revolution" of 1980, as one Republican redistricting consultant put it? My statistical analyses, detailed in other papers, echo a statement that Burton made before he died in 1983: "The most important thing you do, before anything else, is you get yourself in a position (to) draw the lines for (your own) district. Then, you draw them for all your friends before you draw anyone else's." After tailor-making very safe districts for their allies and bolstering other Democratic incumbents, Burton and Berman just did not have enough Democratic voters left to affect the partisan balance markedly. In extremely adverse years for Democratic legislative and congressional candidates, such as 1980, they might have held at most three more seats under the Burton plan, while under very favorable conditions for Democrats, such as 1982, they would probably have won more seats under the 1973 Masters' plans.

Republicans, perhaps deliberately, confused what political scientists would call "bias" with what they term "responsiveness." To get two-thirds majorities in the legislature and widespread support in the congressional delegation, the framers of the 1981–82 plans strengthened incumbents of both parties, making it more difficult for either primary or general election challengers to win. This risk-averse strategy guaranteed California Democrats more power through seniority in Congress, but cost them the ability to make large gains in seats if the political tides shifted in their favor. In a word, Phil Burton was a strategic conservative, and the Burton partisan gerrymander was largely a fiction.

The 1990s: Republican Mastery

Although Democrats in 1991 controlled the Assembly, 48–32, the Senate, 24–15 with one independent, and the congressional delegation, 26–19, the increased importance of the Voting Rights Act and the Republicans' double veto power dictated a simple Democratic strategy: conciliate minorities and make a deal with either extremist or moderate Republicans. Thus, Democrats gave major reapportionment committee and staff positions to Latinos, instructed redistricting technicians to group together nearby areas of ethnic minority concentration, and proposed three complete sets of redistricting plans. "Plan A," the Democrats' preferred districting arrangement, was offered to be bargained away or pressed in court, should negotiations break down. "Plan B," the congressional part of which was endorsed by Newt Gingrich, concentrated Republicans in seats thought to be strongly anti-abortion and anti-gun control, and was designed to appeal to right-wingers. "Plan C," in which Republican seats were created in areas that were considered pro-choice or pro-environment, was believed to be more attractive to the supposedly "moderate" Pete Wilson.

The goal of Republicans, Governor Wilson's aides announced, was a "fair" reapportionment, while the more straightforward spokesman for the Republican congressional delegation said he sought "the maximum number of Republican seats." Wilson's strategy, therefore, was even simpler than that of the Democrats: Refuse to negotiate or to let any other Republican negotiate with any Democrat, appoint a "commission" nominally balanced in partisanship, gender, and race without consulting any Democratic or minority group leader, veto all legislative plans, turn the issue over to the state Supreme Court—which Wilson aides privately referred to as "Pete's law firm"—and suggest that the court's Special Masters use the commission's proposal as a starting point. But the governor's commission took so long to complete its plans that they lost whatever publicity value they might have had if offered in the midst of legislative consideration, and the commission's "pretty" districts so obviously reduced African-American and Latino representation, guaranteeing a likely successful suit under the Voting Rights Act, that Wilson's chief redistricting consultant had to fix up the districts in black and Latino areas before the commission's plans could be made public. Insensitive to minority vote dilution, inefficient, and, as we shall see, radically biased in favor of the Republicans, the commission's performance made the voters' rejections of commission proposals during the 1980s seem prescient.

Faintly hoping that Wilson might accept what he would not negotiate about, the Democrats despairingly passed all three of their sets of reapportionment plans, but the governor immediately vetoed every one, the 6–1 Republican state Supreme Court named as Special Masters three retired appellate judges, all of whom had been appointed by Republican governors, and they, in turn, picked Paul McKaskle as their expert, as the 1973 Masters had. This time, McKaskle's plans delighted the Republicans, promising a "Democratic disaster of major proportions," according to one pundit. Democrats noted that while McKaskle constructed many "majority-minority" districts, which generally help Republicans by concentrating highly probable Democratic voters, he made no effort, unlike the Democrats in 1981 and 1991, to draw "influence districts." Such districts, in which minorities cannot by themselves elect a candidate of choice, but where they can strongly affect the choice of the district winner, often help Democrats by focusing Democratic support on a larger, but still limited number of seats.

Between late January 1992, when the Masters' plan was ratified, in party-line votes, by the state Supreme Court and a three-judge federal panel, and the November 1992 election, Democratic registration surged more than it had in any presidential year since 1976, the California depression caused George Bush to abandon the state as hopeless by October 1, Democratic turnout swelled, and moderate Republican voters frequently abandoned "Christian right" Republican nominees, such as one who accused the U.S. Army of practicing witchcraft. In a very good year for the Democrats, they won 30 of the 52 congressional seats, 48 of the 80 in the Assembly, and controlled 22 Senate seats, with two more independent and three vacant. Although there was only a minuscule shift in party registration percentages from 1992 to 1994, the Democratic percentage of the two-party vote in the average congressional or Assembly district in California dropped to from 57% to 52%, and Democrats held only 27 of the congressional seats, 39 in the Assembly, and 21 in the Senate.

None of these totals, however, captures what those who drew the Masters' plans should have expected to be the political outcomes of their designs when they drew them, or allows a comparison between the effects of the Masters' plan and other proposed plans. Suppose we calculate (again with methods detailed in other papers) what would have happened if the voters had behaved just as they did in November 1992, except that their patterns of registration had been those of February 1992. I concentrate on congressional elections for simplicity. Then with 57% of the vote, Democrats would have probably have elected only 28 members of Congress under the Masters' plan or the Governor's Commission, only 24 under a Republican plan, but 33 under the Democrats' "Plan A."

If voters had behaved as they did in 1994, but with the February 1992 registration figures, then the Masters' Plan would have given them only 22 congressional seats, the Governor's Commission, 19, the Republican plan, the same 24, and Plan A, 28. In a Democratic landslide, in other words, the Masters' Plan, at the time it was put into force, could be expected to give Democrats less than proportional representation; in a year when a Democrat in a typical district won 52% of the vote, the Masters' plan could be expected to award Democrats only 42% of the seats—less than the Republican plan. If the best test of the nonpartisanship of a plan is not the process that produced it or the posts held by its authors, then the 1991 Masters' plans were more favorable to the Republicans than the Burton "partisan gerrymander" had been toward the Democrats 10 years earlier. And the compact-looking Governor's Commission plan was even more skewed, for it would have rewarded the Republicans in 1994 with 63% of the seats, when they received only 48% of the two-party votes in the average district.

2001: A Speculation

The prevailing interpretation of the Voting Rights Act during the redistricting of the 1990s encouraged line drawers in legislatures, courts, and commissions throughout the nation to construct districts, however ungainly they looked on maps, in which African Americans and Latinos had opportunities to elect candidates of their choice, even if voting was polarized by race. The results were the largest upsurge in minority legislators since the First Reconstruction after the Civil War and, in a more than equal and opposite reaction, a condemnation of "racial gerrymandering" by the majority on the U.S. Supreme Court. In the 1993 and 1995 decisions of *Shaw v. Reno* and *Miller v. Johnson*, a 5–4 majority of the U.S. Supreme Court decided that anyone who lived in a particular majority-minority congressional district had a right to challenge its boundaries in court, whatever the district's shape, and that if the "predominant" reason for drawing it was racial, it might be declared unconstitutional and redrawn. Plaintiffs did not have to prove, as plaintiffs usually do, that they were damaged by the action of the defendants or even that they might be injured in the future, and majority-Anglo districts were seemingly immune from attack. (Courts had always largely ignored racial gerrymandering *against* blacks and Latinos, which has been going on since 1871.)

Ironically enough, on the same day that they handed down the *Miller* decision, the justices affirmed a federal district court's refusal to overturn the redistricting of California, even though the published report of the Special Masters, which was quoted extensively in the plaintiffs' briefs, openly admitted that they had first drawn the maximum number of majority-minority districts before beginning to set other boundaries. Race, in other words, was admittedly the predominant reason for drawing these districts. If these directly contradictory precedents are allowed to stand, all that can be said about the extent of protection that the law will provide to ethnic minorities during the 2001 reapportionment is that it will be a lawyers' feast. Should the California decision be ignored or overruled, minorities could lose half or more of their California seats, as they likely would have under the plans of the Governor's Commission in 1991. Some commentators have even suggested that any future attempts by Congress or the states to alleviate the dilution of minority votes will be ruled unconstitutional. On the other hand, if *Miller* is reversed or sidestepped, then minority representation should continue to grow as the minority percentages of California's population do.

Whatever happens to ethnic minorities, term limits are almost certain to undermine any attempt at a bipartisan compromise over redistricting in 2001. Since it seems highly probable that the Republicans will control the state Supreme Court, the only hope for avoiding a bitter partisan conflict will be for that party to win the governorship in 1998 and majorities in both houses of the legislature in 2000.

Even if the Democrats won all three, they could expect the Republican majority on the state Supreme Court, which after all was put into place partly to guard the party during redistricting, to find some reason to unravel the legislative handiwork and substitute a plan of its own. The Democrats' experience with the "nonpartisan" plans of 1991, drawn without any consultation with Democratic legislators, members of Congress, or other officials, will discourage them from putting as much trust in judicially managed redistricting as they did in 1991.

It seems likely, therefore, that the Democrats will sponsor an initiative in 1998 or 2000 to turn redistricting over to a bipartisan commission, ironically probably something resembling the Nielsen Commission that they defeated in November 1982. In a double reverse, the Republicans will probably oppose such a commission, especially if they think that they might control majorities of both houses of the legislature after the 2000 election. Whether the commission, if it is put into effect, will be able to restore any semblance of what in retrospect seems the uncomplicated and benign world of the legislature before those 1971 rifle shots, is extremely doubtful. Perhaps the anarchy, party disloyalty, and bizarre behavior in 1995 that denied the Republicans the Speakership that they had apparently won for the first time since 1970 and corroded what was left of the once-proud Assembly's reputation was an ironic retribution for past dirty tricks perpetrated by the party of Richard Nixon.

Suggested Sources

Butler, David, and Bruce E. Cain. 1992. *Congressional Redistricting: Comparative and Theoretical Perspectives.* New York: Macmillan.

Cain, Bruce E. 1984. *The Reapportionment Puzzle.* Berkeley: University of California Press.

Grofman, Bernard, ed. 1982. *Representation and Redistricting Issues.* Lexington, Mass.: D.C. Heath.

Hardy, Leroy, Alan Heslop, and Stuart Anderson, eds. 1981. *Reapportionment Politics: The History of Redistricting in the 50 States.* Beverly Hills: Sage.

Kousser, J. Morgan. 1997. "Reapportionment Wars: Party, Race, and Redistricting in California, 1971-1992." In *Race and Redistricting in the 1990s,* ed. Bernard Grofman. New York: Agathon Press.

Rush, Mark E. 1993. *Does Redistricting Make a Difference? Partisan Representation and Electoral Behavior.* Baltimore: Johns Hopkins University Press.

Chapter 9

The 2003 Recall Debates:
Issues, Candidates, and Media Coverage

Rachel VanSickle-Ward and Darshan J. Goux

"One of the other candidates would have to douse himself with gasoline and set himself on fire on stage to keep Schwarzenegger's absence out of the first paragraph of the debate coverage.

Dan Schnur, quoted in "Rivals Wrangle, Except One" George Raine, *San Francisco Chronicle*, September 4, 2004

There was substance among the shouting.

Margaret Talev and Alexa H. Bluth, "Candidates Turn Heat on Schwarzenegger: Newcomer is Primary Target During Debate," *Sacramento Bee*, September 25, 2003

Introduction

The 2003 California gubernatorial recall election was a unique period in the state's political history, and voters faced a series of rare choices. In the 10-week campaign, voters had to decide whether or not to take the historic step of recalling the governor, and choose who, from a list of 135 candidates, should replace Governor Gray Davis in the event of his removal. In this abbreviated campaign cycle with multiple unknown candidates, the traditional shortcuts voters use to reach voting decisions, like partisan affiliation, may not have been enough to help them make a decision on either or both of these questions. In confusing elections like this, what campaign consultants refer to as "free media"—debates, public events, and the news coverage of them—can be especially critical to voters' efforts to learn about and evaluate candidates and issues. This chapter analyzes the content of the candidate debates during the 2003 recall election and the print media coverage of those debates. We assess the accuracy of media coverage in this unusual setting, and we investigate which issues, candidates and strategies dominated the news about the debates and the debates themselves.[1]

The Recall

To recall an elected official is to remove him or her from office via popular vote before the duration of his or her term. Along with the initiative and the referendum, the recall represents one of the three mechanisms of direct democracy— the process by which voters decide policy directly rather than delegating decisions to representatives. Recall elections occur frequently at the local level, but only 18 states permit a gubernatorial recall (Bowler and Cain 2004). Securing a recall election against the governor is considerably easier in California than in other states— no malfeasance need be shown, signature requirements for the recall petition are low,[2] and petitioners are given 160 days to collect signatures (Bowler and Cain).

The 2003 California recall election was remarkable for a number of reasons. Governor Gray Davis was California's first statewide official to face a recall election and only the third governor (after North Dakota's Lyn Frazier in 1921 and Arizona's Evan Meacham in 1987) to face such an election in the nation's history (Bowler and Cain 2004). Signature gathering for the recall began only months after Davis had solidly defeated his Republican rival, Bill Simon, by five percentage points (47.3% to 42.4%).[3] A majority of voters (55.4%) voted in support of removing Democrat Gray Davis, despite the fact that registered Democrats outnumbered registered Republicans in the state (44% and 35% respectively).

Among the many striking elements of this unusual political event, one of the most fascinating was the field of 135 candidates vying to replace Davis, including a former child actor, a college student, and, most famously, the candidate who

---

[1] We are grateful to Christian Mejia and Dalia Yadegar for their research assistance and to the Institute of Governmental Studies at the University of California, Berkeley, for financial support of this project.

[2] Twelve percent of the number of voters who voted in the prior election must sign the recall petition to place it on the California ballot.

[3] California Secretary of State Statement of Vote, 2002 General Election.

would win the election handily: movie star Arnold Schwarzenegger. The most viable of those candidates—a mega celebrity, a wealthy businessman, two elected officials, a pundit, and a virtually unknown third-party candidate—were given the opportunity to debate one another. The result was two multicandidate, multiparty forums, unique for a statewide race in our two-party system. In this chapter, we focus on the dynamics of those debates and the press they garnered. First, we provide a brief background on the relationship between candidate debates and media coverage.

Do Debates Matter?

The influence of the media on public opinion and behavior during election campaigns varies significantly according to individual predispositions, political interest and knowledge, and attention to media sources. During campaigns, media are especially influential to voters' political knowledge, and campaign debates can be a significant source of learning (Graber 2002; Weaver and Drew 2001). While the bulk of candidates' financial resources may go to television advertising, debates are a significant component of candidates' earned media strategies.[4] Debates represent one of the few opportunities voters have to hear directly from the candidates.

Interestingly, media coverage and interpretation of debates may overshadow debates' direct effects. Voters, who do not watch the debates, rely exclusively on secondary accounts of the debates to learn about the candidates and their issue positions. Even voters who watch debates in their entirety may reach one conclusion about the candidates at the end of the debate, only to make different evaluations one week later. Voters' impressions and interpretations of debates may change over time as they compare and contrast their impressions with media interpretations. So, for example, viewers may initially have rated former president Jimmy Carter well for his performance in the 1976 presidential debates, but as the media concluded he had underperformed, impressions of his debate performance eroded among supporters and opponents (Lang and Lang 1978). Additionally, media may give a more negative impression of the campaign than is accurate. Media coverage of debates tends to give more attention to the strategy or horse race aspects of the debate than to the issues discussed, and media coverage of debates may make it seem like candidates spent more time attacking each other than they actually did (Jamieson and Hart 1996).

Media may also influence debate effects before a debate has even taken place. Media coverage of campaign debates begins long before the debates themselves. Who will participate, who is expected "to win," and what strategies the candidates are expected to employ preoccupy commentators in the pre-debate time period.

---

[4] Scholarship on political campaigns tends to distinguish between "earned media" (or sometimes "free media"), which refers to press coverage of campaign events, and "paid media," which describes advertisements purchased by the campaign.

The Project for Excellence in Journalism found that media tend to focus on performance, tactics, and strategy in both pre- and post-debate analysis and not on issues or how election outcomes might affect voters (2004). In fact, media expectations shape the context in which a debate takes place and may determine the measures by which candidates are eventually evaluated by that same media and by viewers. A candidate who enters a debate as the underdog, for example, faces lower expectations than the candidate who is considered experienced and skillful.

Despite the importance of media coverage of debates, scholarship on the nature of that coverage is limited. Existing research on debate effects and media coverage of debates tends to focus on presidential election campaigns (Kraus 1962; Bishop et al. 1978; Kraus 1979; Jamieson and Hart 1996). Lower ticket campaigns and campaigns with multiple candidates are rarely examined. Voters may enter these campaign cycles with less information about the candidates and with a limited ability to use traditional shortcuts like party labels to guide their decision making. The extent of media influence on individuals is determined by an individual's exposure to media and by prior attitudes (Zaller 1992), but voters tend to be less engaged in lower ticket races and have fewer preexisting attitudes to guide them.

Understanding the role of media is especially significant in this limited information environment. The absence of scholarship, then, is particularly troubling because candidate debates may play an even more important role in informing voters in lower ticket races than in presidential elections. In the case of the 2003 recall election media attention was heightened but voters had fewer preexisting cues to guide them.

Purpose of This Study

This study of the 2003 California gubernatorial recall debates addresses three basic sets of questions. First, we consider general findings about the debates and the debate coverage: What aspects of the debates did the press choose to focus on? Which candidates garnered the most newspaper coverage? Was this an accurate representation of the debates themselves? Second, we look at the nature of candidate participation: What strategies did candidates employ in the debates, and how were these tactics reflected in the print media? Third, we analyze issue coverage: What issues received the most attention during the debates, and were these the same issues highlighted by the media?

Methodology

Newspaper Coding

The material coded in this project is a "running record" of print media coverage of the 2003 gubernatorial recall debates. We selected three major papers to include in our analysis: *The Sacramento Bee, The San Francisco Chronicle,* and *The Los Angeles Times.* Inclusion of these newspapers has three benefits— geographical variation, wide readership, and significant coverage of state-level political events.[5] We sampled papers with the terms "recall" and "debate" in the headline and/or the lead paragraph between July 24, 2003 (the date the recall was officially announced) and October 7, 2003 (the date the recall election took place). Our search found 72 articles that included debate coverage. For each debate mention we coded the participant referenced, and the nature of mention—issue, ideology, strategy, qualification, personality/style, horse race, direct quote or other.[6] We also recorded whether the article came before or after a debate had occurred.

Debate Coding

We analyzed the two major debates that included at least five candidates. These debates took place on September 3, 2003, in Walnut Creek and September 24, 2003, in Sacramento.[7] In addition to then Governor Davis, six candidates took part in at least one debate. Participants included Lieutenant Governor Cruz Bustamante (Democrat), former gubernatorial candidate Peter Camejo (Green), author and commentator Arianna Huffington (Independent), State Senator Tom McClintock (Republican), businessman Peter Ueberroth (Republican), and actor Arnold Schwarzenegger (Republican). Bustamante, Camejo, Huffington and McClintock participated in both debates.

We analyzed every statement made by the candidates during the debate and coded it according to whether or not the candidate answered the question, whether the statement addressed a specific issue, and if the statement constituted

---

[5] For a complete description of coding schemes and intercoder reliability results, please contact the authors.

[6] *Issue/Policy*—a candidate's position on or statement about an issue or policy. *Ideology*—description of a candidate or debate comments as liberal, conservative, moderate, etc. *Strategy*—references to the statements candidates make (whether or not they are directly quoted) about themselves and/or other candidates. These may be attacking a policy, campaign decision, lack of qualification, etc. in other candidate (Attack), or defending the candidate's own policy or qualification (Defend), or a combination of both. *Qualification*—references to the candidates' background and experience. *Personality/ Style*—references to the candidates' demeanor, whether or not they were confrontational, demure, etc. Importantly, the personality category also includes references to the debate as a whole (e.g., as a circus, a feisty exchange, or a bore). *Horse Race*—references to the stakes of the debate, expectations of the candidates, performance of the candidates, assertions of the "winner" or "loser," and debate relevant references to how the candidates are performing in the polls. *Direct Quote*—references to the candidates that quote them directly. *Other*—references to a debate which do not fall into any of the specified categories.

[7] We were unable to obtain footage of a third "forum" held in Los Angeles on October 2, 2003, which included fewer than five candidates. Very few of the articles we coded referenced this debate

a defense of the candidate speaking or an attack on another candidate. If a strategy (attack/defend) was apparent, it was coded according to whether it was an attack or defend statement based on an issue, ideology, qualification, or personality, which were defined according to the same guidelines as the newspaper codes.[8]

General Findings

In the late stages of a high-profile election we find considerable media attention devoted to issues. Media mentions, both before and after the debates, were more likely to focus on issues than on candidate personality, strategy or horse race coverage. (Figure 1)

Indeed, issue mentions were more frequent than those three categories combined. Grouping categories of coverage broadly as "substantive" (i.e., discussion of candidates that gives voters helpful information about the candidates' priorities and ability to govern—qualifications, ideology, and issues) versus "superficial" (i.e., discussion of candidates that have more to do with style, performance and popularity), substantive mentions were 30% more frequent than superficial references (957 versus 735 mentions). The results suggest that media coverage of the 2003 recall debates gave readers ample opportunity to learn about the policy positions of the candidates.

As striking as the amount of print coverage devoted to issues was, media underrepresented the frequency of issue discussion during the debates. For example, as is discussed in more detail below, when attacking other candidates or defending themselves, candidates mentioned issues about three times more frequently than they mentioned all of the other categories (horse race, personality, qualifications, ideology and other) combined (293 and 97 respectively) or about 75% of all references. Thus, while giving considerable attention to issues, it appears the media overemphasized other categories such as personality and qualifications.

Putting issue coverage aside, media before the debates were most likely to focus on the horse race, followed in order by candidate qualifications, strategy, personality, and ideology. After the debates, candidate strategy dominated media coverage followed by mentions of the horse race, personality, qualifications, and ideology. The decline of media attention to candidate qualifications and the increase in attention given to candidate strategy suggests the debates leveled the playing field for less experienced candidates, giving them the opportunity to gain attention through their debate strategies. These frames paint a fairly accurate pic-

---

[8] In comparing categories to one another we only included the issues counted as part of an attack or a defend, not the general issue category (both were used in breakdown of the types of issues discussed). This is important because we would otherwise have artificially inflated the importance of issue statements in the debates. We noted every time an issue was mentioned, but not, for example, when someone glared or raised his or her voice, which the press may have fairly wanted to cover as "personality."

Figure 1.

Media Coverage: 2003 California Recall Debates
(The Los Angeles Times, The San Francisco Chronicle, The Sacramento
Bee)

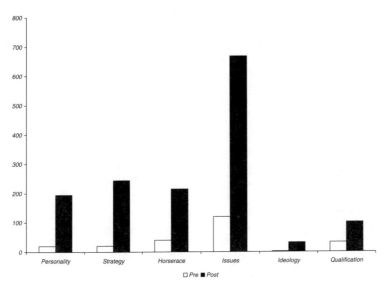

ture of the debates themselves. After issues, comments during the debates focused, in descending order, on personality, qualification, ideology, and horse race.[9] The only difference in order, horse race, is almost certainly a function of the definition of that category, which lends itself more naturally to print coverage than debate comments, since it includes an assessment of how the candidates would or did perform.

The data indicate that in a field of multiple candidates, participating in a debate can reduce differences in the amount of coverage individual candidates receive. Four candidates received the bulk of total candidate coverage, and the amount of coverage each candidate received varied between pre- and post-debate stories. Bustamante (20%), Huffington (18%), McClintock (15%), and Schwarzenegger (26%) earned the most media debate coverage. This is especially noteworthy as Schwarzenegger participated in only one of the recall debates, while Huffington, Camejo, McClintock, and Bustamante participated in both. Ueberroth (4%), Camejo (6%), and Davis (11%) received much less coverage.

---

[9] Since all the attack/defend statements were a strategy, strategy is not considered as a subcateogory here.

The significance of the relationship between candidate participation in the debates and their media coverage is easier to understand when we break down the findings into "pre-debate" and "post-debate" articles. In this way, we can examine whether participating in the debate mattered and, if so, how much.

Pre-debate media coverage centered on Schwarzenegger (39%), Bustamante (23%), McClintock (18%), and Davis (15%). After the debates, the relative coverage of all four of these candidates diminished (Schwarzenegger 25%; Bustamante 20%; McClintock 15%; Davis 11%). In contrast, mentions of Huffington increased to 19% of total candidate mentions (from 2%). Media mentions of Camejo increased from no mentions in pre-debate coverage to 6% of candidate mentions in post-debate coverage. The debates thus gave these lesser-known candidates the opportunity to put themselves on the map if they performed well by increasing their name recognition, a key strategic goal for lesser known candidates. It is worth mentioning that strategies that might earn a candidate more media attention, and thus higher name recognition, are not necessarily the same strategies that earn a candidate positive media attention.

The substantial news ink dedicated to Schwarzenegger does not perfectly reflect the debates themselves. This is hardly surprising, considering his celebrity status. Figure 2 illustrates a breakdown of statements by candidates.

Huffington (97 statements) and Bustamante (93 statements) made more statements in the debates than any of the other candidates and accounted for almost half of all statements made in the two debates. Interestingly, Schwarzenegger managed to make 68 statements in the one debate in which he participated, more than any of the other participants. Compared to Ueberroth (23 statements) and Davis (14 statements), who only participated in one debate, Schwarzenegger was able to earn significant coverage with his performance. In contrast, McClintock (49 statements) and Camejo (44 statements), who participated in both debates, together accounted for only about 24% of all candidate statements.

Despite these discrepancies, when we compare each candidate's debate participation to their proportion of coverage after the debates (Figures 2 and 3), it is not as skewed as one might expect.

Except for Davis and Schwarzenegger, who commanded more coverage relative to the frequency of their statements during the debates, no candidate's proportion of coverage shifted by more than 5%. Media coverage emphasized Schwarzenegger and Davis, but not so much that lesser known candidates were ignored.

Debate Performance

Although they spoke less often, Camejo and McClintock were more likely to address the questions posed by the panel or moderators in both debates. Overall, all of the candidates answered the official questions posed in the debates about 60% of the time. But, that response rate varied dramatically between the

Figure 2.

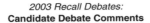

2003 Recall Debates:
Candidate Debate Comments

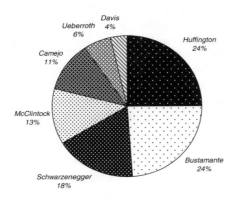

Figure 3.

Media Coverage: 2003 California Recall Debates
Candidates (Post-Debate)

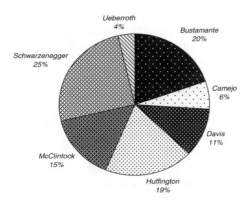

debates—candidates were much less likely to answer the question in the September 24 Sacramento debate than they were in the September 3 Walnut Creek debate. In the Sacramento debate, Schwarzenegger, Huffington, and Bustamante were about as likely not to answer a question as they were to answer it. In the Walnut Creek debate, all candidates who participated were more likely to answer the questions posed than not. It is unclear whether this difference reflects the candidates involved in the debates, the differing formats of the debates, or some other campaign dynamic.

Whatever the candidates' strategies the media seemed determined to emphasize the attacks made in the debates. Overall, candidates were more likely to defend themselves in the debates than they were to attack the other candidates (see Figure 4). While candidates lobbed 123 attacks in the two debates, they defended themselves almost twice as often (236 defends).

Issue positions and references to a candidate's personal characteristics were more frequently the subject of both attacks and defensive statements than were statements about qualifications, ideology, or the horse race. Candidates were most likely to both attack each others' issue positions and to defend their own issue positions. Sixty percent of all attacks were on issues, and 80% of all the defensive statements made in the debates were issue-related. Twenty-eight percent of attacks were on some personal characteristic of another candidate, while candidates were about as likely to defend personal characteristics as they were to defend their ideology or qualifications.

Candidates' strategies within the debates varied significantly. Huffington made more than three times as many attacks overall (47 attacks) as the other debate participants. Although Schwarzenegger and Davis appeared in only one debate (and Davis appeared alone), they made nearly as many attacks in those single appearances as Bustamante, Camejo, and McClintock did in two debate appearances. Perhaps not surprisingly, because of his role in the Davis administration, Bustamante defended himself 54 times, with more defensive statements than any of the other candidates. Davis, on the other hand, made more attacks in his lone debate appearance than he did defensive statements. Camejo, McClintock, and Ueberroth were more likely to offer defensive statements than to attack others, while Huffington was about as likely to defend herself as she was to make an attack. Schwarzenegger offered no defensive statements, but did go on the attack 18 times.

While the candidates' strategies differed within the debates, the quality of the media coverage afforded each of the candidates also differed. Huffington was more likely to attack other candidates in the debates, but her strategy appears to have worked—at least in terms of getting her name in print. Huffington received only one mention in pre-debate media coverage. After the debates, she earned 19% of total candidate mentions in the media and more coverage of her debate strategy than any other candidate (30% of all strategy coverage). (See Figure 5) The majority of this gain came in coverage of her attack strategy (59% of all her mentions) and her personality or style (20% of all her mentions). Although she

Figure 4.

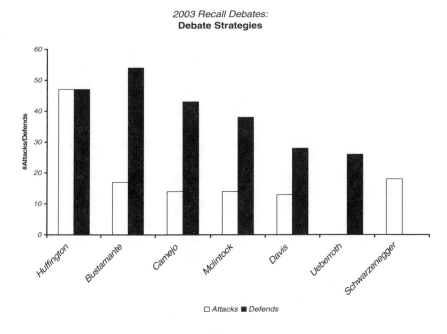

2003 Recall Debates:
Debate Strategies

□ Attacks ■ Defends

Figure 5.

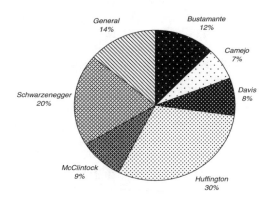

Media Coverage: 2003 California Recall Debates
Debate Strategy
(Attack/Defend)

was as likely to defend herself as she was to attack others, only 1% of all her media mentions noted her defensive strategy.

Similarly, media coverage of Schwarzenegger, who did not appear to make any defensive statements in the debate in which he participated, focused on the horse race and strategic aspects of his performance. Despite participating in only one debate, Schwarzenegger was the subject of 20% of the coverage of candidate debate strategy, and the coverage of Schwarzenegger's debate strategy changed qualitatively before and after debate. Before the debate, media emphasized his defensive strategy; after the debate, his attack strategy received 20% of all his mentions.

Debate coverage of Davis differed from that of the other candidates. In addition to receiving only 12% of total debate coverage, media were more likely to mention Davis's qualifications than any other category in both his pre- and post-debate coverage. There were only nine mentions of Davis in pre-debate coverage. His mentions increased in post-debate coverage (74 mentions), and media continued to give most attention to his qualifications. Like most of the other participants, Davis was more likely to defend himself than to attack others. Unlike media coverage of the other candidates, which tended to overemphasize their debate attacks, Davis's defensive strategy was mentioned twice as often by the media in post-debate coverage as was his attack strategy.

After the debates, media coverage of the remaining candidates, all of whom were more likely to defend themselves than to attack others, tended to emphasize the attacks candidates made rather than their defensive statements. Coverage of Bustamante, who made more defensive statements in the debates than any other candidate, made nearly equal mention of his attacks (15 mentions) and his defensive statements (16 mentions). McClintock, who defended himself more than twice as many times as he attacked other candidates, saw only one mention of his defensive statements and 20 mentions of his attacks. Camejo had no pre-debate media coverage. After the debates, in which he defended himself more than three times as often as he attacked the others, he earned media attention that was dominated by mention of his attacks (16 mentions). And Ueberroth, who participated in only one debate and made no attacks, received much less coverage than the other candidates and no mention of his defensive statements.

Whether or not the candidates chose to use the debates as a chance to defend their own candidacies or as an opportunity to attack their opponents, the print coverage tended to emphasize the latter. And, although a more sophisticated research design is needed to test this, the Huffington case seems to suggest that going on the attack in the debates was a successful strategy for increasing media exposure.

Issues in the Debates and the Media

While the recall of the state's governor was an historic event, the debates and coverage of those debates afforded little opportunity for voters to weigh the pros and cons of the recall question itself. In the debates, only 17 of 785 references to issues focused on the recall question itself. The media apparently had no expectations the recall would be a central aspect of the debates, as none of the pre-debate media coverage carried any reference to the recall question. Post-debate coverage was similarly lacking with only 14 of 639 news mentions of issues after the debate centered on the recall. Rather than allowing voters an opportunity to consider the merits of the recall, the debates seem to have been about candidates vying for the governor's seat, as if it were a more traditional election. Thus, while the paucity of news coverage dedicated to the recall as a debate issue may be disappointing from a civic-minded perspective, it is a fair representation of the lack of attention the recall received during the debates.

The debate agendas may have also been a fair representation of a mood of the electorate. The recall question was ahead among voters since the first polls in April, and on the last Field Poll (August 15) before the first debate, the recall was ahead 58% to 37%. In that same poll, Davis had an approval rating of 20% with a disapproval rating of 70%. It seems that voters had made up their minds, and that the only question was who would replace Davis. This raises a "chicken and egg" problem. Would polling have been less static if the pros and cons of the recall had been more seriously engaged in the debates and in the resultant media coverage?

While the debates and the media coverage of them may have done little to help voters think through the recall question, other issues received much more attention. To assess the nature of media coverage of debates, it is clearly important to consider which issues reporters chose to highlight and compare them to the issues emphasized by the candidates in the debates. In comparing pre-debate coverage to post-debate coverage, the most obvious difference is the sheer growth of mentions.

Figure 6 shows both what issues the media covered before and after the debates and what issues the candidates discussed in the debates. The number of newspaper mentions of issues or policies increased from 134 in the pre-debate articles to 639 in the post-debate articles. On one level this is hardly surprising. Pre-debate discussion of issues was limited to issues that editorial columnists believed should be discussed, expectations of what issues might be discussed and, in the case of one debate, reporting on the questions that would certainly be asked (because these questions were made available to the candidates and the public ahead of time). After the debates, of course, reporters had more material to draw upon.

It is interesting to note the kinds of policies that dominated press coverage, and those that received relatively little attention. Interestingly, two of the major issues that fueled the recall against Governor Davis—the vehicle license fee (VLF) and the energy crisis—ranked fairly low in terms of frequency of mention (18 and 17 respectively, out of 773 total issue mentions). Another issue that seemed to be the focus of public animosity toward Davis, the economy, ranked higher at 53 media mentions, but still received much fewer mentions than immigration (96 mentions) and health care (86 mentions)—issues less notably associated with Davis's supposed failure as governor. On the other hand, the budget,

Figure 6.

2003 Recall Debates:
Issues in the Media and the Debates

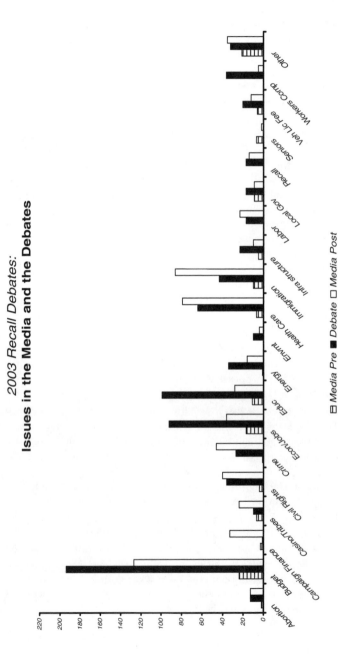

☐ Media Pre   ■ Debate   ☐ Media Post

which received the plurality of issue mentions (151 mentions) was a significant issue motivating the recall.

This partial disconnect between what might seem obvious "recall" issues and the issues that in fact received the most press attention was most pronounced in the post-debate coverage. Before the debates, the vehicle license fee received a small share (5%) of coverage, the economy a moderate share (13%), and energy received less than 3% of coverage. After the debates, energy still comprised less than 3% of media coverage, the VLF similarly dropped down to a negligible proportion, and the economy dwindled to a mere 5% of issue mentions in the media. Budget coverage increased slightly from 18% to 19%. See Figure 7.

So, did the media give readers an accurate reflection of the issues addressed in the debates? The answer is yes and no. Together, the budget (25%), the economy (12%) and education (13%) accounted for nearly half of all the issues raised in the debates. About 20% of post-debate media coverage of the issues in the debates was focused on the budget, but only about 5% was allotted to the economy and 4% to education. Together with the budget, immigration and health care dominated post-debate media coverage. While immigration accounted for only about 5% of the issues raised in the debates, immigration received 13% of post-debate issue mentions. Similarly, health care, which accounted for about 8% of issues in the debates, received 12% of post-debate issue mentions. Crime (3% versus 7%) and Labor (2% versus 7%) also received more attention in coverage of the debates than they did in the debates themselves. The issues that grew in significance in the media after the debates (health care, immigration, crime, and labor) are certainly important issues for the state of California, but they are not the issues most readily associated with the historic drive to recall a popularly elected governor a matter of months after his reelection.

Conclusion

Our analysis of the recall debates shows that in a field of multiple candidates, debate participation can influence both the quantity and quality of coverage a candidate receives. First, candidates who participate in a debate are more frequently mentioned by the media in post- than in pre-debate analysis. For candidates with low name recognition, this coverage may contribute to voter learning. While a celebrity candidate, like Schwarzenegger, earns the most debate coverage, even for participating in only one debate, other candidates like Huffington and Camejo can substantially increase media attention by debate participation.

Issues received considerable attention during these debates. For all the concern about the "circus-like atmosphere" of these forums, those who chose to watch them could learn a significant amount about the candidates' stated policy stances. Those who did not watch, but read newspaper accounts of the debates could also gather meaningful information on candidates' views. We can only speculate at

Figure 7.

2003 Recall Debates:
Issues

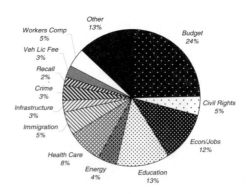

causal mechanisms here, but it is worth considering whether issues matter more in a larger field in which candidates are unfamiliar, and party cues are less helpful to voters because more than one candidate is running under the same party banner.

People often criticize the media for biased, skewed, and inaccurate reporting. While a full discussion of the definitions and evidence of this purported bias is well beyond the scope of this chapter, the role of responsible reporting during an election is obviously critical. As we noted at the outset, media accuracy in covering debates is important because so many voters draw conclusions not on what happens in a debate but on how the media reports it. In the unique case of the recall, voters were more attentive than usual to a gubernatorial campaign, but they had less knowledge going in of the candidates and mechanisms of the election than they normally would, and less time to gather that information.

Comparing the content of the print coverage of the debates to the content of the debates themselves demonstrates that the media's report card in painting an accurate picture of the debates was mixed. The debates themselves offered viewers little opportunity to consider the recall itself, and newspaper coverage of the debates reflected that deficiency. Reporters rightly devoted the majority of coverage to issues but perhaps still not as much as the debates warranted. Media accurately reflected the roles of personality, qualification, and ideology in the debates, but overemphasized attacks against other candidates. Newspapers were off, but not dramatically so, in their allotment of coverage to the various candidates based on their debate participation—skewing attention toward more recognizable candidates but still giving lesser known candidates more coverage than they had had before the debates. They correctly emphasized major issues like the budget, but gave exaggerated coverage to immigration and short shrift to education. While a complex picture emerges from this project, one conclusion is clear. Researchers should continue to analyze debates at the state and local level, with particular attention to multicandidate debates.

References

2004. "The Debate Effect: How the Press Covered the Pivotal Period of the 2004 Presidential Campaign," ed. Project for Excellence in Journalism. Washington, D.C.

Bowler, Shaun, and Bruce Cain. 2004. "Recalling the Recall: Reflections on California's Recent Political Adventure." *Political Science and Politics* 37:1.

Graber, Doris A. 2002. *Mass Media and American Politics*. Washington, D.C.: CQ Press.

Jamieson, Kathleen Hall, and Roderick P. Hart. 1996. "Assessing the Quality of Campaign Discourse." Pp. 31, ed. The Campaign Discourse Monitoring Project: The Annenberg Public Policy Center of the University of Pennsylvania.

Lang, Gladys Engel, and Kurt Lang. 1978. "The Formation of Public Opinion: Direct and Mediated Effects of the First Debate." In *The Presidential Debates: Media, Electoral, and Policy Perspectives*, ed. George F. Bishop, Robert G. Meadow, and Marilyn Jackson-Beeck. New York, N.Y.: Praeger Publishers.

Weaver, David, and Dan Drew. 2001. "Voter Learning and Interest in the 2000 Presidential Election: Did the Media Matter?" *Journalism and Mass Communication Quarterly* 78: 787.

Zaller, John. 1992. *Nature and Origins of Mass Opinion*. Cambridge: Cambridge University Press.

Part III. Policy

Chapter 10

Immigration and California Politics

Jack Citrin and Andrea Campbell[1]

Pushed by the drive to improve their fortunes and pulled by the demand for industrial and agricultural labor, newcomers from within the United States as well as abroad have poured into California for 150 years. These waves of immigrants have produced a diverse society but also engendered economic competition and ethnic tensions that inevitably spill over into the political arena.

By regulating the entry of individuals into a nation's community and establishing the rights and obligations of aliens, immigration policy decides who belongs to America and on what terms. These decisions are made at the national level, but the consequences for states where immigrants settle are profound, if only because the evolution of federal laws concerning their rights has imposed new budgetary obligations on other levels of government.

Immigration is a highly emotional subject that touches on the main policy issues in California today—budgeting, education, affirmative action, health care, and reapportionment. The current makeup of California derives from the impact of the Immigration and Nationality Act of 1965. This opened America to a massive wave of immigration from Asia and Latin America, with California receiving far more of these immigrants than any other state (LeMay 1994). Concern

---

[1] We gratefully acknowledge the valuable assistance of Amy Lerman and Michael Murakami in the preparation of this chapter.

about the cultural and economic threat of immigration led first to an "official English" ballot in 1986 and then, in the context of economic recession, to the passage of Proposition 187, a measure denying *illegal* immigrants access to most government services. Congress and the Clinton administration responded to this popular "message" with proposals to tighten border controls, speed the deportation of illegal immigrants, and limit the ability of *legal* immigrants to receive welfare, supplemental security income (SSI), and food stamps (Lochhead 1996:1). In 1998, California passed an initiative restricting the use of bilingual education in the public schools, purportedly to speed the linguistic and cultural assimilation of immigrant children, and three other states soon followed suit.

This chapter surveys the impact of immigration on California politics and society. It is divided into five sections. Section I summarizes patterns of migration into the state from 1848 until 1965. It describes the recurrent cycle in which California first welcomed immigrants as hard-working laborers and then made them objects of hostility as their numbers increased and their economic competition with "natives" intensified (Olzak 1992). Section II describes the impact of the post-1965 immigration reforms on the ethnic composition of California, with particular attention to increases in the Latino and Asian segments of the population. Section III briefly reviews arguments concerning the economic, fiscal, social, and political effects of immigration. Section IV describes the state of recent public opinion toward immigration. We highlight the ambivalence of attitudes toward legal immigrants and the strong animus against illegal immigrants, examine ethnic differences in attitudes about immigration, and consider the process of immigrant incorporation into the electorate. Section V is a brief conclusion that restates the main policy dilemmas for the future.

I. From the Gold Rush to the Civil Rights Era

The discovery of gold at Sutter's mill in January 1848 spurred the first of many waves of migration to California. Migrants from the hinterland streamed toward the state whose land was advertised by Chambers of Commerce as "flowing with milk and honey" (Southern California Bureau of Information, 1892: 7). In each decade from 1860 to 1930 (with the lone exception of the depressed 1890s), California's population grew by 40% or more. After 1880, migration from other American states was a larger factor in California's population growth than either natural growth (the surplus of births over deaths within the state) or foreign immigration (Commonwealth Club of California 1946: 20–21).

Throughout this period, however, foreign migrants of varied ethnicities also came to California. Initially welcomed, economic competition and racial prejudice typically triggered legislation and public protests that stemmed the influx of one group after another.

The first group of Asian immigrants to come to California in significant numbers was the Chinese, who began arriving during the Gold Rush (Hing 1993). At its height, more than 200,000 Chinese, mostly men, were working in mines and agriculture, on railroads and in small businesses. Initially, public officials promoted Chinese immigration (Hing 1993: 20), but these newcomers became the victims of white antagonism, discrimination, and violence, particularly during economic downturns (Olzak 1992).

By the late 1860s, Chinese immigration was a major issue in California; anti-coolie clubs were numerous and mob attacks on Chinese increased. In 1870, Congress responded by amending the Nationality Act of 1790 to deny citizenship rights to Chinese immigrants. In 1882, the Chinese Exclusion Act effectively halted Chinese immigration and encouraged the deportation of Chinese laborers, who were portrayed as degraded heathens (Fuchs 1992).

Few Japanese came to the United States before the 1880s, but there were increased efforts to attract them after passage of the Chinese Exclusion Act limited the number of Chinese farm workers. Japanese laborers first worked the sugar plantations of Hawaii and then moved to the West Coast, becoming an important force in California agriculture between 1890 and 1910. Like the Chinese before them, the Japanese became targets of racial hostility, not only because they reminded Californians of the earlier "Yellow Peril," but also because they were successful in becoming independent farmers. In 1913, California passed the Alien Land Act, effectively preventing Japanese from acquiring property.

Foreign policy considerations led to the Gentlemen's Agreement of 1908. Under its terms, the Japanese government stopped issuing travel documents to U.S.-bound laborers, while the United States allowed wives and "picture brides" to migrate. Consequently, the Japanese in America could continue to build families and maintain their size over time. As a result, most Japanese Americans in California today come from families who have lived in the state since before World War II (Oliver, Gey, Stiles, and Brady 1995: X).

Filipinos replaced the Japanese as an important source of agricultural labor in California because as noncitizen nationals of the United States since the Spanish-American War, they were able to travel without regard for the immigration laws. Once again, though, anti-immigrant sentiment flared during an economic downturn, with anti-Filipino riots occurring from 1929 to 1934. Between 1934 and 1946, Filipinos in the U.S. were subjected to the restrictive immigration law of 1924 and assigned an annual quota of only 50 visas (Hing 1993).

Mexicans were an important source of agricultural labor in California as early as 1900. From 1900 until 1942, Mexican migration to California was "spontaneous and irregular," supplementing the labor of other ethnic groups whenever needed (Galarza 1964: 14). The government cooperated with growers in regulating the supply of poor, often undocumented, Mexican workers by creating a revolving door that turned seasonally and during economic cycles (Fuchs 1992: 52). After the forced repatriation of more than four hundred thousand Mexicans, including thousands of American citizens of Mexican descent, during the Great Depression (Samora 1971), the federal government responded to renewed demand for farm labor during World War II with the Bracero program. This measure allowed for planned migration and orderly recruiting of Mexican workers who were assembled at recruiting centers inside Mexico and brought to U.S. reception centers (Galarza 1964).

The Bracero program, which lasted until 1964, was supplemented by the continued employment of illegal workers. Thus, official tolerance of a dual legal-illegal system of immigration (Rojas 1996a; 1996b; 1996c) dates back to the 1950s. When the Bracero program ended, established patterns of migration and lax border controls meant that high levels of both legal and illegal immigration from Mexico continued, a pattern persisting to this day.

Indeed, the dialectic of accepting newcomers whose labor was needed and rejecting them when the costs of immigration seemed to rise even applied to the influx of the 300,000 white "Okie" migrants from the South Central states of Arkansas, Oklahoma, Texas, and Missouri. With the onset of the Great Depression, urban relief authorities, particularly in Los Angeles, had pressured Mexican residents to leave, (Stein 1973: 37), so worried California growers turned to the desperate Okies for needed agricultural labor. By 1938, though, there was an immense oversupply of such workers and anti-Okie hysteria erupted. The Okies tended to concentrate in just a few counties in the San Joaquin Valley (Commonwealth Club of California 1946: 6), where they used public health services, filled the public schools, and collected relief. This generated complaints about the tax burden that are remarkably similar to contemporary protests about the costs of providing government services to illegal immigrants from Mexico.

African Americans followed the Okies as the next wave of internal migrants to California. During the 1940s, California's black population increased more than four-fold. World War II-era black migration differed from that of previous years in both composition and pace. Again, the availability of jobs, this time in industry, was the spur. Due to labor shortages among whites in the shipyards and munitions plants and to Franklin Delano Roosevelt's Executive Order 8802 banning racial discrimination in the defense industries, a large movement of African Americans to California started in 1942. During the 1940s, California had the largest net in-migration of blacks of any state in the country (Johnson and Campbell 1981).

II. Immigration Reform and the New California.

The war against the Nazis discredited racist thinking, and in its aftermath the civil rights movement established the norm of opposition to discrimination based on race or ethnicity. In a context of Cold War competition for the loyalty of the Third World, an immigration system based on national preferences could not be sustained. The 1965 Immigration and Nationality Act abandoned the national origins system and replaced it with an open system giving primacy to family reunification (Fuchs 1990).

As noted, this opened the door to immigration from Asia and Latin America. The emphasis on family reunification meant that the ethnic composition of the first wave of new arrivals would have a potent multiplier effect on the future shape of American society as their relatives followed them to the United States. For example, a frequent pattern is for an Asian student to come to the United States, acquire Department of Labor certification, and become an official resident entitled to bring over a spouse and children. After becoming citizens, both husband and wife are able to sponsor parents and siblings. The same provisions of the law enable the brothers and sisters to bring their spouses, children, and parents. Under the family provisions, nonquota immigration of Asians has been over 100,000 per year since 1970 (Auerbach 1994).

The unintended consequence of immigration reform, then, was significant change in the ethnic composition of the United States, and of California in particular. After 1970, California actually became a net exporter of people to other regions of the U.S., and international immigration was responsible for nearly half of California's population growth (Vernez 1993: 148). While until 1965 the vast majority of immigrants to the United States were from Europe, now 80% arrive from Asia or Latin America (U.S. Bureau of the Census 1993). As a result, California has replaced New York as the main destination of newcomers. Indeed, of the 5.6 million foreign-born who moved to the United States between 1995 and 2000, 1.2 million, or one in five, settled in California. However, California also experienced out-migration during the same period, with 518,000 of its native-born population and 237,000 of its foreign-born residents leaving the state (U.S. Census Bureau).

Foreign policy pressures were another stimulus of immigration to California. Following the Korean War in 1953, Korean immigration to the United States began with the entry of "war brides" and students who stayed and then brought their relatives under the family reunification provisions of the 1965 reform. Following the end of American involvement in the Vietnam War, large numbers of Vietnamese, Laotian, Cambodians, and Hmong tribes came as refugees from the new communist regime. Those who became permanent residents or citizens could sponsor family members for immigration (Oliver, Gey, Stiles, and Brady 1995: XI). And while American policy sought to disperse the Indochinese refugees across the country, many returned to California.

California also received an influx of refugees from Central and South America (LeMay 1994: 15). Legal arrivals were joined by a soaring number of illegal immigrants. More than two-thirds of the illegal immigrants to the United States since 1970 come from Mexico, with many driven across the porous border to California by unemployment and the end of the Bracero program (LeMay 1994: 21).

In the early 1980s, a growing sense of anxiety about the impact of such massive immigration on the nation's economic and cultural fabric engendered more legislation. In 1986, Congress passed the Immigration Reform and Control

Act (IRCA). This law attempted to curb the rise in illegal immigration through two new provisions: employer sanctions and a program that allowed certain illegal immigrants to become lawful residents and, eventually, citizens. But despite IRCA, it is estimated that during the 1990s 300,000 illegal immigrants continued to enter the United States every year, with about half coming to California (U.S. Commission on Immigration Reform 1994). Today, President Bush is proposing a guest worker program to address the present flow of illegal aliens into the country.

The interplay of immigration reform, international events, and the relatively high fertility rates of Latino and Asian immigrants has transformed California's ethnic makeup. Table 1 shows that the Anglo (or non-Hispanic white) segment of the California population declined from 77% in 1970 to 47% in 2000—a proportion estimated to decrease further to 40% by 2020. The black population has remained stable at 7%. In contrast, the share of Latinos in the California population rose from 12% in 1970 to 32% in 2000. By 2020, it is projected to increase to 39%. The Asian population in California is growing most rapidly, increasing from 4% in 1970 to 14% in 2000. Taken together, these trends made California America's first majority-minority state outside of Hawaii.

The central role of immigration in this process of change is clear. In 1960, 8.5% of the residents of California were foreign-born, compared to 5.4% in the country as a whole. By 1990, 26.2% of Californians (almost 8.9 million) were foreign-born, compared to only 10.4 nationally (U.S. Census). By 2004, one out of every four Californians were foreign-born (Johnson 2005).

The following examples illustrate the magnitude and diversity of recent immigration. In 1960, the census reported there were 695,643 foreign-born residents of Mexican origin in California; in 2000 this group numbered almost 3.8 million. In 1960, there were only 20,000 foreign-born residents in California from Guatemala, Nicaragua, and El Salvador; in 2000, there were roughly 635,000—more than a 30-fold increase. Over the same period, the number of residents born in mainland China, Taiwan or Hong Kong grew by more than six-fold from 85,000 to more than 570,000 residents (Lopez 2003).

Latino and Asian immigrants are younger and have more children than native-born Americans, creating a disparity that significantly increases the share of California's minority population even further. Moreover, the relative youth of these ethnic groups has important consequences for overcrowding schools, bilingual education, and white flight. The March 2004 Current Population Survey of the U.S. Census Bureau found that while 20.8% of all California residents were second generation immigrants—i.e., individuals born in the United States with at least one foreign-born parent, fully 41.5% of children under 18 were second-generation immigrants. In Los Angeles County, second generation children from Mexico make up an astounding 55% of all children under 18, a fact reflected in the composition of the public school population. Still, immigrants do learn English. The 2000 Census reports that of the third-generation Latinos in

Table 1. California Population by Race and Ethnicity, 1970–2020

	1970 (000s)	%	1980 (000s)	%	1990 (000s)	%	2000 (000s)	%	2020 (000s)	%
Anglo	15,392	77	15,704	67	17,489	57	20,170	47	18,123	40
African American	1,400	7	1,784	8	2,199	7	2,263	7	2,806	6
Hispanic	2,369	12	4,544	19	8,111	26	10,966	32	17,778	39
Asian & other	792	4	1,575	7	3,077	10	4,741	14	6,740	15
Total	19,953	100	23,608	100	30,826	100	33,871	100	45,448	100

Source: Kitty Calavita, "U.S. Immigration and Policy Responses: The Limits of Legislation," in *Controlling Immigration: A Global Perspective,* ed. Wayne A. Cornelius, Philip L. Martin, and James F. Hollifield (Stanford: Stanford University Press, 1994). 2000 data projections for 2020 from U.S. Census Bureau, 2000.

California, 75% speak only English compared to only 5% of first generation
Latino immigrants.

III. Debating the Impact of Immigration.

The unprecedented level and the changed composition of immigration after
1970 prepared the ground for an upsurge of "restrictionist" sentiment.[2] As the
main terminus of the new immigration, it is not surprising that immigration issues
were particularly salient in California and that this state emerged as the main bat-
tleground in the current policy debate. For example, when the recession of the
early 1990s heightened concerns about the economic and fiscal impacts of immigration (Citrin, Green, Muste, and Wong 1997), Governor Pete Wilson led the
attack on the federal government for failing to fund mandated expenditures for
refugees and illegal immigrants (Nakao, 1991). Similarly, after the bombing of the
World Trade Center in February 1993 and interception of ships smuggling immigrants from China later that year triggered new fears that the nation had lost control of its own borders, U.S. Senator Dianne Feinstein (D-CA) suggested the im-
position of a border crossing toll to obtain revenue for bolstering Border Patrol
forces. Fellow senator Barbara Boxer (D-CA) went even further and proposed that
the National Guard be deployed to stem the flow of illegal immigrants at the U.S.-
Mexican border. Today it is Republican Governor Arnold Schwarzenegger who
has campaigned against legislation granting state drivers' licenses to illegal immigrants and who advocates stricter border control.

Jobs and the Economy

One important concern in the debate over immigration reform is the effect
of immigration on the state and national economy. Since immigration can
clearly affect the size and quality of the labor force in the receiving country,
how have recent immigration trends influenced the jobs, wages, and working
conditions of Americans, particularly poor Americans? Historically, fears of job
displacement, unemployment, and pressure on earnings reinforced nativist attacks on immigration (Higham 1955). These anxieties help explain the frequent
tendency of labor unions to oppose immigration, while business groups traditionally favor a more open door for entrepreneurial, lower-cost workers
(Kirschten 1990). When Congress considered a law to limit the level of legal
immigration in 1996, among the strongest opponents were high-tech industries
in California concerned about their ability to recruit foreign engineers and scientists.

---

[2] We use this term to refer to support for cutting the level of immigration, both legal
and illegal.

Unfortunately, there are no generally accepted conclusions about the economic impact of immigration. Economists reach contradictory results, partly due to whether they focus on long-run or short-run effects, distinguish among national and local impacts, and consider illegal as well as legal immigration. For example, Simon (1989) asserts that, in the long run, benefits of immigration for economic growth and productivity outweigh any costs to local and state workers and governments. Muller (1985: 118–19) concluded that immigrants to southern California during the 1970s replaced rather than displaced native-born workers; native-born job gains were almost exclusively in white-collar occupations, while recent immigrants, mostly Mexicans, generally took unskilled jobs. Borjas (1990: 219) and Butcher and Card (1991) agree that "immigrants have little impact on the earnings and employment of natives," and this result was confirmed by a more recent study. These latter economists argue that immigrants, including illegal aliens, fill an "economical wage niche" by working hard at jobs native workers disdain at wages low enough for the employer to make a profit.

But others counter that the availability of such cheap labor discourages investment in technology and also takes jobs away from low-skilled, low-paid workers, particularly blacks (Papademetriou and Miller 1984; Briggs 1992; Miles 1992). Indeed, interviews with employers indicate that they often prefer immigrants to the available native labor pool and so recruit workers through informal networks of immigrants that exclude potential black hires (Glazer 1995).

The educational attainment, skills, and financial resources of immigrants raise another policy question. Under the 1965 immigration law, one category of visa preference is for immigrants who have special skills not available in the domestic workforce or who intend to start a business and have a certain amount of money to invest. But most recent immigrants have come as a result of the family reunification provisions. And while some immigrant groups, primarily those from Asia and Africa, are more likely than the native-born population to have college and postgraduate degrees, the large majority of the heavier influx from Mexico in recent years has tended to come from rural areas with little formal education, few job skills, and no capital (Borjas and Freeman 1992, LeMay 1994).

The economic consequences of this pattern of immigration seem mixed. On the one hand, specialization of unskilled immigrants in particular industries reduces the prices of those goods to the benefit of American consumers. On the other hand, an increase in the number of unskilled rather than skilled immigrants reduces potential national income because the unskilled are relatively less productive (Borjas 1990: 222). The poverty and illiteracy rates among immigrants also affect the nature of government spending and thus have implications for public finance.

"Designer" immigration is one proposed response to these trends; the entry of those with desired economic skills would be encouraged, while the number of poor, uneducated immigrants would be sharply curtailed. Until now, the opposition of immigrant advocacy groups and public support for family reunification have prevented this kind of reform from being institutionalized, but pressure from high-tech industries largely located in California have produced more visas for software engineers and other specialized workers from Asia.

Taxes versus Services

Whatever the overall contribution of immigrants to the economy in the long-run, there can be short-run costs that burden the public treasury, particularly in states, like California, and localities, like Los Angeles, with large concentrations of new arrivals. Indeed, with the expansion of the American welfare state after 1965 and the concomitant blurring of the line between citizen and alien as a result of liberal legislation and Supreme Court decisions, the fiscal impact of immigration became a more prominent political issue than the effect on employment patterns.

Since 1991, the cost of immigration, particularly illegal immigration, has been a central theme of budgetary politics in California. Governor Wilson raised the issue in the early 1990s by arguing that immigration contributed to a growing imbalance between the number of residents receiving services and those paying taxes. He indicted the federal government for its failure to fulfill funding commitments made in the Refugee Act of 1980 and in IRCA to support immigration and resettlement decisions (California Health and Welfare Agency 1993.) Specifically, the governor identified the costs of incarcerating illegal immigrant felons, state supplementary payments to refugees and elderly immigrants, and health, welfare, and education benefits to immigrants as fiscal drains on the state.

In August 1993, Wilson laid out his policy agenda in an open letter to President Clinton. The governor proposed cutting services to illegal immigrants, including access to public education required by the 1982 Supreme Court decision in *Plyler v. Doe*. He also advocated a constitutional amendment to deny birthright citizenship to children of illegal aliens. In April 1994, California filed suit against the federal government to recover several billion dollars; Florida and Texas, two other states with large numbers of illegal immigrants and refugees, took similar action.

Crafting a cost-benefit ratio for immigration is a difficult enterprise, and the conclusions reached depend on the specific immigrant groups considered and the methodologies used in estimating taxes paid and services consumed. In addition, the overall "cost" of immigration will reflect changes in federal and California laws governing entitlements, shifting rates of utilization of public services by immigrants and the degree to which illegal immigrants obtain benefits, such as AFDC, they are denied by law.

A study by Julian Simon (1989) concluded that during the first 12 years of U.S. residence, the typical immigrant uses substantially fewer public services overall than a native-born resident and is a net contributor in terms of federal taxes paid. A study by the Urban Institute estimated immigrants generate a $25 to $35 billion public assistance annual surplus, but Rice University economist Donald Huddle reached a radically different conclusion concerning the cost of immigrants to all levels of government and projected a $42.5 billion annual deficit (Huddle 1995).

Whatever the impact on the federal government's budget, it does not help states with large numbers of immigrants meet their short-run expenditures. Because immigrants to California are younger on average than natives, they are more likely to have school-age children and require state spending for education. Moreover, this cost to the state in California includes the expense for programs aimed at the burgeoning number of schoolchildren with limited proficiency in English, a group that by now includes more than one in five youngsters.

Even strong advocates of the economic benefits of legal immigration usually accept that the costs of education for the children of illegal immigrants and the eligibility of citizen children for public assistance represent a net fiscal drain in a state with a generous welfare system such as California (Passel and Fix 1994: 158). This belief underlies Governor Wilson's characterization of the cost of illegal immigration as a large, unfunded federal mandate (Wilson 1996). It should be noted that as the 1996 presidential election approached, the Clinton administration and Republican Congress did agree to provide California more than $2 billion toward the cost of services for refugees and illegal immigrants, slightly more than half the amount demanded by the state.

Recent public opinion has favored limiting the access of immigrants to public services for several years, and there have been numerous studies of trickery in making elderly immigrants eligible for Medicaid assistance (Citrin, Green, Muste, and Wong 1997). Welfare reform legislation passed in 1996 prohibits future immigrants from receiving federal benefits during their first five years in the United States and bars most legal immigrants in the United States from receiving food stamps and supplemental security payments. But it is unlikely that changing the level of public assistance available to immigrants will reduce the desire to come to the United States. Economic opportunity rather than the availability of government benefits is the truly powerful magnet that attracts immigrants, legal and illegal alike.

Cultural Assimilation

Anxiety about national unity rose during each major wave of immigration into the United States. In the early twentieth century, there was deep concern about whether Poles, Italians, and Jews would assimilate, but economic mobility, intermarriage, and Americanization quickly worked to achieve the linguistic and cultural integration of these groups. Is there reason to believe that things would be different for the more recent wave of immigrants?

Critics of current immigration policy (Brimelow 1995) suggest that the racial and cultural differences between today's immigrants and the native population are greater than in the past. They argue further that the ability of Mexican and Asian immigrants to maintain ties with their home countries, due to the proximity of the border in one case and access to cheap air travel in the other, also inhibits assimilation. Moreover, neither assimilation nor Americanization are popular ideas among elites today (Glazer 1994). In his recent book, *Who Are We? Challenges to American National Identity* (2004), Samuel Huntington worries that the large influx of Mexican immigrants geographically concentrated in the Southwest raises the possibility of an American Quebec, a Spanish-speaking enclave that rejects traditional American values and promotes allegiance to Mexico as well as, if not instead of, the United States. An empirical test of Huntington's thesis by Citrin, Lerman, and Murakami (2005) found that a traditional pattern of assimilation continued to prevail, with each succeeding generation of Mexican immigrants assimilating both linguistically and psychologically, in the sense of identifying as Americans and espousing patriotic sentiments. Until now, the economy, popular culture, and increasing rates of intermarriage have been assimilative forces strong enough to counter any challenges to the traditional American ideal of *e pluribus unum* posed by multiculturalism's emphasis on the maintenance of distinct ethnic political identities. Nowhere is this clearer than in language policy, where public support for linguistic assimilation is pervasive.

In the context of increasing immigration, critics charged that the spread of bilingual programs reduced the incentive to learn English and retarded the process of assimilation by segregating immigrant children in inferior classroom settings. They argued further that the development of multicultural curricula in the public schools deliberately erodes the traditional role of this institution in inculcating a common set of "American" values. In 1986, Californians overwhelmingly voted for an initiative designating English as the state's official language and forbidding the passage of any law that "diminishes or ignores" the role of English (Citrin, Green, Reingold, and Walters 1991). The effect of this measure has been largely symbolic, but the popular vote for official English was an early sign of the widespread anxiety about the impact of ethnic diversity on social cohesion that resurfaced in the campaign for Proposition 187 in 1994.

In 1998, Ron Unz, a Silicon Valley entrepreneur, sponsored a ballot initiative that limited bilingual education to just one year of an English immersion program. He stated that the existing programs kept non-English speaking students in bilingual settings for many years, limiting their acquisition of English, a necessary step toward upward economic ability. Although immigrant rights groups, Latino activists, and the education establishment vigorously opposed Proposition 227, it passed by a large margin, with majorities of white, black, and Asian voters voting in favor. Whatever the ultimate impact of this reform on the speed with which English is learned, the evidence suggests that today's immigrants continue to learn English at roughly the same rates as earlier, European immigrants (Glazer 1995; Portes and Rumbaut 1990).

Political Effects

The population growth resulting from foreign immigration into California has increased the state's representation in the House of Representatives. The reapportionment of congressional seats that occurs after each decennial national census is based on changes in the number of residents, not citizens, across districts. Accordingly, California gained seven new House seats (and electoral college votes) after the 1990 reapportionment. Most of these seats were located in southern California, the area with the largest concentration of new immigrants. Following the 2000 census, California gained one more congressional seat. Immigration enhances California's political importance in the national arena, both in Congress and in presidential elections. Within the state, immigration bolsters the influence of southern California on policymaking, and voters from this region traditionally have differed strongly from the rest of the state's electorate on issues like water rights.

By increasing the size of the Latino and Asian populations in California, immigration has influenced the pattern of ethnic competition for political offices and power. In some locales such as Los Angeles, the emergent issue is the conflict between "blacks and browns" (Miles 1992); in others, such as the suburb of Monterey Park, the electoral struggle pits Anglos against a diverse group of new Asian residents (Wood 1990). More generally, the Mexican-American Legal Defense and Education Fund (MALDEF) has spearheaded legal and political efforts to increase the election of minority candidates at the state and local levels through redistricting and replacing at-large local elections with district elections that favor residentially concentrated minority groups.

Redistricting and affirmative action in government jobs and contracts are issues that potentially pit Hispanics and Asians against the declining number of blacks in the state (Matloff 1996: 69–70; Miles 1992). The civil rights movement resulted in black political and economic gains, particularly in the metropolitan areas where recent immigrants have settled. Affirmative action rules designate Hispanics and Asians, regardless of their immigrant status, as groups deserving of "representation," enabling advocacy groups to challenge the black political establishment to allocate benefits to their own ethnic group (DelVecchio 1996).

Despite the increasing numbers of Asians and Hispanics in California, their share of the eligible electorate and regular voters is significantly lower than their proportion of the population as a whole (Citrin and Highton 2002)). One obvious reason is what might be termed the citizenship ratios of different ethnic groups. Many Asians and Hispanics are recent immigrants without the right to vote; others have chosen not to become naturalized citizens (Citrin 1987; Pachon 1991). In addition, the relative youth, low income, lack of formal education, and attitudes toward political engagement among recent immigrants help diminish their rate of voting (Uhlaner, Cain, and Kiewiet 1989).

To illustrate, in 2000 Hispanics made up 26% of California's adult population, 18% of its adult citizens, but only 14% of those who voted in the 2000 general election (Citrin and Highton 2002:17). Asians comprised 13% of the state's adult population but only 7% of its voters in 2000. Particularly in statewide elections for candidates or on ballot initiatives, voters in California are as a group older, wealthier, more educated, more likely to be white, and more conservative than the overall state population.

In legislative elections, the ethnic homogeneity of many districts ensures a level of minority representation in the California legislature. Increasingly, however, direct democracy is the mechanism for settling important issues in the state. To the extent that the preferences of immigrants differ from the opinions of the demographic groups more likely to vote on statewide initiatives and referenda, this trend weakens their influence and that of the ethnic minorities to which they generally belong.

The impact of immigration on the balance between Republicans and Democrats is another salient political issue. On the surface, the growing number of Hispanics and Asians would seem to benefit the Democrats, as the party that traditionally champions the cause of minorities and more strongly defends the idea of immigrant rights. Survey data do show that by a margin of two-to-one or more, Mexican Americans and Filipinos in California tend to identify and vote as Democrats (Jackson and Preston 1991). But Chinese, Korean, and Vietnamese voters are much more evenly divided and frequently give majority support to Republicans whose foreign policy and economic attitudes they tend to share (Cain and Kiewiet 1986; Nakanishi 1991). In addition, there is evidence of differences within the Latino and Asian communities due to the voters' age, social status, and recency of immigration. In particular, the partisan affiliation of new immigrants is less established and predictable. Among the native-born public, attitudes toward immigration are related to party identification and ideology, with conservatives and Republicans more likely than liberals and Democrats to express restrictionist sentiments (Citrin, Green, Muste, and Wong 1997). These differences are quite attenuated, however, and immigration is an issue dividing both political parties.

Democratic politicians tied to the labor and environmentalist movements often support restricting immigration, arguing that unskilled foreign workers reduce the jobs and earnings available to native workers and that an overcrowded America lacks the space and natural resources to sustain additional population growth (Kirschten 1990). On the other hand, Democrats who represent Hispanic constituencies and are strongly oriented toward civil rights have allied themselves with pro-growth, pro-business Republicans who view immigrants as a source of needed labor and entrepreneurial energy. In 1996, this bipartisan coalition succeeded in blocking legislation to reduce the level of legal immigration and amend the provisions governing family reunification.

IV. Public Opinion.

In democratic societies, public opinion constrains the course of public policy, if only by placing limits on the choices officials who must face reelection can safely contemplate. When immigration becomes a salient issue arousing substantial citizen interest, political realities may dictate official actions, whatever the private belief of elites. In the 1870s, for example, widespread anti-Chinese sentiment in the western states led the national Republican party to retreat from its egalitarian commitment and support exclusionary legislation aimed at Asian immigration (Hutchinson 1981).

In 1965, before the passage of liberal immigration reform legislation, only 33% of a national sample surveyed by Gallup said that the level of foreign immigration into the United States should be decreased; this proportion reached a high of 65% in 1993 (Simon and Alexander 1993) and was reported at 46% in June of 2005. Similarly, the 2000 American National Election Study (ANES) found that 48% of the public favored decreasing the current level of immigration. In 1994, when political events in California had raised the salience of the issue nationwide, 63% of the ANES national sample expressed this restrictionist opinion. A Field Institute poll conducted in the same year found that 55% of Californians agreed that immigration should be curtailed.

Public opinion data in California indicated an ambivalent outlook toward legal immigration. While a majority of those surveyed by Field in 1994 (and 45% of the Hispanic respondents) wanted to cut back on the influx into California, almost three-fourths believed that foreign-born residents make just as good citizens as those born here, and almost two-thirds agreed that it is beneficial for immigrant groups to preserve their own languages and customs. Opinions about the economic and social impacts of Asian immigrants are more positive than those concerning new arrivals from Mexico (Citrin, Reingold and Green 1990; Espenshade and Belanger 1996). The overall attitude toward legal immigrants thus seems to be: "They tend to be good people, but I wish there were fewer of them here."

The focus of the 1994 election in California, however, was *illegal* immigration. Over one-half of the estimated four million illegal aliens in the United States live in California. In Governor Wilson's attacks on the fiscal impact of immigration, he carefully distinguished between illegal immigrants and those "who came here the right way," and Proposition 187, the so-called "Save Our State" initiative, specifically targeted benefits provided to illegals.

Opinions about illegal immigrants are decidedly more negative than for immigrants as a whole, partly because of prevailing stereotypes of this group as poor, unskilled, and prone to be a public burden, and partly because the term "illegal" connotes criminal tendencies.[3] In 1994, Field found that 72% of the California public believed that illegal immigrants have had an unfavorable impact on the state and 88% viewed illegal immigration as a serious problem. Given these feelings, it is not surprising that there was widespread support for strong measures to stem the tide of illegal immigration. Two-thirds of respondents to the 1994 Field Poll on immigration policy favored the use of National Guard troops to guard the border and 73% approved of a border crossing toll to raise money to fund more border protection. On the other hand, only 42% thought that it would be a good idea to issue special identification cards to all persons living in the United States, arguably a more effective way "to tighten up on immigration."

This climate of opinion provided the backdrop to the heated campaign over Proposition 187, a ballot measure denying state health and education benefits to anyone in California who is not a U.S. citizen, legal permanent resident or a legal temporary visitor. The framers of Proposition 187 strategically tapped into the fiscal concerns of California voters living through a recession. Governor Wilson had made the cost of immigration a salient issue several years earlier. Trailing behind Democratic challenger Kathleen Brown in the polls, he tied his 1994 reelection campaign to Proposition 187. Despite the opposition of most of the state's major newspapers, establishment interest groups, and President Clinton and other top Democrats, the anti-immigrant initiative passed by a margin of 59 to 41%. Wilson went on to win reelection, 55 to 40%.

Proposition 187 passed in all regions of the state except the liberal San Francisco Bay Area; the initiative received its strongest support in the Los Angeles suburbs. Exit polls indicated substantial ethnic differences in voting: 63% of whites, 55% of blacks and Asians but only 31% of Hispanic voters voted for Prop 187.[4]

Ethnic interests play a role in shaping opinions on immigration policy. In a 1994 Los Angeles survey, 41% of the black respondents and 32% of the whites said that legal immigration should be decreased "a lot," compared to 17% of the Asians and 12% of the Hispanics. However, when it comes to policies regarding illegal immigrants, a predominantly Mexican group, Asian attitudes more closely resemble those of whites and blacks. For example, more than 70% of blacks, whites, and Asians strongly opposed a policy of issuing work permits to illegal immigrants, while 75% of Hispanic respondents favored such an entitlement. Similarly, 92% of the Hispanic respondents in this Los Angeles survey favored citizenship rights for the children of illegal immigrants, compared to

---

[3] Factor analysis, a statistical technique that assesses the extent to which opinions cluster along a single dimension, suggests that attitudes toward legal and illegal immigration are distinct, though interrelated.

[4] These figures are the results of a Voter News Survey Exit Poll.

only half of the remaining racial groups in the sample (Sears, Citrin, Vidanage, and Valentino 1994: 14).

On balance, then, Hispanics are much more opposed than members of other ethnic groups to limiting legal immigration, tightening controls against illegal immigration, and limiting entitlements for immigrants (Sears, Citrin, Vidanage, and Valentino 1994; Citrin, Green, Muste, and Wong 1995).[5] Given that the U.S.-Mexican border is the only one in the world where citizens of one country openly mass to wait for their chance to illegally enter another, the special interest of immigration issues to Mexicans and Mexican Americans is clear. In this regard, there is renewed interest in a guest-worker program to allow migrants who will inevitably cross the border seeking work to do so legally.

The pattern of ethnic differences in opinion on immigration issues points to cleavages among minority voters. Despite the tendency of ethnic activists to cooperate in supporting immigrant rights, among the general public, black preferences are closer to those of whites than to the opinions of Asians or Hispanics. Indeed, blacks are particularly concerned about the negative impact of immigration on their job opportunities (Citrin, Green, Muste, and Wong 1995). Immigration has increased the diversity of California's population and the complexity of building coalitions among its minority ethnic groups.

V. Conclusion

International migration is a complex phenomenon that no single country can control. Even during the deep recession that beset California from 1991–94, foreign immigration into the state increased due to sectoral labor needs and the persistent push of poverty in Mexico. But because regulating the flow of immigrants to one's country lies at the heart of national sovereignty, in the United States, state government policies are simply the tail on the federal government dog.

Immigration brings "strangers" into our midst and inevitably a certain degree of instability. Do more people add to our economic and environmental problems? Do immigrants add to the cost of the welfare state? Does the influx of people of different races and languages threaten national unity? Glazer (1995) concludes that in an era of pessimism about the economy and a lack of national self-confidence, uncertainty about the answers to these questions seem to lead a majority of Americans to yearn for more cohesion and thus to desire less immigration. A look at history shows that this is not a novel reaction (Higham 1955).

The U.S. Commission on Immigration Reform acknowledged popular fears when it titled its 1994 Report to Congress "U.S. Immigration Policy: Restoring Credibility." This document emphasized the need for drastic measures to control illegal immigration. How to reform legal immigration is more controversial, but

---

[5] This pattern emerges in national, California-wide, and Los Angeles County surveys.

at the level of national policy, the most critical decisions concern: (1) the overall level of immigration; (2) the relative weight of skills as opposed to family ties in the allocation of visas; and (3) the entitlement of immigrants and refugees to government benefits.

Whether the current level of immigration is reduced or not, a compact between federal, state, and local governments that aligns policies and fairly allocates the fiscal burden of immigration is imperative. As the state with the largest number of immigrants, California must be especially concerned with their impact on the cohesion of the community. The state can assist in the cultural and political integration of immigrants with programs that facilitate learning English and speed the process of naturalization. Even if international conditions and national policies change, immigration to California will only slow, not end, with continuing implications for the state's economy, culture, and politics.

References

Auerbach, Susan, ed. 1994. *Encyclopedia of Multiculturalism*. New York: Marshall Cavendish.

Borjas, George J. 1990. *Friends or Strangers: The Impact of Immigrants on the U.S. Economy*. New York: Basic Books.

Borjas, George J., and Richard B. Freeman. 1992. *Immigration and the Work Force: Economic Consequences for the United States and Source Areas*. Chicago: University of Chicago Press.

____. 1996. "Punish Employers, Not Children." *New York Times* (July 11): A23.

Briggs, Vernon M, 1992. *Mass Immigration and the National Interest*. Armonk, NY: M. E. Sharpe.

Brimelow, Peter. 1995. *Alien Nation: Common Sense about America's Immigration Disaster*. New York: Random House.

Butcher, Kristin F., and David Card. 1991. "Immigration and Wages: Evidence from the 1980s." *American Economic Review* 81: 292–96.

Cain, Bruce, and Roderick Kiewiet. 1986. "California's Coming Minority Majority." *Public Opinion* 9: 50–52.

California Health and Welfare Agency. 1993. *A Failed Federal Promise*.

Citrin, Jack. 1987. "Public Opinion in a Changing California." in *The Capacity to Respond*, ed. Ted K. Bradshaw and Charles G. Bell. Berkeley, Calif.: Institute of Governmental Studies.

Citrin, Jack, Beth A. Reingold, and Donald P. Green. 1990. "American Identity and the Politics of Ethnic Change." *Journal of Politics* 52: 1124–54.

Citrin, Jack, Beth Reingold, Evelyn Walters, and Donald P. Green. 1990. "The 'Official English' Movement and the Symbolic Politics of Language in the United States." *Western Political Quarterly* 43: 535–59.

Citrin, Jack, Donald P. Green, Christopher Muste, and Cara Wong. 1997. "Public Opinion toward Immigration Reform: The Role of Economic Motivations." *Journal of Politics*, forthcoming.

Citrin, Jack, Donald P. Green, Christopher Muste, and Cara Wong. 1995. "Public Opinion toward Immigration Reform: How Much Does the Economy Matter?" Berkeley: Chicano/Latino Policy Project.

Citrin, Jack, and Benjamin Highton. 2002. *How Race, Ethnicity, and Immigration are Shaping the California Electorate*. San Francisco: Public Policy Institute of California.

Citrin, Jack, Amy Lerman, and Michael H. Murakami. 2005. Paper presented at the annual meeting of the Midwest Political Science Association. The Palmer House Hilton, Chicago, Illinois.

Citrin, Jack, Amy Lerman, Michael Murakami, and Kathryn Pearson, "Testing Huntington: Is Hispanic Immigration a Threat to American National Identity?" unpublished working paper, Institute of Governmental Studies.

Commonwealth Club of California. 1946. *The Population of California*. San Francisco: Parker Printing.

DelVecchio, Rick. 1996. "Unusual Suit Stirs Racial Questions in Oakland." *San Francisco Chronicle*, August 13, 1996, A13-A14.

Espenshade, Thomas J., and Maryann Belanger. 1996. "U.S. Public Perceptions and Reactions to Mexican Migration." Paper prepared for the Conference on Mexican Migration and U.S. Policy, Center for Strategic and International Studies, Washington, D.C., June 14–15, 1996.

Field Institute. 1995. "A Summary Analysis of Voting in the 1994 General Election." *Califonia Opinion Index* 1: 1–6.

Field Institute. 1994. "A Digest on How the California Public Views a Variety of Matters Relating to: Immigration."

Fuchs, Lawrence H. 1990. *The American Kaleidoscope*. Hanover, N.H.: Wesleyan University Press.

Fuchs, Lawrence H. 1992. "Thinking about Immigration and Ethnicity in the United States." in *Immigrants in Two Democracies: French and American Experience.*, ed. Donald L. Horowitz and Gerard Noiriel. New York: New York University Press.

Galarza, Ernesto. 1964. *Merchants of Labor: The Mexican Bracero Story*. Charlotte: McNally and Lofton.

Glazer, Nathan. 1995. "Immigration and the American Future." *The Public Interest* 118: 45–60.

Higham, John. 1955. *Strangers in the Land: Patterns of American Nativism 1869–1925*. New York: Atheneum.

Hing, Bill Ong. 1993. *Making and Remaking Asian America through Immigration Policy, 1850–1990*. Stanford: Stanford University Press.

Huddle, Donald L. 1995. "A Critique of the Urban Institutes Claims of Cost Free Immigration: Early Findings Confirmed." *Population and Environment* 16: 507–19.

Huntington, Samuel. 2004. *Who Are We?: Challenges to American National Identity*. Cambridge, Mass.: Harvard University Press.

Hutchinson, Edward Prince. 1981. *Legislative History of American Immigration Policy,1798–1965*. Philadelphia: University of Pennsylvania Press.

Jackson, Byran O. and Michael B. Preston, eds. 1991. *Racial and Ethnic Politics in California*. Berkeley: Institute of Governmental Studies.

Johnson, Daniel M., and Rex R. Campbell. 1981. *Black Migration in America: A Social Demographic History*. Durham: Duke University Press.

Johnson, Hans. 2005. "California's Population in 2025" in *California 2025: Taking on the Future,* ed. Ellen Hanak and Mark Baldassare. Public Policy Institute of California.

Kirschten, Dick. 1990. "Come In! Keep Out!" *National Journal* 22: 1206–11.

Lopez, Alejandra. 2003. "The Foreign-born in California: Place of Origin, Region of Residence, Race, Time of Entry, and Citizenship." *CCSRE Race and Ethnicity in California: Demographics Report Series,* Stanford University.

LeMay, Michael C. 1994. *Anatomy of a Public Policy: The Reform of Contemporary American Immigration Law*. Westport, Conn.: Praeger.

Lochhead, Carolyn. 1996. "Clinton Backs Welfare Overhaul." *San Francisco Chronicle*, August 1, 1996, A1, A8.

Matloff, Norman. 1996. "How Immigration Harms Minorities." *The Public Interest* 124: 61–71.

Miles, Jack. 1992. Blacks vs. Browns. *The Atlantic Monthly* 270: 41–59.

Muller, Thomas. 1985. "Economic Effects of Immigration." In *Clamor at the Gates: The New American Immigration*, ed. Nathan Glazer. San Francisco: ICS Press.

Nakanishi, Don T. 1991. "The Next Swing Vote? Asian Pacific Americans and California Politics." In *Racial and Ethnic Politics in California*, ed. Byran O. Jackson and Michael B. Preston. Berkeley: Institute of Governmental Studies.

Nakao, Annie. 1991. "Assessing the cost of Immigration." *San Francisco Examiner*, December 1, 1991, B1, B3.

Oliver, J. Eric, Fredric C. Gey, Jon Stiles, and Henry Brady. 1995. *Pacific Rim States Asian Demographic Data Book*. Oakland: Pacific Rim Research Program.

Olzak, Susan. 1992. *The Dynamics of Ethnic Competition and Conflict*. Stanford, Calif.: Stanford University Press.

Pachon, Harry. 1991. "U.S. Citizenship and Latino Participation in California Politics." In *Racial and Ethnic Politics in California*, ed. Byran O. Jackson and Michael B. Preston. Berkeley: Institute of Governmental Studies.

Papademetriou, Demetrious G., and Mark J. Miller, eds. 1984. *The Unavoidable Issue*. Philadelphia: Institute for the Study of Human Issues.

Passel, Jeffrey S., and Michael Fix. 1994. "Myths about Immigrants." *Foreign Policy* 95: 151–60.

Portes, Alejandro and Ruben G. Rumbaut. 1990. *Immigrant America: A Portrait*. Berkeley: University of California Press.

Rojas, Aurelio. 1996a. "Border Guarded, Workplace Ignored." *San Francisco Chronicle* (March 18): 1.

_____. 1996b. "Growers Hire Illegals with Impunity." *San Francisco Chronicle* (March 19): 1.

_____. 1996c. "Boomtowns Count on Illegals." *San Francisco Chronicle* (March 20): 1.

Samora, Julian. 1971. *Los Mojados: The Wetback Story*. Notre Dame: University of Notre Dame Press.

Sears, David O., Jack Citrin, Sharmaine Vidanage, and Nicholas Valentino. 1994. "What Ordinary Americans Think about Multiculturalism." Paper presented at the annual meeting of the American Political Science Association, New York City, September 1, 1994.

Simon, Julian S. 1989. *The Economic Consequences of Immigration*. Oxford: Basil Blackwell.

Simon, Rita J., and Susan H. Alexander. 1993. *The Ambivalent Welcome: Print Media, Public Opinion, and Immigration*. Westport, Conn.: Praeger.

Southern California Bureau of Information. 1892. "Southern California."

Stein, Walter J. 1973. *California and the Dust Bowl Migration.* Westport, Conn.: Greenwood Press.

Uhlaner, Carole J., Bruce E. Cain, and D, Roderick Kiewiet. 1989. "Political Participation of Ethnic Minorities in the 1980s." *Political Behavior* 11: 195–231.

U.S. Bureau of the Census. 1993. "We the American Foreign Born." Washington, D.C.: Government Printing Office.

U.S. Commission on Immigration Reform. 1994. U.S. Immigration Policy: Restoring credibility: 1994 report to Congress. Washington, D.C.: U.S. Commission on Immigration Reform.

Vernez, Georges. 1993. "Mexican Labor in California's Economy: From Rapid Growth to Likely Stability." In *The California-Mexico Connection,* ed. Abraham F. Lowenthal and Katrina Burgess. Stanford: Stanford University Press.

Wilson, Pete. 1996. "Piety, But No Help, On Illegal Aliens." *New York Times* (July 11): A23.

Wood, Daniel B. 1990. "Monterey Park Seeks Harmony." *The Christian Science Monitor,* October 18, 1990, 6.

Chapter 11

Water in California:
A Case Study in Federalism

Megan Mullin

California's water problem can be described simply. The state does not have enough water to meet human, agricultural, and environmental demands, and the water California does have is not located where the demand is. Much of the state enjoys a seasonal Mediterranean climate with warm, dry summers that provides ideal growing conditions for fruits, vegetables, and nuts and contributes to Californians' high quality of life. However, careful management of water resources is needed to sustain large human populations in this environment. Cycles of flooding and drought are inherent to Mediterranean climates, but large cities and businesses cannot tolerate these cycles. They import water from other parts of the state in order to secure a more reliable supply.

In some regions, water is abundant: rainfall is plentiful in the northern part of the state, and snowpack in the Sierra Nevada serves as an excellent water storage system. But almost all human demands for water reside elsewhere—along the coast, in the southern desert, and in the fertile Central Valley—creating the need for an enormous infrastructure to transport water to where people live and crops are grown. The infrastructure that has developed over the last century is precarious, with aging pipes and treatment facilities that might not withstand damage from earthquakes or climate change. Moreover, the mass diversion of water away from its natural course has had significant environmental consequences that create an obstacle to further infrastructure expansion. Projected population increases in the coming decades will place even greater pressure on the state's water resources.

The root cause of California's water problem may be simple, but its manifestations are complex. Water scarcity forces choices about how to allocate water among competing demands, how best to protect water quality and natural ecosystems, and who should pay for securing a safe and reliable water supply. Battles over water underlie much of California's most contentious politics. Water shapes the state's history and explains many contemporary schisms and alliances. With insufficient water resources, different user groups must compete to acquire enough supply to meet their demands. The state's agricultural industry has benefited over time from an ample allocation of water at extremely low prices. Agencies representing urban water users have long challenged these subsidies and fought to increase the amount of water dedicated to business and residential use in metropolitan areas. In recent decades, environmentalists have become important players in water politics by demanding that more water remain in streams and wetlands in order to protect water quality and wildlife habitat. These three groups operate in a complex legal and institutional environment, changing strategies and shifting coalitions across water policy issues and questions.

California's water problem is a public policy problem; it cannot be resolved wholly in the marketplace. Water is an essential good, and governments have an interest and duty to ensure that all state residents have enough water to meet their basic needs. If water were managed like any other commodity, with price mechanisms alone determining allocation, some residents or communities might be excluded from the marketplace. The quality of water service also might suffer. Indeed, governments first stepped in to manage local water resources in California when customers became dissatisfied with the high rates and poor service provided by private water companies.

A marketplace also can fail to protect common assets. Too many users drilling wells into an underground aquifer or diverting water away from a running stream will collectively damage the environment. Ultimately, they may reduce the capacity of that source to store and transport future water supplies. The power and resources of the state may be necessary to coordinate the actions of private individuals and enforce limits on water use. The public sector can protect state assets in whose benefits all residents share, such as clean and scenic rivers and beaches, wetlands that provide habitat for migratory birds, a sound economy that provides jobs and security, and a diverse agricultural industry that allows state residents to enjoy fresh produce and local wine.

The government's multiple interests in water management—the provision of safe drinking water, the control of negative externalities from private water use, and the protection of public assets—leads multiple levels of government to participate in water policy. Water policy in California is a case study in federalism. The involvement of many governmental bodies across jurisdictional levels has both advantages and disadvantages for resolving questions about water policy. In some cases the multiplicity of public actors makes it difficult and costly to arrive at a policy decision. Often, however, greater resources and expertise become available than if a policy question resided at just one level of government. Federalism provides a greater number of checks to make sure that no issue or interest is overlooked in reaching a policy solution. Finally, a federalist approach to water management can help to overcome stalemate when governments offer incentives and penalties that encourage other governments to act. The remainder of this chapter explores how federalism influences the development and resolution of water policy conflicts in California.

California's Water Supply

California has a complex hydrological infrastructure of rivers, lakes, snowpack, and groundwater basins to store and transport its water supply, but this natural system is not enough to support millions of residents and a booming economy given the state's climate. Most of the state's precipitation falls in the winter months, primarily in the north and in the mountains. Drought cycles produce large annual fluctuations in rainfall, so even wet regions have an unpredictable water supply. The deficiency of precipitation at the time and place where users require water creates the need for a built system of reservoirs, dams, and aqueducts to supplement the state's natural hydrology.

Natural groundwater basins are an important part of the state's water conveyance and storage system. Approximately a third of the state's precipitation contributes to the water supply by running off into rivers and streams or seeping through the ground to recharge a groundwater basin; the rest either evaporates or gets consumed by vegetation.[1] The 431 groundwater basins throughout California help to distribute seasonal rainfall and store it for use throughout the year. Groundwater basins also can be artificially recharged to store additional water beyond what seeps in naturally. Pumping groundwater is a relatively low cost method for obtaining water, and approximately 30% of the state's urban and agricultural water use in an average year comes from groundwater.

Snowpack is another natural contributor to the water storage system. Precipitation is heaviest throughout the state in winter; snowpack stores water in the mountains while rain is falling in the valleys and along the coast. The majority of winter snowfall in the Sierra Nevada does not run off until after March, with snowpack runoff peaking in May. This runoff contributes to the flow of rivers and streams long after the rainy season has ended throughout the state.

Groundwater and snowpack are critical elements in the state's water supply system, but both resources may be in jeopardy. Groundwater basins are a common good shared by owners of land overlying the basin and consequently are subject to

---

[1] Most of the following figures regarding water supply and use come from the 1998 California Water Plan, prepared by the state Department of Water Resources. At the time of this writing, the 2003 update was still in draft form.

exploitation. Private actors have an incentive to maximize their individual water use, even though overuse produces a collective harm. If users extract more water than seeps in over the long term, the basin may suffer saltwater intrusion or even land subsidence—the land literally sinks, diminishing the basin's future storage capacity. Paving over open space and agricultural land affects groundwater supply by reducing the amount of water that flows into basins, and contamination from toxic chemicals can restrict groundwater usage. As a result, some counties in California regulate the drilling of new wells to control groundwater consumption, and many communities are beginning to consider groundwater recharge in their land-use decisions. Climate change poses a further threat by reducing snowpack and spring recharge of groundwater basins.

Since groundwater is not sufficient to meet California's water demand, and precipitation does not fall where and when the state needs it most, a developed infrastructure of reservoirs, dams, canals, and aqueducts stores surface water from rivers and streams across seasons and transports it throughout the state. The largest single project is the Central Valley Project (CVP), a set of dams and canals operated by the federal Bureau of Reclamation. California took the lead in planning the CVP, but the Great Depression interfered with the state's ability to sell bonds for construction. A project that would provide water to farmers and develop public power while creating jobs fit nicely into President Roosevelt's New Deal program, and the president authorized an emergency allocation to begin construction in 1935 (Hundley 2001). The CVP taps northern California rivers to supply an average of seven million acre-feet of water annually, primarily to agricultural users.[2]

California has its own large water project, aptly named the State Water Project (SWP), which was built by the Department of Water Resources after voters approved its construction in a 1960 statewide vote. The state project is less than half the size of the CVP, with original long-term contracts to deliver 4.2 million acre-feet a year to urban and agricultural users. The project has never been completed as planned, however, and existing facilities allow delivery of approximately three million acre-feet in a normal year.[3]

---

[2] An acre-foot of water covers the area of an acre to a depth of one foot and supplies enough water for two households per year. California's total supply available in a typical year is 78 million acre-feet, about half of which is used for environmental purposes and the rest for urban and agricultural consumption.

[3] Unfinished portions of the CVP and the SWP continue to ignite controversy in the water community. Congress authorized construction of Auburn Dam in 1965 as one of the final facilities to complete the CVP. The dam was intended to provide flood control and new water storage on the American River. Construction halted after a 1975 earthquake, and since then environmentalists seeking to preserve the American River Canyon have successfully blocked repeated efforts by project proponents to secure funding to finish the dam. Another project proposal that periodically reappears is the Peripheral Canal, a canal that would take water from the Sacramento River and carry it around the eastern edge of the San Francisco Bay Delta to pumping plants in Tracy. The Peripheral Canal originally was proposed in 1965 as a SWP facility that would help restore the Delta

Many local water agencies operate their own surface water projects, which together provide more than a quarter of the total state water supply dedicated to urban and agricultural uses. The largest of these local projects is the Los Angeles Aqueduct, which delivers water to the city of Los Angeles from Owens Valley and Mono Basin. Los Angeles first began importing water from Owens Valley in 1913 and extended its aqueduct to the Mono Basin in 1940.[4] The aqueduct has an annual delivery capacity of 550,000 acre-feet, but Los Angeles has had to reduce its draw in response to judicial and regulatory decisions that call for environmental restoration in the two source regions. San Francisco's Hetch Hetchy system delivers water from the Tuolomne River in Yosemite National Park to San Francisco and surrounding cities. Congress authorized flooding of the Hetch Hetchy Valley in 1913, 23 years after the park's establishment, over the bitter opposition of John Muir and other preservationists. Other large local projects include the East Bay Municipal Utility District's Pardee Dam and Mokelumne Aqueduct.

The final major water source for California is the Colorado River, whose north and south basins provide 15 million acre-feet annually to the seven states along its course. A 1922 agreement among these states, later codified in federal law, gives California a legal right to 4.4 million acre-feet of Colorado River in an average year. A subsequent treaty with Mexico committed the United States to assuring that 1.5 million acre-feet would flow to its southern neighbor each year. California routinely overdraws from the Colorado, however, tapping into Arizona's and Nevada's unused allocations to divert as much as 5.2 million acre-feet annually. Within California, Colorado River rights are shared by three irrigation districts and the Metropolitan Water District of Southern California, with agriculture receiving approximately 80% of the supply.

Together, the facilities described above currently supply enough water to meet statewide demand in a typical year. California lacks sufficient supply to carry it through dry years, however, and projected population growth will put enormous pressure on the state's water systems. California is expected to grow by one-third between 2000 and 2020, gaining more than 11 million new residents (California Department of Finance 2001). This population increase will create greater demand for water in urban areas and will add to the challenge of maintaining adequate water quality and groundwater recharge. Without substantial reductions in demand or sources of new supply, California is expected to

---

and provide increased water supply to the CVP and SWP. In one of the biggest water battles in California history, voters in 1982 repealed the legislature's authorization of the project. The vote divided north and south, with northern Californians charging that the canal was just another water grab by the southern part of the state. The proposal reappeared during the 1990s in CALFED negotiations over Delta restoration, but the option was rejected in CALFED's final plan.

[4] For more on the colorful and tragic history of Los Angeles' quest for water, see Kahrl (1982), Reisner (1986), and Hundley (2001).

experience shortages of 2.4 million acre-feet in a typical year by 2020 (California Department of Water Resources 1998). Given current usage, that is the amount of water consumed by five million households.

Options for increasing water supply are limited. Many groundwater basins already have suffered damage from overuse. New surface storage proposals face overwhelming political opposition, primarily from environmentalists, who have successfully built coalitions to block construction of Auburn Dam and the Peripheral Canal. Other options for expanding water supply include recycling and desalination. These currently account for 1% of the state's supply, and both face important hurdles to widespread use. Approximately 200 water reclamation facilities currently recycle water, but public concern about the safety of recycled water restricts its application to nonpotable uses. Even for applications such as landscape irrigation, recycled water faces some opposition based on fears that it will contaminate groundwater. Desalination is very expensive and energy-intensive, the latter an especially important obstacle considering the state's limited electricity supply.

Without substantial increases in system capacity, major conservation initiatives will be needed to reduce demand for water. Approximately half the state's water is dedicated to environmental purposes such as maintaining minimum levels of water instream for fisheries and recreation, preserving flow to dedicated wild and scenic rivers, and protecting wetlands and the San Francisco Bay-Delta drainage system. Water that is designated for environmental use in one local area may be available for another use downstream, however. Once water becomes available for consumptive use, agriculture accounts for approximately 80% of consumption. Opportunities exist for reducing agricultural use through conservation, because heavy subsidies through the CVP and SWP have led to substantial waste and inefficiency in irrigation practices.[5] The remaining 20% goes to urban uses, primarily residential consumption but also commercial, industrial, and public sector water use. Urban water users reduced their per capita consumption in response to a prolonged statewide drought in the late 1980s, but analysts estimate that conservation-oriented policies could produce an additional 30% reduction in urban water use with currently available cost-effective technologies (Gleick et al. 2003).

In some ways, conservation is a more difficult political challenge than expanding supply. Technological improvements can achieve some amount of conservation; these require funding but generate little political opposition. Substantial progress in reducing demand requires changes in how we use water, however, and few politicians are willing to mandate those changes. Water might not

---

[5] In 1990, farmers paid between $2.50 and $19.31 per acre-foot for untreated water from the CVP and $62 per acre-foot for untreated SWP water. The Metropolitan Water District of Southern California paid $123 per acre-foot to the SWP in addition to transportation costs (Hundley 2001, 465). These price differences have grown smaller in the past decade as the CVP's 40-year water delivery contracts have come up for renewal.

be a high-profile issue in most elections, but it becomes salient when constituents learn that they cannot wash their cars on certain days or that they will pay higher rates to water a large lawn, or when farmers are told that they must allow land to lie fallow. With fragmented control of the state's water system, politicians often avoid making those hard decisions by passing responsibility to another level of government.

Water Federalism

Discussions of federalism often concern how multiple levels of government should divide responsibility for some function. One might ask whether states should exert influence over local land-use decisions, for example, or if welfare programs are better administered by state or federal government. This type of discussion suggests that governments make clear choices about how to allocate responsibility for programs and services. In fact, a government's authority in a given policy area may emerge from historical legacy or political convenience rather than careful consideration of appropriateness, and frequently the boundaries of authority for any individual government are less than clear. In a complex policy area such as water planning, issues have too many natural, social, cultural, and economic dimensions to be managed by any single jurisdiction. When we consider how federalism affects water governance, therefore, it is useful to think about how different levels of government cooperate to produce policy outcomes rather than focus on how they divide responsibility.

Current institutional arrangements for water governance are in large part a function of existing commitments and investments by individual governments. As long as a government has a role in operating one of the state's water projects, it has an interest in a wide range of water policy decisions throughout the state. But justification for the involvement of multiple levels of government in California's water planning reaches beyond their ownership of water projects. Even if all projects were managed by the state, local and federal agencies still would have important influence over water policy. The complexity of water issues draws in a wide array of public actors. Federal and state agencies charged with protecting the environment and local governments responsible for land-use decisions all must play a part in water planning, since the activities they regulate have important effects on water quality and supply. State and local governments have an interest in promoting economic development and maintaining a water infrastructure adequate to serve all residents. The value of California's agricultural industry as a national resource contributes to federal involvement. Moreover, California's choices about water policy have effects that extend beyond the state's borders. Rivers and groundwater basins do not respect political boundaries, so it is impossible to address California's water policy questions in isolation from surrounding states and Mexico.

In addition to these functional grounds for water federalism, there are political reasons for multilevel governance in water issues.[6] Elected politicians have an incentive to distribute benefits to their constituents in order to claim credit and win reelection; for the same reasons, they often seek to shift burdens to other levels of government. Federal officials view major investment in a large water project as attractive if it benefits residents in several states, as in the Colorado River projects, or if there is a national interest at stake such as protecting California's valuable crops. State officials can receive credit for winning federal approval for these projects and passing the cost burden up to the national level. On intrastate water disputes that position one group of stakeholders against another, the federal government has every reason to stay neutral. The state will only get involved if its participation is unavoidable, or if state officials think they can receive credit for resolving the dispute. Otherwise, they may pass responsibility on to local governments and the private actors involved in the issue.

Thus for historical, functional, and political reasons, water governance in California is divided among multiple jurisdictions and many agencies at each jurisdictional level. Table 1 shows the federal and state agencies involved in water management. Of the federal agencies, those with the biggest roles include the Bureau of Reclamation, which operates the CVP; the Environmental Protection Agency, which regulates water quality; and the Fish and Wildlife Service, which is charged with protecting wildlife and habitat. In addition to managing water projects and enforcing regulations that restrict water usage, the federal government is responsible for interstate and international agreements that affect California's allocation from the Colorado River.

At the state level, 14 different government agencies oversee water quality and supply. The primary state actors are the Department of Water Resources, which oversees the SWP and is responsible for overall water planning, and the State Water Resources Control Board, which regulates water rights and water quality. The nine regional Water Quality Control Boards enforce water quality standards. The state has its own set of environmental laws—the California Endangered Species Act, the California Environmental Quality Act, the California Wild and Scenic Rivers Act, as well as others—that in many cases are stronger than their federal counterparts, so state environmental regulation is an important constraint on water policy choices. The state also has a regulatory duty to control prices charged by private water companies. Finally, the state coordinates thousands of local agencies that take part in water delivery.

Local governments involved in water policy include cities and counties as well as independent special districts that provide water as part of a limited package of services. Native American tribes have water rights and play a role in some water disputes. Local governments manage delivery of both drinking water and irrigation water, and they are responsible for most of the water treatment and

---

[6] See Peterson (1995) for a full explanation of functional and legislative theories of federalism.

Table 1. Government Agencies Involved in Water Management

Federal Agencies	State Agencies
Bureau of Reclamation	State Water Resources Control Board
U.S. Environmental Protection Agency	Regional Water Quality Control Boards
Fish and Wildlife Service	Department of Water Resources
U.S. Geological Survey	Department of Health Services
National Oceanic and Atmospheric Administration	Department of Fish and Game
Bureau of Land Management	Reclamation Board
National Park Service	Department of Food and Agriculture
Department of Agriculture	California Environmental Protection Agency
U.S. Army Corps of Engineers	Delta Protection Commission
Western Area Power Administration	Colorado River Board
	California Bay-Delta Authority
	Department of Pesticide Regulation
	Department of Toxic Substances Control
	California Integrated Waste Management Board

Source: Draft California Water Plan Update, January 2004.

wastewater management in the state. In addition, local land-use and development decisions have important consequences for overall water management. As water has become more scarce, water availability in many cases has become an obstacle to growth. Recent debate at the state level over the linkage between water and land use has drawn attention to the complex negotiations that occur in local communities over how to distribute water and who should bear the costs of system expansion.

In this complex institutional environment, lines of authority frequently are uncertain and decision-making processes rely on negotiation and collaboration. As in many other policy areas, federalism means more than the division of responsibility among multiple nested governments; it is a mode of political decision making that involves extended relationships among political actors (Elazar 1966). Governments themselves become stakeholders in debates over policy questions, and agency officials may join in coalition with advocacy groups to contend with other governmental actors (Sabatier and Jenkins-Smith 1999). The fragmentation of responsibility for water policy creates a variety of different decision-making venues at all jurisdictional levels. Interests and groups often enjoy an advantage in certain venues—urban water users exert substantial influence in the state legislature, for example, while environmentalists often have greater success pursuing their agenda in the courts—so the venue in which a policy question is considered may influence its outcome (Baumgartner and Jones 1993).

Water federalism can create coordination problems that increase the time and cost required for reaching decisions, but it also can help to overcome stalemate and stimulate action. Political obstruction that occurs in one venue can be overridden by action elsewhere. The possibility of preemption by other jurisdictions may prompt governments to act. Rules and incentives exist that encourage governments to cooperate rather than obstruct one another. State and local governments may be required to operate within the constraints of federal law, or they may comply in order to benefit from federal programs. On some particularly complicated water issues, multiple agencies and stakeholders across jurisdictional levels have come together to collaborate on a solution, bringing more resources and expertise to the issue than would otherwise have been the case.

These features of water governance help to overcome the constraints on policy making that arise from historical behavior and long-established patterns of water use. The state's legal system of water rights locks in levels of consumption by providing an incentive for holders of a water right to use the maximum amount of water allowed. Holders of appropriative rights have to "use it or lose it"; if they do not put their water to beneficial use for five consecutive years, the amount of water they have a right to receive in future years may shrink.[7] Until recently, conservation and environmental uses were not treated as "beneficial use," so farmers had an incentive to flood their fields even in a wet year in order to ensure that they would have the water they needed in future dry years. Appropriative rights give greatest priority to the earliest users of a water source, locking in water usage for subsequent generations. Land-use decisions at the local level lock in patterns of water use: building houses with large lots creates demand for outdoor irrigation that will last for the life of the house. Decisions by farmers to specialize in a crop similarly comprise a commitment to a certain level of water consumption—high consumption if the crop is cotton or alfalfa, lower for fruits and vegetables. Once patterns of usage have been established, constituencies arise to defend those uses and it is difficult to construct political agreements that shift water from one use to another.

The challenges for policy makers grappling with conflicts over water are substantial, and the stakes are high. California's economy and the quality of life of its residents rely on a vast infrastructure to store and transport water so that a safe, clean supply is available where and when humans demand it. This infrastructure

---

[7] California's system of water rights recognizes both appropriative rights, which are based on actual use of water, and riparian rights, which grant a right to use water based on ownership of property that abuts a natural watercourse. As a general rule, riparian rights are not lost through nonuse.

has reached its capacity, but the state's population continues to grow. Californians must learn to control their consumption through conservation or find a way to expand the developed water supply. Substantial hurdles stand in the way of either solution. Political rivalries, long established behaviors, locked-in institutions, and the potential for environmental damage all constrain the options available to policy makers. On top of all this, the cost of any solution is high and there is no consensus on who should pay to secure future water supply. Is it the obligation of future residents to pay for the conservation and system expansion that is necessary to meet their water demands? Or should all Californians share these costs, since existing residents benefit from an earlier generation's willingness to subsidize water use? These questions arise in almost every water conflict, and local issues frequently reflect larger statewide battles.

The divided, federalist system of water governance sometimes complicates decision making in water policy, but it also can provide opportunities and incentives that make it easier to find solutions. The following section describes three contemporary water policy challenges and shows how the interplay among governments at different jurisdictional levels can facilitate, rather than impede, policy making.

Water Transfers

As demands for water begin to put pressure on the state's developed water supply, many policy makers are looking to water markets as a tool for reallocating existing supplies to the places with the greatest need. Water markets supplement California's rights-based system for water allocation with one that relies on price, giving farmers with historical water rights the opportunity to profit from them by selling water to urban and other users who are willing to pay higher prices.

Water trading first captured the attention of state policy makers during a drought in the mid-1970s, but it did not become an important element in water management until another multiyear drought prompted the state to establish an emergency water bank in 1991.[8] In that time of extreme water scarcity, the Department of Water Resources (DWR) served as a clearinghouse for water trades. The current water market is less centralized. Transfers among contractors within the same water projects made up more than half of all water traded in the state between 1988 and 2001. Direct state and federal government purchases of water make up another 31% of the total volume traded. This water primarily goes to environmental uses and, in dry years, to offset lower deliveries from government projects. Only 15% of water transfers occur among private and local government users not associated with the same project. Water trades currently account for approximately 3% of water use in the state.

---

[8] The following description of the current water market relies primarily on Hanak (2003).

Agricultural users are the leading source of supply in the water market, providing at least 90% of traded water. This is not surprising, since agricultural users hold most of the water rights and entitlements in the state and obtain their water at a very low price. Irrigation districts and individual farmers make conservation improvements or allow land to fallow in order to make water available for sale. They also may transfer groundwater, either directly or by using groundwater on-site in order to transfer a supply of surface water. Most transfers are short-term transactions that keep the water in the same region.

Although many policy makers view water transfers as the best option to meet growing demand in urban areas, in normal years urban agencies have not been an important part of the water market. Almost all the long-term and permanent water transfers that have taken place involve sales from agricultural to urban users. Urban agencies attempting to secure water supply for growing populations cannot rely on temporary contracts, but long-term commitments can be very difficult to negotiate. They involve many parties, including buyers, sellers, conveyers, and agencies that regulate water along the path of the transfer. They also raise concerns on the part of the seller about how the transfer will affect viability of the water source; whether the seller will have some unforeseen need for the water in the future, perhaps for environmental mitigation; and what negative "third-party" effects the transfer might have on economic health in the source region if farmers allow land to lie fallow. All of these issues can create obstacles for large-scale, long-term water transfers.

Although a water transfer usually is an exchange involving private and local government entities, state and federal actors play an important role in the water market. They are a leading buyer, and both state and federal governments have taken action to promote and facilitate water transfers. Transfers must clear state and federal environmental regulation, and those involving surface water rights must obtain approval from the state. State and federal authorities get involved if the transfer requires conveyance through one of the major projects. In short, it is likely that any major water transfer will simultaneously fall under federal, state, and local jurisdiction.

Recent events surrounding a proposed transfer from the Imperial Irrigation District (IID) in the southern California desert to San Diego highlight the complexity of a major agricultural-urban water transfer. Initially negotiated between IID and the San Diego County Water Authority in 1998, the proposed transfer soon captured federal and state attention as an important element in California's plan to reduce its Colorado River consumption to the 4.4 million acre-feet per year the state is allowed under federal law. Imperial Valley farmers' Colorado water rights date back to the 1880s. IID holds rights in trust for individual farmers, so an elected board rather than individual farmers makes decisions about using those rights. One of four agencies that hold all the state's rights to the Colorado, IID alone has rights to 65% of the state's allocation. Consequently, Imperial involvement is critical if California is going to achieve a reduction in its use of Colorado River water.

The state is running out of time to achieve this reduction. In late 1996, the federal government began to put pressure on California to comply with legal limits on its use of Colorado water. The following year, the state released the California 4.4 Plan, which relied on agricultural-urban transfers among Colorado River users as a key strategy for reducing usage of Colorado water. The U.S. Secretary of the Interior determined that if parties could come to an agreement on a major water transfer by the end of 2002, the state would get another 15 years to lower its Colorado consumption to the legal level. Without a deal, the federal government would immediately limit California to the 4.4 million acre-feet the state was allowed.

In the initial transfer proposal, San Diego would pay for conservation projects in the Imperial Valley in exchange for 300,000 acre-feet of water. Environmental review of the plan revealed that increasing conservation would damage the Salton Sea, a lake created in 1905 when a levee broke and Colorado River water rushed in to the desert basin. Now the lake is almost entirely fed by agricultural runoff, and with the loss of wetlands in California the lake has become critical habitat for wildlife and an important sanctuary for migratory waterfowl. The Salton Sea is growing increasingly polluted and saline, and its survival depends on the flow of runoff. Ironically, increasing conservation in the Imperial Valley would harm the environment by increasing the lake's salinity and exposing more of the lakebed, potentially triggering dust storms.

By the time the environmental costs of the initial transfer proposal became apparent, state and federal officials had taken an interest in the IID-San Diego transfer plan and encouraged the parties to find another alternative. Negotiations turned to IID reducing its water consumption by taking some agricultural land out of production. An October 2002 proposal included land fallowing as a source of water savings, despite concerns in the Imperial Valley about the effect of fallowing on the local economy. Closing in on the December 2002 federal deadline, IID and San Diego came under intense pressure from state and federal authorities to reach agreement. In December, IID's governing board voted 3–2 to reject the proposal based on concerns about the deal's effects on the local economy and the district's liability for damage to the Salton Sea (Hanak 2003; Kris 2003). In response, the federal government unilaterally cut the state's allocation of Colorado River water by nearly 15%, enough water for 1.2 million households, and state officials proposed legislation to further reduce IID's water supply.

Talks continued into 2003, involving the Coachella Valley Water District and the Metropolitan Water District in addition to IID and San Diego. At the same time, IID went to court to challenge the federal government's authority to cut the district's water allocation. In August, federal officials stepped in again, this time with a promise to restore some of the water it had taken away and extend California's deadline for reducing Colorado withdrawals if the parties could reach agreement on a transfer. The parties finally signed a long-term transfer deal in September; state lawmakers quickly passed legislation affirming the deal and the governor signed it into law. The final agreement allowed Imperial to reduce its water usage through a combination of conservation and land fallowing. It established state responsibility for restoration of the Salton Sea and set up a restoration fund. Federal officials applauded the agreement, and Interior Secretary Gale Norton restored California's access to surplus Colorado River allocations for 13 more years while the state continues to work towards consuming within its legal limit.

Water markets offer much promise for promoting more efficient water use and better matching supply with demand. The ideal of a water market involves exchange between willing buyers and willing sellers with prices set by the market-place. In fact, any water transfer is likely to be much more complicated and far-reaching than this ideal. The initial exchange between IID and San Diego offered benefits to both parties: urban residents would receive a secure water supply, and conservation investments in the Imperial Valley would boost the local economy and stimulate job growth. The potential for environmental damage extended the impact of this transfer beyond the two parties, however, introducing a state and federal interest in the trade and increasing the potential cost to IID. In this way, expanding the scope of the transfer beyond the immediate buyer and seller created an obstacle to its completion. But state and federal interest in reducing California's Colorado River consumption helped to secure a deal when negotiations otherwise would have fallen apart. Using its control over the source of Imperial water supply as leverage, the federal government pushed local actors towards a policy solution.

Bay-Delta Restoration

In the case described above, threats and incentives from higher levels of government prompted local actors to reach an agreement. In the case of Bay-Delta restoration, state and federal agencies collaborated directly with local governments and nongovernmental actors to reach a solution to a complex water policy problem.

The problem was the degradation of the San Francisco Bay-Delta, the largest estuary on the West Coast and the backbone of California's water system. The estuary's watershed drains 40% of the state's rainfall and snowmelt. Fed by the Sacramento and San Joaquin Rivers, the Delta historically was a wetland before settlers diked it off and converted it to farmland. Today, the Delta covers 700 square miles with interconnecting marshes, islands, and channels. It provides critical habitat for fish and wildlife and serves as a migration corridor for two-thirds of the state's salmon. The Delta is the center of the state's developed water supply. Huge pumping stations near Tracy capture water from the Delta and send it through the pipes and aqueducts of the CVP and SWP to farms and communities throughout the state. The Bay-Delta provides drinking water for 22 million Californians.

Over time, the Delta's central role in quenching the state's thirst damaged the health of its ecosystem. Drought and excessive diversion of the Delta's freshwater caused saltwater intrusion, deterioration in water quality, and farmland subsidence. Fish populations declined due to poor water quality and growth in the population of introduced species. Continuing demand for water by agricultural and urban users made it difficult to increase freshwater flow to the Delta in order to address these problems. Efforts by the State Water Resources Control Board to address Delta outflows met resistance by stakeholder groups and the public (Wright 2001). On top of all this, the levees providing flood protection for the Delta's homes and farms deteriorated and became vulnerable to earthquakes.

Beginning in the 1980s, environmental groups turned to federal statutes to win protection for the Delta. They sued the U.S. Environmental Protection Agency for failing to enforce Clean Water Act standards, and they petitioned the U.S. Fish and Wildlife Service to protect declining fish populations. When federal officials moved to establish federal water quality standards for the Bay and Delta and list the Delta smelt as endangered, shutdowns of the state's massive water projects became a real possibility to restore Delta flows. Agricultural and urban users that relied on water supply from the CVP and SWP recognized they needed to help find an alternative solution.

Facing a court-ordered deadline for resolution of the water quality lawsuit, in December 1994 all the major stakeholders in Bay-Delta restoration—including federal and state agencies as well as urban, agricultural, and environmental interests—announced agreement on the Bay-Delta Accord, a statement of principles for Bay-Delta management that included a commitment to a long-term planning process. State and federal officials had spent the previous year laying the groundwork for the accord by coordinating their efforts on the Bay and Delta to make sure that agencies responsible for water quality and species protection were working in concert with one another (Wright 2001). The U.S. Department of Interior played a particularly important leadership role in developing a collaborative process among the many agencies and parties involved in water policy. The threat of court-ordered system shutdowns brought the nongovernmental stakeholders to the table for the final round of intense negotiations that led to the accord.

The CALFED Bay-Delta program was established the following year as a cooperative effort among 23 state and federal agencies and dozens of local and nongovernmental stakeholders to improve the environmental health of the estuary while ensuring the reliability of water supplies. In bringing together rival interest groups to work on Bay-Delta issues, CALFED was a landmark achievement. The planning process was complex and contentious, however, and the enthusiasm of many participating groups waned over time (Wright 2001). Ongoing disagreements among stakeholders threatened to jeopardize the entire process. In 2000, CALFED produced a framework for a 30-year plan for Bay-Delta management. Reflecting the consensus-based approach that generated it, the framework did not embrace any single strategy for addressing water supply but rather endorsed a range of strategies including conservation, trading, and groundwater and surface storage expansions. The plan put off decisions about new storage projects until its second phase beginning in 2010, although feasibility studies are currently underway.

Attention now has turned to implementing the CALFED framework. The plan lays out $8.7 billion in projects over the first seven years, with costs shared among federal, state, and local authorities. Funds from statewide bond measures have supported projects to reinforce levees, provide safe fish passages, improve water quality, and promote conservation. One of the biggest accomplishments has been development of the Environmental Water Account, which acquires water from willing sellers for use in fish protection. The account has improved water supply reliability to farmers and urban areas by preventing emergency water system shut-downs to protect fish species. State legislation in 2003 established the California Bay-Delta Authority as the oversight and implementing agency for Bay-Delta restoration.

In some respects, CALFED represents an ideal case of interjurisdictional collaboration on water management. The CALFED process assembled expertise and resources from dozens of agencies, and it prompted cooperation among histori-cally rivalrous private actors. As a consequence, issues surrounding environmental restoration of the Bay-Delta received more sustained and thorough attention than would have been the case under normal politics. It is important to note, however, that CALFED never would have existed without the threats and deadlines pro-duced by interest groups pursuing their goals through normal politics. Moreover, there is no guarantee that the policy solutions identified through the CALFED process will receive the funding and attention needed for implementation.

The challenge for water stakeholders now is to maintain the interest and sup-port of federal authorities. Having established a collaborative governing process across jurisdictional levels, success in restoring the Bay-Delta depends on contin-ued participation by all parties. Yet Congress has stalled on reauthorizing federal participation in the Bay-Delta process, and the federal government has failed to provide its portion of funding for restoration projects. Some stakeholders also have raised concerns about recent federal decisions that are not seen to be in the spirit of CALFED collaboration (Robitaille 2003; Zakin 2002). In the case of Bay-Delta restoration, federal authorities were critical to establishing a cooperative, cross-jurisdictional approach to resource management that helped to overcome historical antagonisms and stalemates. Waning interest on the part of the federal government raises questions about whether it will carry out its commitments, and reduces the level of trust and collaboration among all participants.

Water Supply and Land Use

The final case involves the introduction of water availability into the land-use planning process. Here, the state played an important role in forcing local govern-ments to consult and share information when planning for the growth of a com-munity.

Authority over land-use policy historically has resided firmly with the na-tion's municipalities. As public concern about sprawl and other negative consequences of development heightened in recent decades, however, many states stepped in to improve coordination of local land-use planning. In California, state law lays out requirements for local planning processes, but leaves cities and counties to make actual planning and development decisions. The state may further influence local decisions through tax codes and environmental regulations. In specific regions, such as along California's coast, the state takes a more active role in approving development proposals, but in general questions about the amount and type of development that should be permitted in a given location are left to localities. Efforts in the 1970s to create a role for the federal government in land-use regulation were unsuccessful (Popper 1981).

Local responsibility for land-use planning allows communities to respond to residents' needs and shape their own future growth, but there are costs. Local control makes it difficult to address issues such as transportation, air quality, and water supply that spill over local boundaries. Lack of coordination among neighboring cities and counties can produce collective harms such as traffic congestion and air pollution. Where resources or infrastructure are limited, as in the case of water, one jurisdiction's decision to expand its population can jeopardize services to a neighboring community. In some cases, division of responsibility for local services among multiple, specialized governments produces even greater fragmentation in decision making. Clashes can occur between cities and counties that approve new development and special districts that are expected to provide services to the incoming residents.

One of those clashes in the early 1990s ultimately led to an important set of changes in how water is treated in the land-use planning process throughout California. In 1992, Contra Costa County supervisors amended the county's general plan to allow construction of 11,000 new homes in Dougherty Valley. The county expected East Bay Municipal Utility District (EBMUD), the special district that supplied water to the surrounding area, to expand its boundaries to include the new development. EBMUD declined, arguing that it did not have enough water supply to extend service to the development and protect its existing 1.2 million customers in the case of a water shortage. The district sued the county in order to avoid being forced to expand its service area, and at the same time pursued legislation that would give water agencies statewide a role in approving new development.[9]

Surprisingly, despite the shortage of water resources in California, prior to this time there existed no requirement that developers or local governments identify a water source for new development. Cities and counties would approve a development project and expect the local water agency to extend service to the new residents. A few northern California cities enacted moratoria on new building in the 1970s and 1980s after experiencing severe water shortages, but in most cases water was not a factor in land-use decisions. For water agencies with a lim-

---

[9] In 1999, after lengthy legal battles, Dougherty Valley developers finally reached a deal with two other water agencies for water service to the proposed development.

ited supply, expanding service to new residents put service to existing businesses and residents in jeopardy.

The disconnect between water and land-use planning created a particular challenge in communities where an independent special district was responsible for water service. In cities and counties that have their own water departments, the approval of new development without sufficient water to serve it may frustrate water department personnel, but the same local officials who approve the development will be held responsible if it leads to water shortages for existing residents. If a water district provides service to the community, it enjoys none of the tax or other benefits of new development and bears the burden of trying to stretch limited supplies to meet the demands of new and existing customers. Moreover, there is likely to be greater information sharing and cooperation between land-use and water planners in cities that have their own municipal water departments (Hanak and Simeti 2004). EBMUD turned to the state legislature in order to find a solution to this fragmentation in local decision making.

In 1991, the district teamed with Assembly Member Dominic L. Cortese (D-San Jose) to introduce a one-sentence bill that would prohibit approval of a development project unless the applicant identified a long-term, reliable source of water. That bill finally passed in a much weaker form to require general consultation with the public water agency before a city or county could amend its general plan. Three years later, Cortese and EBMUD argued that consultation and referral were not enough and proposed another bill that would require a city to obtain proof that water supply was adequate to serve new development before the city could amend its general plan. A broad coalition backed the legislation, including agricultural and environmental groups that historically fought with EBMUD. The state was just emerging from a long period of drought, and all the major water user groups agreed with the principle that existing water users must be protected before making commitments for expansion in water service. Developers and the Chamber of Commerce were the bill's primary opponents, as well as the League of California Cities and the California State Association of Counties, which fought their loss of autonomy over land-use decisions. They succeeded in blocking the Cortese bill, but the following year a weaker version passed over their opposition. Senate Bill 901 (Costa) required cities and counties to obtain a 20-year commitment for water supply for projects of 500 units or more during their environmental review. It also provided a number of ways that a municipality could go forward with the project even if the water district forecast a water shortage.

EBMUD returned to the legislature in 1999 with evidence that few development projects approved after the passage of SB 901 were fully in compliance with the law. It proposed a new package of legislation to strengthen the linkage between land-use and water planning. The district and its new ally in the legislature, Sheila Kuehl (D-Santa Monica), fought for the next two years to win passage of the legislation, amending bills in order to satisfy the concerns of their opponents.[10] This time EBMUD faced opposition not just from the development community and cities and counties, but from its own professional association, the Association of California Water Agencies (ACWA). ACWA raised concerns that providing a greater role for water agencies in development approval would make them a target for developers and force them to spend time in litigation defending their judgments about water supply.

In 2001, a decade after EBMUD first took the problem to the legislature, a pair of bills establishing a strong link between land-use and water planning finally passed and were signed into law. One of the bills, SB 610 (Costa), closed the loopholes in the law passed six years earlier requiring a water supply assessment for large-scale development projects during the projects' environmental review. In addition, the bill required a detailed assessment of the state of the groundwater basin if groundwater was identified as the water source, and it tied state funding to the adoption of an urban water management plan. The second bill, SB 221 (Kuehl), prohibited a city or county from making final approval of a large development project unless the local water agency or the city or county itself found that a sufficient water source would be available by the time the homes were ready to be built.

With passage of these two bills, the state added some steps to the planning process and placed constraints on the ability of cities and counties to approve new development for which adequate water supply is not available. When considering a large development proposal, cities and counties must consult with the local water agency at two stages in the process: first to obtain a detailed assessment of water supply, and later to obtain written verification that water supply is available to serve the new development. Without these laws, it is likely that the economic incentives for cities and counties to approve new development would continue to outweigh consideration of water supply—with consequences that would extend beyond local borders when drought dries up water supplies for all the state's residents.

The disconnect between water supply and land use was a local problem that required a local solution. But local governments refused to act on their own: cities and counties opposed any loss of autonomy over the planning process, and many water districts resisted an expansion of their authority. The state stepped in not to expand its own role in land-use planning, but rather to force greater coordination among local governments.

---

[10] Kuehl was an Assembly member when she first sponsored her bill, but she had been elected to the state Senate by 2001 when the legislation passed.

Conclusion

Water management in California is by necessity an intergovernmental endeavor. It is part historical legacy and part inherent to the resource itself that federal, state, and local governments all should have an interest in water policy decisions. Water flows across political borders, and its use in any one location has effects that spill over to neighboring communities. The complexity of water issues and scarcity of the resource give rise to conflict that may play out in a variety of political venues.

As we see in the cases above, participation by multiple governments can have a positive effect on the design and implementation of California water policy. Water federalism ensures consideration of both local and global interests; local governments can respond to their constituents' demands while higher levels of government coordinate fragmented local decisions and protect the state's collective assets. On individual water issues, a combination of cooperation and competition among governments can produce an effective policy solution. The federal government's obligation to fulfill commitments to Mexico and other western states prompted it to issue threats and incentives that led to a deal on the Imperial-San Diego water transfer. The threat of legal action against federal and state agencies brought about the multistakeholder CALFED negotiations. And with the help of a state mandate, local governments finally are cooperating and sharing information on development decisions.

The question remains whether the current system of water federalism is adequate to address California's future water challenges. Public officials must find a way to meet the water demands of a rapidly growing population while coping with continued deterioration in the existing water infrastructure and potential reductions in water supply due to the effects of climate change. Unfortunately, while the problem of water in California grows more difficult, the pool of possible solutions shrinks. In the short term, it is possible to make substantial gains in water conservation by adopting cost-effective technologies. Piecemeal decisions by individual governments can help postpone the need for new supply. As water-saving technologies become more widespread, however, reducing per-capita water use requires behavioral changes that affect Californians' quality of life. Similarly, the first major long-term water transfers are likely to be the easiest, because they target the greatest discrepancies between supply and demand. Negotiating trades from regions that have no excess supply, or where conveyance facilities are not readily available, will be much more challenging.

California's water problem is an institutional problem. A more coherent process for water policy making is necessary if the state is to secure a reliable water supply for coming generations. Some have called for more collaborative efforts like CALFED, which attempt to build consensus among competing interests. We have seen, that this type of effort depends on a long-term voluntary commitment by all parties, which is difficult to secure and maintain. In reality, the tangle of federal, state, and local authority allows elected officials to ignore water problems until some external threat or incentive forces them to act. Given this pattern, the solution to California's water problem may lie in making those threats and incentives more available. It may be that contention, rather than cooperation, is what forces governments and other stakeholders to find a way to manage California's water resources.

References

Baumgartner, Frank R., and Bryan D. Jones. 1993. Agendas and Instability in American Politics. Chicago: University of Chicago Press.

California Department of Finance. 2001. "Interim County Population Projections." Sacramento: Demographic Research Unit, Department of Finance.

California Department of Water Resources. 1998. "California Water Plan Update." Bulletin 160–98. Sacramento: Department of Water Resources.

Elazar, Daniel J. 1966. American Federalism: A View from the States. New York: Crowell.

Gleick, Peter H., Dana Haasz, Christine Henges-Jeck, Veena Srinivasan, Gary Wolff, Katherine Kao Cushing, and Amardip Mann. 2003. "Waste Not, Want Not: The Potential for Urban Water Conservation in California." Oakland, Calif.: Pacific Institute for Studies in Development, Environment, and Security.

Hanak, Ellen. 2003. Who Should Be Allowed to Sell Water in California? Third-Party Issues and the Water Market. San Francisco: Public Policy Institute of California.

Hanak, Ellen, and Antonina Simeti. 2004. "Water Supply and Growth in California: A Survey of City and County Land-Use Planners." Occasional Paper. San Francisco: Public Policy Institute of California.

Hundley, Norris, Jr. 2001. The Great Thirst: Californians and Water, A History. Revised edition. Berkeley: University of California Press.

Kahrl, William L. 1982. Water and Power: The Conflict over Los Angeles' Water Supply in the Owens Valley. Berkeley: University of California Press.

Kriz, Margaret. 2003. "Water Wars." California Journal 47:40.

Peterson, Paul E. 1995. The Price of Federalism. Washington, D.C.: The Brookings Institution.

Popper, Frank. 1981. The Politics of Land-Use Reform. Madison: University of Wisconsin Press.

Reisner, Marc. 1986. Cadillac Desert: The American West and its Disappearing Water. New York: Penguin Books.

Robitaille, Stephen. 2003. "Water War Talk." California Journal 52:12.

Sabatier, Paul A., and Hank Jenkins-Smith. 1999. "The Advocacy Coalition Framework: An Assessment." In Theories of the Policy Process, ed. Paul A. Sabatier. Boulder, Colo.: Westview.

Wright, Patrick. 2001. "Fixing the Delta: The CALFED Bay-Delta Program and Water Policy under the Davis Administration." Golden Gate University Law Review 31:331–50.

Zakin, Susan. 2002. "Delta Blues." High Country News, September 30.

About the Authors

A. G. Block is director of the public-affairs journalism program at the University of California Center Sacramento. Prior to his position with the university, he spent 22 years on the staff of *California Journal*, a monthly magazine devoted to nonpartisan reporting of California public affairs and politics, where he served as managing editor, editor, and publisher. He is editor of the *California Government and Politics Annual*, co-editor and principal author of the *California Political Almanac*, and a columnist for the Sacramento-based *Capitol Weekly* newspaper. Before moving to California, Block was a columnist and editor of *Ketchum Tomorrow*, a weekly newspaper in Ketchum, Idaho, and a reporter for the Boise-based *Idaho Statesman*.

Bruce E. Cain is Robson Professor of Political Science at the University of California, Berkeley, director of the Institute of Governmental Studies, and director of the University of California Center in Washington. His writings include *The Reapportionment Puzzle*, *The Personal Vote*, written with John Ferejohn and Morris Fiorina, and *Congressional Redistricting*, with David Butler. He edited *Developments in American Politics*, Volumes 1 and 2, with Gillian Peele. Cain has served as polling consultant for state senate races, redistricting consultant to the Los Angeles City Council and the attorney general of the state of Massachusetts, consultant to the *Los Angeles Time,* and commentator for numerous radio and television stations in Los Angeles and the Bay Area.

Andrea Campbell is associate professor of political science at MIT. She received her B.A. from Harvard College and her Ph.D. from the University of California, Berkeley. Before joining the MIT faculty she was assistant professor of Government at Harvard University. She has written *How Policies Make Citizens: Senior Political Activism and the American Welfare State* (2002) and other articles and book chapters on American public policy.

Jack Citrin is professor of political science at the University of California, Berkeley and associate director of the Institute of Governmental Studies. He is an author of *Tax Revolt: Something for Nothing in California, California and the American Tax Revolt, The Politics of Disaffection among British and American Youth* and *How Race, Ethnicity, and Immigration Shape the California Electorate* as well as numerous papers on American public opinion and behavior. His new book, *American Identity and the Politics of Multiculturalism*, will be published next year by Cambridge University Press.

John Decker is a visiting fellow at the Institute of Governmental Studies. He has served as chief fiscal advisor to two Speakers (Antonio Villaraigosa and Robert Hertzberg), and the Senate Minority Leader (Senator Kenneth L.

Maddy). He also served as staff director to the Senate Budget and Fiscal Review Committee. He successfully negotiated major changes in state taxes, local finance, and pension policy. He is a visiting lecturer at the Goldman School of Public Policy at the University of California, Berkeley. In 2004, Decker was a Rockefeller Fellow at the Bellagio Study Center in northern Italy.

Darshan Goux is a Ph.D. candidate in political science at the University of California, Berkeley. She studies American politics, political behavior, and methods, specializing in voter behavior, public opinion, and campaigns. Goux received a B.A. from Yale University in 1995. She has worked as a political consultant and public opinion researcher for a variety of officeholders, Fortune 500 companies, and nonprofit organizations in the U.S., New Zealand, and Australia.

John Jacobs was political editor and columnist for McClatchy Newspapers, based at the *Sacramento Bee*. He spent a year reporting for the *Washington Post* and 15 years reporting for the *San Francisco Examiner*; his last seven as chief political writer. He is the author of *A Rage for Justice: The Passion and Politics of Phillip Burton*, and co-author, with Tim Reiterman, of *Raven: The Untold Story of the Reverend Jim Jones and His People*. Jacobs died in 2000.

Patrick Johnston served in the state Assembly from 1981 through 1990 and in the state Senate from 1991 through 2000 where he chaired the Appropriations Committee for six years. Currently he is member of the California Bay Delta Authority that oversees the state's water system. A resident of Stockton, Johnston is a government affairs consultant and teaches state politics at UC Berkeley's Goldman School of Public Policy. Johnston was IGS's first legislator in residence.

J. Morgan Kousser is professor of history and social science at the California Institute of Technology and the author of *The Shaping of Southern Politics: Suffrage Restriction and the Establishment of the One-Party South, 1880–1910* and *Colorblind Injustice: Minority Voting Rights and the Undoing of the Second Reconstruction*, and numerous scholarly articles. *Colorblind Injustice* was co-winner of the 1999 Lillian Smith Award of the Southern Regional Council and of the Ralph J. Bunche Award of the American Political Science Association.

Thad Kousser is assistant professor of political science at the University of California, San Diego. His research interests include legislative politics, policy-making, and political regulation. His publications include work on the initiative process, term limits, reapportionment, campaign finance laws, the blanket primary, health care policy, and European Parliament elections. His book, *Term Limits and the Dismantling of State Legislative Professionalism*, won the APSA Legislative Studies Section's Alan Rosenthal Prize.

Karl T. Kurtz is director of state services for the National Conference of State Legislatures and has been studying and working with American legislatures for over 30 years. He is coauthor of *Republic on Trial: The Case for Representative Democracy.*

Eugene C. Lee, a retired political science professor, was director of the Institute of Governmental Studies at UC Berkeley from 1966–88, following service as a vice president in the UC system. A student of California government and politics for over 50 years, Lee served as consultant to the California congressional delegation in 1979 and to the special masters on reapportionment in 1991. In addition to books and articles on California politics, Lee has written extensively about issues of university governance and has been an advisor to university systems, both in the United States and abroad.

Gerald C. Lubenow retired as director of publications at the Institute of Governmental Studies in 2005, but continues to oversee the Berkeley Public Policy Press. He received his B.A. from Harvard and did graduate work in journalism at the University of Wisconsin. He joined *Newsweek Magazine* as a correspondent in 1965 and served as bureau chief in San Francisco and London. He received the Gavel Award of The American Bar Association and two Page One Awards from the Newspaper Guild of New York.

Megan Mullin is assistant professor of political science at Temple University. She received her Ph.D. from the University of California, Berkeley. Her research interests include federalism, policymaking, and political participation, and currently she is working on a major project investigating the policy effects of special district governance.

Susan Rasky teaches at the University of California, Berkeley, Graduate School of Journalism. She graduated from UC Berkeley with a degree in history and holds a master's degree in economic history from the London School of Economics. Rasky served as congressional correspondent for *The New York Times* and won the George Polk Award in 1990 for her coverage of the federal budget.

Preble Stolz, who died in June 1996, was a professor of law emeritus at UC Berkeley. He did his undergraduate work at Reed College and his law studies at the University of Chicago, where he served as editor-in-chief of the *Law Review*. He joined the Berkeley faculty in 1961 after clerking for Justice Harold Burton of the United States Supreme Court and serving as a deputy attorney general of California. In 1975 and 1976 he served as director of program and policies for Governor Jerry Brown. He was an expert on California government and its judiciary, having authored a major book in 1981 entitled *Judging Judges—The Investigation of Rose Bird and the California Supreme Court.*

Revan Tranter received a law degree from Oxford and a master's degree in public administration from the University of Pittsburgh. He joined the Institute of Governmental Studies, UC Berkeley, as a visiting scholar in February 1995, upon retiring after 22 years as executive director of the Association of Bay Area Governments. In 1990–91 he served as president of the International City/County Management Association, whose distinguished service award he received in 1996. A senior fellow of the National Academy of Public Administration, he is the author of articles in several countries' local government publications.

Gerald Uelmen is professor of law at Santa Clara University School of Law, where he served as dean from 1986–1994. He is an active appellate practitioner, and served as co-counsel for the defense in the cases of *People v. O. J. Simpson* and *People v. Christian Brando*. He is a past president of the California Academy of Appellate Lawyers and of California Attorneys for Criminal Justice. Uelmen serves on the board of directors of the Sixth District Appellate Project, the California Habeas Corpus Resource Center, and the National Association of Criminal Defense Lawyers. He also chairs the editorial advisory board of *California Lawyer Magazine*, and is the author of *Drug Abuse and the Law Sourcebook*; *Lessons from the Trial*; *The Wizard's Guide to California Evidence*, and a one-man play on the life of William Jennings Bryan, which was produced in Omaha, Chicago, and San Jose. He is co-author of two collections of legal humor, *Disorderly Conduct* and *Supreme Folly*.

Rachel VanSickle-Ward is a Ph.D. candidate in political science at the University of California, Berkeley. Her research interests are in public law and public policy, particularly social policymaking and regulation at the state level. In 2005 she collaborated with Robert Kagan on a book chapter on Supreme Court case *Marshall v. Barlow's*. Her dissertation, "Explicit Language: Fragmentation and Policy Specificity in the U.S. States," treats the effects of institutional and political fragmentation on policy construction. She graduated from Pitzer College with a degree in political studies and English literature and served as a legislative consultant for California State Assemblymember Helen Thomson.

Index

Appendix

Internet Resources on California Government and Public Policy

Ronald J. Heckart

California state and local agencies, research institutes and advocacy groups routinely post topical information, statistics, and policy papers on the World Wide Web. The Institute of Governmental Studies Library at UC Berkeley maintains a links gallery to a selection of key Web sites that provide this information. The URL is: http://igs.berkeley.edu/library/gallery-ca.html

The links gallery has 10 broad subject categories, with many subcategories, and many entries have brief annotations. The broad subject categories are:

Gateway Sites
Academic and Research Sites
State Agencies
State Legislature and Law
Local and Regional Government
Media
Political Parties, Campaigns and Elections
Public Opinion
Public Policy
Statistics

It is important to remember that the World Wide Web is in a constant state of flux. New sites appear all the time, and existing sites change their URLs and content. It may be advisable to supplement a search of the links gallery with a key word search on one of the major Web search engines such as Google or Yahoo.